I Could've Been

Christopher Drake

Copyright © 2021 Christopher Drake
All rights reserved
First Edition

PAGE PUBLISHING, INC.
Conneaut Lake, PA

First originally published by Page Publishing 2021

ISBN 978-1-6624-2605-6 (pbk)
ISBN 978-1-6624-2606-3 (digital)

Printed in the United States of America

Dear Vanessa,

    I love you more than I value what most perceive as life. I have enjoyed a beautiful journey that has led me in and out of depression as I continue to face the realities. I was born alone; I will die alone. The only things that I own are my perception of happiness and the knowledge that I procure making sure that I learn something new every day my eyes open. You are my gift from God that keeps my fire burning looking for a solution for real freedom as I struggle in this rat race. As a baby, your provoking perspective inspired me, blowing my mind when you would ask, "Can I go to Grandma's world?" Reminding me that while we all live on this planet, we create our own worlds divided by wealth, education, and technology. There's an old saying, "It takes money to make money!" The question of my journey has always been choosing the right investment. Trying from every angle to get ahead, *I have sold everything that I could without selling my soul.*

    You will never understand how many times I have had to start over learning something brand-new. You will never understand how many worlds I've been through in this one lifetime, such as nerd, jock, and even an entrepreneur. I learned at a young age through a drug-infested, gang-controlled city that either you *adapt or die.* Educating myself in every venture, realizing that nothing is personal. *It's all business. You are my blood.* Since your existence, I pushed myself to find a legal way to provide. Loyalty is a value important in life. Blind loyalty is faith in someone or something to give you what you want. My soul doesn't desire anything any man has. This story is my life. I wrote this to you. In writing this, I found the desires of my soul. Literature has given me my freedom. I pray that you can read through all my failures with a new perception, valuing them as lessons. Life is a learned experience which pushes me to try to be the best daddy I can be despite never learning what a daddy is supposed to be. Obstacles are a part of life. Every day will be a challenge. Challenges build character.

Push yourself to do things that you would never think that you could do. When I started writing this novel, I couldn't see the finish line. Loving you, wanting to provide a better life made me push myself to do something most black men don't have time to conceive dealing with the pressures that life already places on us. Being someone that's never been "normal," I tried to fit in, but God continued to make me uncomfortable, forcing me to change daily. When you start doing the same thing every day, you're preparing for death instead of living. Born to die. What's life if you don't live it. My only request in life or death is that you search for knowledge in everything that you do. Your grandmother raised me preaching a lot of things. I hold on dearly to "When you know better, you do better!" Relative to her continually saying, "What you know no one can take from you!" From which I evolved writing something that I never thought in a million years that I would write, a novel. Love will make you do some crazy things. After reading this, I hope that you understand that no one will love you unless you love yourself. Never value someone else's love over loving you. Own your path in whatever world you create for yourself, trust your gut, and don't let anyone take you from your world.

I could say I love you until I'm blue in the face, being the man that started my own quote at twelve, "Words are words, what I like are verbs!" I invested two years of my life in faith, hoping to be the only man you ever need. I know what it means to need a daddy. I can't fix that, but I can make sure that I exhaust every avenue to prove to you how much being your daddy means to me. I love you. I want the world to love you like I do.

Love you,
Daddy

Special Child

"Momma, who invented time?"

One of the many questions that I would often ask your grandmother. Starting back as early as I could verbally communicate my own thoughts. My actual memory goes back as young as the age of two, when your grandmother tried to rekindle an old flame, leaving Kansas City to move back to Arkansas. I can see our cat like it was yesterday. Your grandmother named him Romeo after Shakespeare's *Romeo and Juliet*. She always had a book in her hand. Whenever she would be distracted by reading, I would chase after Romeo's tail. That cat was my first test in life. He was smarter than I was at the time. He discovered that if he went under the coffee table, that I was too stupid to stop my pursuit of his tail, causing me to bump my head. The pain on the soft spot of my head would stymie me to leaving him alone. She risked it all trying to believe in the Disney version of love, believing in her Prince Charming, who was destined to sweep her off her feet while overcoming all obstacles to prove his devout love. After two years of trying, the magic died, leaving her broke and jobless. When we moved back to Kansas City, she left Romeo in Arkansas. We moved in with her father (my grandfather). Having family that she could lean on gave her an opportunity to start over from scratch trying to reinvent herself and give me stability with a place of protection. A place where I could just be a normal kid. Surrounded by a village of children and a community of strong values. I forgot I was an only child. With the nature of the inner city beast around us. The nurture of the neighborhood had an energy all its own. On Twenty-Fourth and Wood, the community was united. Respect and fear were tools used to build the children's understandings in our neighborhood for our future. Even with vivid nightly dreams (which scared me sometimes because they seemed so real), my old soul was able to find peace. I was just another kid among many. I just felt like a special child.

My grandfather was a man who believed strongly in the word of God, named James Edward Weaver, known by all as Jack. His nickname personified he was a jack of all trades. Remarried to his new wife, Ester, who also had three of her youngest girls still living at home. Every day there were seven mouths to feed. My mom and I had moved into his basement and shared a room. Our quarters were just big enough for us both to have twin beds with enough space for a nightstand between the two beds where our heads laid. At the foot of my mom's bed, there was a television stand consisting of two milk crates where our nineteen-inch television sat on top of my mom's VCR. At the foot of my bed was a dresser that we split equally, the room seemed like it was divided, but it was more united. Your grandmother had a TV tray that fit between the beds that she used as a table. If she wasn't reading, she would spend time with me teaching me to play card games. Like a nervous tick, anytime I would say "I want," your grandmother's response was "People in hell want ice water." Which made me search for other words or ways to express myself in our room.

Outside the door to our room, my grandfather was inventive splitting the rest of his basement into multiple use rooms. Next to our room was a laundry room / playroom /overflow closet. The space directly outside our bedroom door was turned into a makeshift closet for hanging clothes only. My two older aunts, Nora and Leah, kept the two upstairs rooms. In most houses it would have been considered the attic because the roof was immediately above the rooms. Nora was a teenager, and Leah was preteen, so they stayed isolated upstairs. The only time I saw them was dinner or when they wanted control of the living room television. On the main floor, the living room couches were covered in plastic. Floor runners covered the carpet from the door through the living to the kitchen. It was all around the dining room table, continuing a path to the bedrooms on the north side of the house. My grandfather's only daughter with Ester had a room directly across the hallway from the master bedroom being the youngest in the house. Between the rooms was a full bathroom.

Daily, our home was full, especially if anyone came to visit or play. In the summer, my other three aunts (by my grandfather's first wife) would come visit, forcing Nora and Leah to share a room. While my three aunts Harper, Casey, and Vanessa from Arkansas split the last room in the house. Being the first boy born in the family in twenty years, I was enamored with women. Grandpa, being my only daily male role model, was the king of his domain. Like a lion, his seat positioned at the end of the dining room table was a central location where he could keep tabs on everything. Six feet tall with a slender build, he could hide behind an opened newspaper, only letting you know he was there by the turning of the page about every ten minutes. He worked the second shift at General Motors. He was usually up by 9:00 a.m. Sitting at the head of the table, reading the newspaper, drinking his coffee. By 9:30 a.m. he was on to paying bills. Some days at 10:00 a.m. he would take a two-hour nap. Most days he would just move from the bills to either a puzzle book solving crossword problems or an actual puzzle. It was normal to see a five-thousand-piece puzzle laid across one-half of the dining room table. Every day about one o'clock, he would get up from the table and fix his lunch, followed immediately by a shower. You could set your watch by his routine, after his shave and shower. He would sit back at the table dressed and ready for work. From 1:50 p.m. to 2:15 p.m., he would read his Bible before heading to the plant. On his days off between garage sales and flea markets, he was always working on an outside project. Looking back, it was like he stayed looking busy so his wife wouldn't give him something to do. With one child in common with Ester, he worked hard to provide for everyone. If overtime was offered, he was working it. During the cold winter months preparing for snow any given day, it was typically too cold to play outside. Luckily I had a live-in playmate.

My youngest aunt, whom I affectionately called Boo-Boo, was a year and four months younger than me. I chose her nickname from the cartoon that we watched daily. Seeing that Yogi was the leader, I saw myself as him, and I wanted a sidekick just like him. Never ever giving into my cartoon delusions, my aunt never called me Yogi. She in turned called me Bubba from one of her favorite shows, *The Beverly Hillbillies*. Most days we ate breakfast lying on a floor runner, watching television as we ate our cereal. After our bellies were full, we would try to watch cartoons as long as we could. If we remained quiet, we could watch until one of Ester's soap operas came on. Once either *As the World Turns, Another World,* or *All My Children* came on, we were banished from the living room, left to our own devices. Most days we would end up downstairs playing in the basement, outside the room shared by your grandmother and me. We felt the only way to keep fairness between us was to let her pick our games or toys one day and me the next. She was a girly girl just like you, Vanessa. She loved dolls and dress up. She was big into Barbie. This meant that to get her to play He-man, GI-Joe, or A-team with me, I had to play with her dolls and occasionally play dress-up with her. Luckily, because we were too young to protect ourselves, we played in our basement, where none of the other kids in the neighborhood knew that I fairly split days to play either being dressed by Boo-Boo to whatever her liking, playing with Barbie dolls or playing with the paper dolls that you could change their clothes because they were only maintained by tabs folded over in specific spots. We both had to be in control, being two people that liked to control all the rules. We also had to be someone who followed all the rules. We could only play with each other if the rules stayed fair.

Summertime the temperatures of Kansas City could grow extreme, boasting temperatures averaging 90 to 110 all summer long. Every day me and Boo-Boo played outside we ended up wet from the water hose. We weren't allowed to go in the house more than three times before we had to stay there. Ester kept tabs, reminding us, "I don't pay to cool the outside." Being quick learners, we learned to drink water from the water hose, which always turned into us playing in the water. My grandfather being a forward thinker invested in a swimming pool. In actuality, it was a huge circle metal trough with a half-inch plug. It would take hours to fill and drain, but in the summers, it got us out the basement. As young as we were, it was genius. We could have twelve kids our size swimming at the same time. All

I COULD'VE BEEN

the neighborhood kids saw it as a pool, not a horse trough. With the slope of the hill in the backyard, it created a deep side of three feet and a shallow side with a little over a foot of water. Allowing any kid to find a comfort zone. The only real problem that we ever had was getting in and out on a sunny day. If we didn't wet the side we got out of, we could burn ourselves on the metal. It was our childhood utopia making us the most popular kids in the neighborhood being the only house for ten miles with a "pool."

With summer winding down, I grew eager for the new school year, until your grandmother learned that in the State of Kansas, you have to be five years old before August 1 to start school. Since my birthday was in October, I couldn't start until the following year. Two months and six days kept me from starting school when your grandmother expected. She felt that I was prepared and stayed on the principal at Chelsea. After school started, your grandmother gave me an hour each day to teach me something new. Your grandma made sure she instilled some commonsense rules to help me survive when I did get to attend school. Most of it was simple moral principles: treat people the way you want to be treated, don't hit anybody unless they hit you first and then whoop their butt. Lastly, don't lie. She told me that if I told the truth, she would defend me. If I lied to get out of trouble, she swore the punishment I got at home would be the worst ever. Since one of her favorite saying was "I brought you into this world, so I can take you out," I didn't want to press my luck.

After my birthday, time flew so fast, I spent any spare time playing hide-and-seek with Boo-Boo. I was sent to Oklahoma to my aunt Vanessa's house for Thanksgiving. It was the first trip I made anywhere without your grandmother. The day after Thanksgiving, my aunt Vanessa had to call your grandmother because I refused to eat leftovers. After the phone call, my aunt had her husband drive us to McDonald's despite his discernment. When I returned back to Kansas City, the Christmas tree was up with tons of presents underneath. Every day when the adults weren't looking, Boo-Boo and I would shake the boxes to guess what might be in them. Each day the massive pile of gifts grew until Christmas eve. Christmas day Boo-Boo and I spent hours opening our gifts as we revisited our guesses before opening anything. After Christmas we both were spoiled with so many gifts that we had plenty to occupy us anytime we were told "Go play!" through the cold winter months. When summer came around again, the popularity of the only pool in the hood flooded my grandfather's backyard with kids. The rules of the neighborhood were when you were at someone's house, you followed their rules. So just like Boo-Boo and I, anyone swimming with us drank out of the water hose when they were thirsty. We could have so much company that we could stay in the pool from 11:00 a.m. until the sun started setting, rotating friends around their parents' schedules like a neighborhood day care.

Happily entering school in the fall, Boo-Boo lost her daytime playmate for me to attend Chelsea Elementary right down the street from the house. I thought my teacher was the sweetest, smartest person I'd ever met. Mrs. Brooks had a birthday cake on the wall for each of her students. For the life of me, I could not remember my birthday. Every morning before I got out of your grandmother's car, I would ask, "Momma, when is my birthday?" I would get out her car heading straight to class. The only problem I had was retaining the month and day through the announcements and the pledge of allegiance. For several months I tried daily to obtain my birthday cake cutout. Inverting the month and the day, totally forgetting the year. One day Mrs. Brooks gave us the opportunity to earn our cakes one day after lunch. I had been trying for so long I broke out into tears when I couldn't get it right. When the rest of the class went to recess, she let me stay behind and worked with me. She became concerned that I was possibly dyslexic and started spending extra time with me on getting the date correct. It only took me seven months to get it right. After school I caught the bus to the boy and girls club on Ninth and Minnesota as my after-school day care until your grandmother got off work. From three until six Monday through Friday, I played pool by myself in the game room, while the other kids stayed downstairs. With only two adults to watch ten kids, I was allowed to play upstairs alone. Once every half hour, one of the adults would check on my safety. After being picked up by your grandmother at 6:15 p.m., we normally would pick up fast food to make the evening easier. Ester, like my grandfather, was from Arkansas and she cooked like it. Your grandmother loved me too much to make me eat livers and onions, chitterlings, or whatever my grandfather had time to kill. His country motto was "If you kill it, you eat it."

Over the summer my grandfather discovered that I was too tall to ride on his knee like my auntie and cousins my age. Whenever it was more than four of us, he would sit us on his knee, grab the back of our shirts, and try to make us fall off his knee. We called it rodeo. Being too tall to participate, he had to find something else to keep me engaged. Knowing that he was responsible for teaching us as children how to be better and more successful than he was, he started teaching Boo-Boo and me about money. He would pay us to do simple tasks around the house. On Fridays, he would take us to 7-Eleven to spend what we had earned. My grandfather was very generous in his payment. My aunt Boo-Boo would spend every dime, while I was stingy spending my money. It got to the point that I had fifty dollars at six years old. My grandfather's lesson wasn't going over on me so well. He started inviting me to join Ester and him for their hobby of garage sales. He kept a pen nearby whenever he would read the newspaper to circle the sales. On Saturdays he would wake me at five in the morning trying to make every garage sale first. He was constantly trying to encourage me to spend what I earned, but I would have no part in it. I liked the way the money looked more than what was for sale. My grandfather's determination to teach me that money wasn't as important as people went unsatisfied. Refusing to be defeated, he started taking me to swap meets, trying to give me more options to spend my money on. We could spend hours walking up and down the aisles for me to spend less than five dollars. The only thing he could get me to spend money on was baseball cards.

Your grandma was stuck in her country ways and didn't trust banks. She kept three piggy banks. They were all shaped like cats. She used one for silver dollars; one for quarters, dimes, and nickels; and the last one for pennies. Every day she got home from work, she emptied her pockets, going straight to the piggy banks. Seeing her daily practice made me want to save my money. It was what I saw from your grandma. She worked, paid her bills, and saved the rest. Even though your grandma was living with her father, Ester was determined to make sure that no adult got a free ride in her house.

Your grandma was working for a company called CECO. Working 8:00 a.m. to 5:30 p.m. When she wasn't at work, she had all eyes on me for most of the evening until she was ready to wind down with a book. She kept a bookshelf of the books that she had conquered and finished, announcing almost daily that she had finished another one, adding it to the bookshelf. Every couple of weeks she would get a new box of books. Her favorite books to read were romance novels. She would constantly share with me the stories of her books and the sacrifices made for real love. She could easily spend three or four hours a night reading with the touch light between our beds on the lowest setting possible while I slept.

Monday through Friday I learned morality and integrity playing with Boo-Boo. She taught me that my feelings weren't more important than hers. Right was right. If it came out of your mouth, you better be ready to stand on it. Early in my childhood she taught me that my word represented me. Without standing on my promises, she refused to play with me. We were both stubborn and pigheaded with what we learned from the Southern influences in our lives. Every day we negotiated equality and fairness in order to play together. After a year and a half of playing with my militant auntie, I was convicted with principles and refused to let anyone play with mine.

With all the women in the house, my grandfather had one son. My uncle would stop by once a week just to see me. He was a rebel that didn't fear rules or laws. On one of his visits, he bought me a cap gun and some plastic boats. While he taught me to steady my hand by taking a breath before pulling the trigger, he was also sharing his beer with me. I didn't like the taste of the of it. I did like the power I felt squeezing the trigger. My uncle would line the boats up near the bushes to catch the ricochet if I missed, but I was a sure shot at six years old. He was so impressed with my shooting that he started inviting friends over to wager on me to hit the target from multiple distances. My neighbor Jacob would always appear out of nowhere when my uncle came around. My uncle always included him, making him my instant friend.

I COULD'VE BEEN

If I wasn't playing inside with Boo-Boo, I was out exploring the neighborhood with Jacob. He was a year older and more exposed to the neighborhood. His mother, Mrs. Stark, was a beautician. She turned her dining room into her salon. With dozens of women a day in and out of his house, he was around salon talk regularly, unless his mother, Emma, caught him eavesdropping, trying to be grown. Then she would send him outside to play until the streetlights came on, using whatever we could to entertain ourselves. Grocery store paper bags seemed to entertain us the most. We would tear the bags and make planes or dice. If we could sneak scissors out the house, we would cut it and make cards. After stretching a paper bag into more entertainment than you could ever imagine, we eventually ran out of ideas and started emulating our parents rolling up the paper bags into cigarettes. It started as a contest of whose cigarette was the biggest. After mastering every way possible to outdo each other, Jacob decided that fake smoking was cool, but we needed a lighter. I was okay with fake smoking, but Jacob wasn't satisfied. Raised to always make people prove what they say, I snuck in the back door. I headed downstairs to your grandma's stash of lighters. When I got back outside, Jacob lit his bag. He hit it four times without a hitch, encouraging me to join him. We played as if we were gangsters like Al Capone or Bugsy Calhoun. Ester saw us from the kitchen window and yelled for us to pick our switches off the weeping willow tree. We lined up for our punishment. Of course I was first. She took her time cleaning the switch of any extra leaves with my backside to her. When she finished, she tore me a new behind. The whole time she was spanking me I was saying, "But you do it," which made her even more upset. She realized that every Sunday and Wednesday, when she took Boo-Boo and me to church, I was paying attention to the pastor's examples of leading people to Christ through actions and works. I also wasn't afraid to call her out. She couldn't even spank Jacob after that. She took his switch and walked him next door. After spending about ten minutes inside talking with Mrs. Stark, I didn't see Jacob for a week. The rest of my summer I spent attending church whenever Ester went. She was the lead usher and had to get to church before anyone else to make sure that it was set for service. She also was the last to leave, making sure that whatever messes were made were cleaned. With three out of seven days a week, I was her tagalong since I was trying to use the preacher to save my behind.

Your grandmother took me to class on my first day of first grade. The teacher had put name tags on the desk. Her instructions were to find our seats. I walked around the class until every seat was full. There was only one desk left with a name tag. I refused to sit at the desk because it didn't say Chris. My teacher pulled out her roster. As I broke down in tears, she said, "Christopher Drake." With your grandmother seeing me crying she came to me. Seeing the desk, she explained that it was my name on the desk, my full name, Christopher. I cried and carried on until my teacher made me a new name tag that only said Chris. My first-grade teacher was Mrs. Morris. She was very plain and looked like a giant doll. Her hair was cut perfectly at shoulder length. Her skirt was always matching her blouse and shoes. She looked like she went home to a giant doll house. She never seemed happy or able to smile. Distracted like most first graders, it didn't take me long to understand that Mrs. Morris's face kept the same expression no matter her mood. Like a doll, she had one facial expression. My first-grade school year was great. Recess twice a day was the best part. On Tuesdays and Thursdays, we had our "special classes," rotating gym, choir, and art. My favorite extra was gym. It was the coolest class in the school. Our teacher bought juggling scarves and taught us all to juggle. He kept us with new games that taught us cool stuff every class.

A few months into first-grade year, your grandmother met a man named Bill. He was a truck driver by occupation. Even though he was barely six feet tall, he was strong and intimidating. The rough ride of the road made his shell hard, making him a real tough guy. I was afraid of him until he started spending time with me doing things I liked to do. He was out of town all week. On the weekends he would take me to see his horse, Spooky. Anytime the weather was nice enough, he would put a saddle on him and let me ride. After Bill educated me on Spooky's diet and grooming, he could do no wrong in my eyes. We went to visit Spooky almost every weekend. Bill was truly a cowboy in spirit. He was also a forward thinker like

I COULD'VE BEEN

my grandfather. He was leery of the grocery store, paranoid of the government's FDA.

With the resources around him, he decided to start his own garden in the back of his mother's house. He already owned the plot of land directly behind her house. The house that once existed had been cleared for years, and it was a vacant lot. His father had raised chickens, producing his own eggs, when Bill was a kid and the coops were still standing and in decent shape. Being the mastermind he was, he decided to make use of the old chicken coops, repurposing them for rabbits. After we spent a weekend reassuring the cages, he went to the City Market, the largest outdoor market in Kansas City. We started with a male and female Flemish giant. My job was to feed the rabbits on Saturday and Sunday morning at 6:00 a.m. It started with me filling a ten-gallon bucket half full of rabbit feed to carry to their trough. With my weekdays consumed with school, I was always shocked when I showed up and there were new rabbits. After reconditioning the rest of the cages, Bill bought another male and female New Zealand red hair. He segregated the rabbits by pedigree, saying, "They have to be purebred to be worth anything." I was too consumed with school to realize how fast rabbits multiply. I just know that we started the first day of spring. By the end of May, when school let out, we had almost forty rabbits.

Since it was summer, your grandma decided that she would split her time between his mother's house and her father's house. Which in turn split my time as well. Every morning I had to carry fifty pounds of rabbit feed on my shoulders to the cages. I learned to tear the corner of the bag and pick it up, pouring the feed in the troths. Allowing me to feed all the rabbits in ten minutes. The city finally demolished the house next to Bill's mother's house, clearing the land. As fast as they could clear out the trash dumpster, Bill bought it. The neighborhoods in downtown Kansas City, Missouri, were full of vacant lots where houses were burned down and later demolished by the city. Now between Bill and his brother, who lived next to his mother, they owned half of the block. Bill's brother had a ten-foot privacy fence around his oasis. Bill didn't believe in fences; he believed in guns. After investing in a walk-behind tiller, he started in the plot of land behind the house. He would wake me every morning to feed the rabbits while he went down the hill to turn the ground. After more than a few morning of the same routine, I went to report that the rabbits were fed and watered. Bill stopped the tiller, and he walked me back up the hill, handing me yard gloves, with two new ten-gallon buckets, with a stick as wide as my shoulders. He said, "I need the rabbit shit to fertilize the garden." He instructed me that he needed me to crawl under the cages and collect the rabbit feces in the buckets. After filling the buckets, he told me that I needed to carry them downhill to him so he could get the ground ready for things that had a short harvest. More importantly, he was starting to prepare the ground for next year. Bill negotiated with his job to only deliver loads that would allow him to be home in the evenings. All summer long I would awake at 6:00 a.m. to feed the rabbits with him. After we finished, he would head to work. I only had to go under the cages when Bill had time to work the land. After your grandmother kissed Bill goodbye, she would drive me from Missouri to Kansas to my grandfather's before she headed to work. After work, she would come get me, and we would head back to Missouri to Bill's mother's house. Every time we would pull up to him always in the garden, which would put me back to work until sundown.

  The house was huge, right in the heart of downtown Missouri. Three stories above ground as well as a basement. The front porch was a beautiful open design that covered the full width of the house. Past the French doors was one of the most immaculate handrails I had ever seen, hand crafted. It appeared to be one solid oak log from the first floor to the second. The stairs were immediately to the right of the door. To the left was the living room. If you walked the hallway from the foyer, it led you past a restroom to the kitchen. Pass the bathroom, if you took the path to the left, it would lead you to Bill's mother's room. The other side of that hallway was a locked door to the basement. The second floor consisted of four bedrooms and a bathroom despite having six doors. The sixth door was a small twisted stairway up to the third floor, which was one room with a one-half bath. It was Bill's room. Splitting my time between houses, my room was on the second floor. Bill's niece had recently

I COULD'VE BEEN

moved in with her father, which left one room available. Bill moved his daughter, Hazel, into his mother's house as well, giving her the last room in the house. Bonding with the girls playing games, they became my family. They couldn't replace Boo-Boo or the neighborhood, but they were my new daily companions. With the summer ending and the garden preparation for next spring winding down, I was exhausted of daily 6:00 a.m. wake-ups. Your grandmother told me that I was going to be sleeping at my grandfather's house because school was starting. She said, "Some nights you might be at home without me, but Grandpa will be right upstairs." I was so tired of rabbits and rabbit poo I didn't care. I wasn't afraid to stay in the room I normally shared with her by myself. As school started, she decided that getting to work would be easier from home. Staying with me all week. As luck would have it, my second-grade teacher was Mrs. Morris again. Knowing how she operated her class, I was excited for the school year. On Friday after school, your grandmother told me that they were giving me a Saturday off from my duties for Bill to take her to the hospital. She said, "To make things easier. I'm going to spend the night at Bill's house." She sat on her bedside reading until I fell asleep.

Born to be Wild

The next morning, I awoke to the rambunctious playing of Boo-Boo and Mya, Jacob's sister. They were playing hide-and-seek in the basement, which had five rooms. Our bedroom, two storages one on both sides of the stairs. Half of one of those storage rooms was filled with the furnace and water heater. There was also laundry room with clothes that hung from the ceiling around the room. Minus the washer and dryer on one side and the deep freezer and refrigerator on the other, it was like a giant walk-in closet because clothes hung on the opposite wall as well. Leaving a perfect four-foot walkway or play area in between. On the left side of the room under the hanging clothes was one of the biggest toy boxes ever. My grandfather made it by hand. There was also a bathroom with a shower that had a three-quarters brick wall separating the shower from the toilet and sink. My grandfather explained that since there wasn't proper ventilation, he couldn't build the wall to the ceiling. He said the heat from the shower needed a place to escape. The privacy door for the restroom was the same for the shower. When you opened the bathroom door, you blocked the entry to the shower. Knowing all the good hiding spots, I joined their game of hide-and-seek. When it was my turn to hide, I chose the bathroom.

Mya counted, "One, two, three…ten. Ready or not, here I come." It took her literally three minutes to find Boo-Boo hiding in the toy box. Teaming together, they searched everywhere for me. Even taking a quick look in the bathroom. Remaining undetected, I was hiding quietly in the shower. They continued to search until Boo-Boo heard me laugh. When they figured out that I was in there, I was able to hold the hook on the back of the door to keep them out. Boo-Boo refusing to accept defeat, she changed the game to hold me

I COULD'VE BEEN

in the shower. After a standoff of what seemed to be an eternity, I got bored, realizing that they couldn't tag me standing in the shower. I decided to succumb to their game change. With both off them leaning on the door, I couldn't overpower them to escape. Refusing to submit, I decided to be wild and climb over the wall to prove my dominance. Just as I had one leg over the wall, it collapsed. At the mercy of the wall between my legs, I fell in the direction that the wall collapsed. I felt my left leg touch the ground before the collapsing concrete split it in two.

Being a jokester, I was always telling Grandpa that one thing or another was broken. When both Mya and Boo-Boo ran upstairs to inform him of my unfortunate accident, he didn't move a muscle. They both returned to me twice as frantic, saying, "He said quit playing!" It was hard for him to believe.

I looked my aunt directly in the eyes and said, "Boo-Boo, go back to my grandpa, tell him it's serious this time." It didn't take but a second before he and his wife came down to see the bone poking at my skin as if it wanted to penetrate it. My grandfather carefully scooped me up in his arms. Cradling me to his chest, he carried me to his Cadillac. Ester sat in the back seat. My grandfather laid me across the back seat with my head in her lap and drove me to the nearest hospital. I calmly listened to everything they said as I stared at the ceiling of the car. Reaching Bethany hospital, I still had not shed a tear. My grandfather pulled directly to the curb. He ran into the hospital, and seconds later, he was being followed out by a nurse with a hospital bed. After carefully placing me on the hospital bed, they rolled me to the emergency room waiting area. In a circle of rooms all divided by curtains, as luck would have it, your grandmother was already there to be seen for a serious sinus infection. She looked down the emergency room bay and noticed my shoes. Trusting her gut, she walked down the bay, pulling back the curtain. We were both shocked to see each other. Thinking she would be disappointed, I cried. The shock had carried me almost an hour without a tear, but as soon as I saw your grandmother, the tears ran like a faucet. After x-rays, the doctors announced to my family that I had broken my femur. He explained that after surgery, I would need to remain at the hospital for at least two months. With the placement of the break, they were going to install a pin in my leg to relieve the stress and allow it to heal faster. At the age of seven I was sequestered from all my friends as I laid in a hospital bed with my leg hanging in the air. Grandma still had to work. The hospital became her second home around her schedule. Every ten days I went for an x-ray. On my third x-ray, the doctor said that my leg was healing faster than expected. Twenty-one days later I was released from the hospital. School was already a few months underway. I was in a cast from my left ankle all the way to my waist. I was gifted a wheelchair that Grandma's insurance provided. Unable to attend school in my wheelchair, my school gave Grandma resources to get me a home school teacher to keep me caught up with my teacher's curriculum.

Home school was great. Because of my wheelchair, my grandfather gave me Boo-Boo's room, while she slept in his room with Ester at night while he was working. Her room became my everything. As my classroom, the one-on-one setting showed my teacher all my strengths; however, it also exposed my weaknesses. My teacher had me tested for dyslexia. Her encouragement and patience helped me to work on it, and soon she taught me to manage it. She discovered that half of the problem was that I needed glasses. I had an astigmatism which effected my reading as well. Home school lasted about four months before my cast was reduced, and I converted from the wheel chair to crutches. Just before Valentine's Day, I got my cast removed. I returned to class and started rehab three days after Valentine's Day on Monday. It was easy for me to find comfort in the classroom because Ms. Morris had not changed a bit. Her even-keeled personality kept the classroom calm. She did seem to perk up when we played classroom Jeopardy. She really went all out for the game. With five school categories to choose from. Some of the questions exposed my dyslexia. We were split into two teams with two buzzers. Racing against my classmates made me feel socially awkward. If the person buzzed in before you and got the question right, you were out of the game. Not being one to accept defeat, I could survive until she wrote an English question on the board. Every time it would put me out the game to a classroom full of laughs. Since she knew something about me, I went to school every day with a purpose to make her smile. My daily attempts eventually landed me in the principal's office. After that, I tried to stay off her radar.

As my leg grew in strength, your grandmother had two ideas. Her first idea, I think, was to defy Bill. She enrolled me in karate class. Which filled my schedule two days a week on Tuesdays and Thursdays. She also thought roller skating would be great exercise for both of us. Trusting her more than I trusted anyone, I had no reason to argue. We started going skating every Saturday morning, even though it was time to start tending to the garden. The weather bought me the first few weeks in March. Our first snow of the year was late January, which your grandmother said was the reason for March snow. I blamed the groundhog for seeing his shadow. After I got my GI, the traditional karate class uniform, my desire to be accepted shined in class. Sensei Penny would use me for all her demonstrations, giving me a front row seat to her knowledge. She would always say, "Force is not a sign of strength but rather a sign of weakness." She brought to life the concept of energy and control of energy. Doing more damage with a punch from two inches than with a fully extended punch. As the person whom she demonstrated on, it gave me complete understanding. "Karate is not to attack. It is to defend." The class taught me to anticipate potential dangers. We started each class with the greeting we were taught followed by ten different stances. As we did each position, we counted in Japanese. *Ichi, ni, san, shi, go, ruku, shichi, hachi, kyuu, juu.* Every day I learned something new. Halfway through my five weeks of classes, your grandmother came to pick me up from class, saying the weather man projected no more winter weather. Which meant this weekend it would be back to work in the garden. After I started back in the garden, I made Grandma promise that if I kept my grades up that she would continue to take me skating. Every Saturday, I would wake at 5:45 a.m. to be outside at 6:00 a.m. With the amount of rabbits we now had, I carried two fifty-pound bags to the cages. One on each shoulder. My disgust for rabbit poo was gone. Bill's moto sang in the back of my head. "It's a job, someone got to do it. If you're going to do it, be the best." During the week with school still in progress, Bill's brother fed the rabbits. Which allowed me to make all my karate classes. With no one going under the cages but me, every Saturday it was so much poop that I could make five trips down the hill. My new understanding of discipline taught me that pain and strength were in the mind. With my new mental conditioning, I would rush to finish as fast as I could. Most Saturdays I could be finished and in the shower by 9:00 a.m. With the skating session being from 10:00 a.m. until 3:00 p.m., I found a way to do both.

After a couple of weeks skating forward, admiring all the skaters that could skate backward, I begged Clark, who was the Skateland DJ, to teach me how to skate backward. Being blessed as a fast learner, I was able to figure it out with a few minutes of explanation from Clark. Your grandmother couldn't skate backward either. While I mastered it right away, she struggled. With a new skill in my bag, it allowed me to flirt with all the girls in the skating rink. When I wasn't skating backward, winking at girls, my rehab coach had helped me build my strength to be one of the fastest skaters my age. With the skater community being small, my new talents allowed me to make a lot of friends. Every Saturday I would see this same beautiful young lady. Not being shy when it came to flirting, I skated up to her, asking her name. Not knowing what to do next, I skated off as she told me her name was Lisa. She chased me around the rink until she got close enough to me to ask me my name. She became my Saturday skate buddy. She was just as competitive as me, playing every game Skateland played. More often than not she was the person I would be competing with at the end of red light, green light. I would be the person she was competing with in the limbo. I couldn't do the splits like her, which made me admire her and want to learn. With all my basement playtime, I didn't see it as just for girls. Lisa practiced with me until I to could do the splits on skates. I could never get all the way split, but I could get low enough to be one of the last three. Realizing that I couldn't win every game, hating to lose at anything, I decided to work/referee the games. Using my friendship with Clark, who announced the games over the microphone, I was able to work any game I wanted.

I COULD'VE BEEN

With school almost out for the summer, Cole, my neighbor from across the street, came over to play. He told me that he could not stay long because he had baseball practice. Being someone who always wanted to be a part of things, I asked my grandma Ester while she was on the phone, "Can I go with Cole Hall?" Off of the last name alone, she said, "Yes." His father was a pastor whom she trusted. Knowing my mom would not get off until six, I knew I would be back before she got home. The team was a part of the city youth initiative. When the coaches signed up to be a coach, the league provided jerseys to them. I sat in the bleachers as they took the field for practice. With parents still working, there were only eight players at practice, so no one was in right field.

As the coach hit the ball around, it kept getting past the first and second baseman. After the fourth time of someone having to chase the ball into right field, the coach saw me sitting in the stands and asked, "Son, do you want to play baseball?"

Excited, I said, "Yes, but I don't have a glove."

He told his son who was on the pitcher's mound to get me a glove. After I got my glove, he told me to go to right field. He said, "Don't let the ball get past you. When you get it, throw it towards home plate, where I am." Standing in right field, the bugs were really bothering me. I was no better than the empty position that he started with. When I chased down the first baseball hit my way, I did exactly as I was instructed. I picked up the ball and threw it as hard as I could. Never having aimed before, I threw the ball into the bleachers. Coach Brown, impressed with the distance of my throw, said, "Good job," as he sent the catcher (who was shaking his head) to chase down my wild throw. Once the catcher returned with the ball, he purposely hit it to me again. Afraid of the ball, I avoided it until it stopped rolling. Picking it up, I tried to put every ounce of me into tossing it to him. I went to throw the ball to home plate, but as it slipped out of my hand, I threw the ball behind me. Everyone on the team laughed except the coach. He encouraged me to pick it up and try again. Upset after the laughs, I threw the ball so hard. Still without guidance. It took two hops and the coach's son caught it on the pitcher's mound. As the other players showed up, he moved me to the dugout. After practice, I got a uniform. He told me to hold on to the glove and bring it to the next practice. Knowing your grandmother's love for me, I knew if I told my her that I made the team she couldn't say no. Her only rebuttal was my commitment to Bill and the garden. With an agreement that I would not let baseball interfere with Saturday mornings in the garden, she agreed to let me play.

With a couple of practices under my belt with more than a few batting attempts, I still had not lost my fear for being hit with the ball. As I stood in the batter's box running from every pitch, Coach Brown realized that I would do whatever he asked, so he stopped practice, instructing the catcher to remove his gear, telling me to put it on. Petrified but wanting his approval, I did as I was instructed. He said, "The only way to lose fear of the ball is to be hit with the ball. So you are going to play catcher for the rest of practice." As I crouched behind the plate, I brought my fear with me. I would take off running as soon as the batter started to swing his bat. Coach Brown, committed to ridding me of my fear, grabbed an umpire's mask and crouched behind me like an umpire. He said, "All I have is a mask, son. If you let me get hit, you're going to run all the way home." Knowing that he was our ride, I tried my hardest to protect him. Some of his son's pitches were so fast that I couldn't help my desire to run. With Coach holding me in place like I was his shield, it happened. A ball bounced right in front of the plate, out of the dirt, and hit me square in my nuts. He tried to hold me up as I buckled in pain. Most of the team felt my pain and groaned for me. The pain took my voice away. Coach, realizing what happened, let me go. Hitting the dirt in agony, I flopped around like a fish out of water. On the ride home, he let me sit in the front seat. The next practice I told him that I wanted to be a catcher. With only twelve players on the team, he started training me for the backup. Listening to everything Coach Brown said, I became a decent catcher. By the end of the year, I got the start by default. Our other catcher got hurt. Knowing that my team was counting on me, you could have thought I was the starter all along. I had already faced the worst thing that could happen. I went from scared rookie to fearless vet in our ten-week season.

I COULD'VE BEEN

With the baseball season over, the garden was in full bloom because Grandma gave me what I wanted and let me play baseball. I couldn't say no when she said that we were going to spend the last few weeks of the summer at Bill's mother's house. Bill was still driving his truck around the city even though the money was better for the out-of-town trips. The money kept calling, pushing him to more and more overnight trips. With him not able to be there all the time, the garden became my primary responsibility. With the harvest time almost near, all I had to do was feed the rabbits, pull some weeds, and irrigate the garden. Bill already had the water system set up, I just had to turn the water on and off and switch two different hoses from the original hose. Over the summer, the rabbits had multiplied. Now there was over two hundred rabbits of eight different breeds. With Bill's math of a pound of food per rabbit, I was carrying four fifty-pound bags of rabbit feed every day. He had created a compost area at the bottom of the hill for their poop. When I told him that he had been through a pallet of rabbit feed, he lost his mind. The next time I saw Bill, he was separating the males from the females. On Saturday, we hung fliers that said, "Rabbits for sale for 10 dollars live or 20 dollars gutted and clean." Against murder, on Sunday, when Bill had time to be in the garden with me, I voiced my disdain. My voice and opinion were not appreciated, earning me a butt whooping from Bill. Your grandmother sometimes would ground me or spank me with a switch from the weeping willow tree in Grandpa's backyard. Bill thought that was too small for me. He found a wooden paddle and drilled holes in it that he used to punish me. The quiver in my cry with his third swat at my bottom made your grandmother upset. She jumped between his arm and my butt, saying, "DON'T YOU HIT MY SON AGAIN." From that day forward, your grandmother dished out the punishment.

The garden was ripe with so many fruits and vegetables that we had planted. The next Saturday we worked hard all day pulling weeds, running new irrigation lines. Bill had been designing a new pipe fitting that he thought would help cut down the watering time. He said, "Tomorrow we will harvest tomatoes, beans, peppers, cucumber, strawberries, and all beans. Next weekend we will harvest the corn, all the melons, onions, potatoes, squash, zucchini, and anything I forgot." Eager to be finished for the summer, I couldn't wait. Wrapping up the day, excited for tomorrow, we headed up the hill toward the house. As we walked, he asked, "Do you think you could break a rabbit's neck?" I replied no. It didn't stop him. Apparently, he had made some changes in the cages. He had two cages of the adult rabbits. One of males from different breeds. Also one of the females of different breeds. Putting his gloves back on, he reached into the female cage. Grabbing a red hare by the neck, holding her right in front of my face, he broke her neck. Since he couldn't spank me anymore, he had to show me who's the boss. Trying to be his son, I watched as he pulled his pocketknife. He slid his knife under the skin of the rabbit, rendering it hairless, and removed his head. As he gutted the rabbit, I puked. After he stopped laughing, he said, "This is life, get used to it. If it wasn't this rabbit, it would be a chicken or cow." With that rationality, I tried to help him skin them. It was just really hard skinning animals I had just named a few weeks ago.

Sunday dinner at his mother's house was a scheduled event. The entire family knew that his mother always had dinner ready by 4:00 p.m. With the harvest finished, Bill was laid up in his room on the third floor waiting on dinner to be prepared. Every Sunday after church, his mother would start cooking. No kids were allowed in the kitchen ever. When we tried the excuse of wanting something to drink, his mother would say, "There is a water hose outside." Not having any energy because we worked from sun up to sundown Saturday, the girls and I were allowed to watch the television while Mrs. Dunson prepared dinner. Smelling the grease getting hot, I walked toward the kitchen and asked, "What's for dinner, Mrs. Grey?"

She said, "Fried chicken, mashed potatoes, and green beans."

Then I was quickly sent out of the kitchen back to play with the girls.

With my stomach touching my back, all I could think about was food. As the smells of dinner started to permeate the air, something didn't smell normal. I love chicken. I also love mashed potatoes. As we sat around the table, Mrs. Grey fixed our plates. Today with every spoon she scooped on my plate, it smelled as if someone

I COULD'VE BEEN

had farted. I leaned in to try and to smell the spoon. The pungent odor seemed to be coming from the bowl. After we blessed the food, I dug in to the potatoes hard and immediately spit them back on the plate, exclaiming, "Those are not mashed potatoes!" Mrs. Grey broke her own rule and argued with a child.

She said, "Yes, they are, now shut up and eat!"

Being a child, I didn't go back to them but instead picked up my piece of the beautifully fried chicken leg. I took the biggest bite I could. After the taste hit my tongue, I immediately spit that out too! One of the rules in her house was you couldn't get up from the table unless you were completely done or full. After dinner, the refrigerator was off-limits until breakfast. Knowing that it was not even 6:00 p.m. and breakfast would be at least twelve hours, I took my chances and excused myself from the table. Going upstairs, I told my mom, "I don't know what that was, but it's not fried chicken or mashed potatoes."

To which Bill replied, "You're right, it was squash and rabbit."

I spent the next four hours in the bathroom washing my mouth out and brushing my teeth, swearing to never eat another meal in his mother's house again.

Monsters Aren't Born, They're Created

Third grade was beginning, and my teacher had a reputation for being the meanest teacher in the school. Mrs. Crew was an urban legend among students. Legend had it that she was a witch who kidnapped bad kids and tortured them in her basement. The stories were passed down from her previous classes, provoking even the bad kids act good in her class. Most of the kids who survived her class affectionately called her Mrs. Crew-Ella. My first day of class once laying eyes on her, I was convinced that all the rumors were true.

The third day after school, I got home, did my homework, and went next door to Mrs. Stark's house. Her shop was always busy. Trying to be respectful, I didn't speak to Mrs. Stark because she was having a conversation. As I tried to pass her to enter Jacob's room, Mrs. Stark said, "Excuse me, did I sleep with you last night?" After she explained that I needed to speak when I walked into her house, I was embarrassed. Fearful of never letting that happen again, I started speaking to everyone everywhere. When I got to Jacob's room, the Atari distracted me from my fear-filled living room experience. As we started playing Atari, Jacob informed me that he couldn't play long today because he was starting football practice. Grandpa was already gone to work and not wanting to call my mom, so I did the next best thing. I ran next door and asked Ester. Instead of asking if I could go to football practice, because I knew she would say no, I simply asked if I could go watch Jacob practice. She knew that I played baseball, so she didn't think twice about saying okay.

I COULD'VE BEEN

The team was for Jacob's age. When the coach saw my size, he recruited me. I told him that I was a year younger. He didn't believe me. Even though I was younger, my size was equal because of my garden work, and my core was solid from carrying rabbit feed and rabbit poop. Before I knew it I was walking in the house at 7:00 p.m. an hour after my mom got off with a full set of pads and a helmet. Your grandmother looked at me like not only no, but HELL NO! like I had lost my cotton-picking mind. All she could talk about was me braking my leg again. I begged and begged before she told me to let her sleep on it. Always a woman of her word, I knew it wasn't up for discussion the rest of the evening. The next morning before school, I took my chances with an inquiry. She said, "If you so much as twisted a muscle, you are done!" She also said that she had to meet the coach. Once she met Coach Green, it sealed the deal. Coach Green with his military background appealed to your grandmother's trust. With my grandfather having served in the air force, your grandmother felt like I was with family. With his positive, fun-loving energy, I had a role model. I wanted to be just like Coach. His beautiful wife and his beautiful family made me respect his every word.

Now Monday to Friday I would get out of school and try to finish my homework as fast as possible so that there was no interference in Coach Green's lessons in practice. In class I was learning that Mrs. Crew wasn't the witch everyone said. She was all about discipline, rules, and respect. She didn't joke around to keep her respect. As long as you followed her rules, class was a breeze. In practice, I was learning that other kids can be monsters. I didn't own a pair of football cleats, so while I waited for my mom to get paid, I wore the same cleats that I wore for baseball, which were worn and dusty. Every day between drills, someone had something to say about my cleats. My teammates joked on me for the first two weeks of practice, and even after I got cleats, they would remind me that I was only allowed in their club because coach said so, which made me work hard to prove myself. With direction and hard work, Coach Green made me look like an all-star because he taught good technique. Through my standout play in practice, I earned my respect. I rode to practice with Jacob and Dylan. Dylan was the biggest kid on the team. He was six feet tall, weighing almost three hundred pounds in the fourth grade. With us carpooling to and from practice, the talented athletes on the team accepted me and started sharing their knowledge. With all the jokes directed at me, I learned how to have tough skin. I also learned to joke very well myself.

    Coach Green coached me to play running back. He said, "The holes on the right are even numbers, and the holes on the left were odd numbers." He also taught me that when I ran to the right side, I made a basket with my left arm on top. When I ran to the left, I made a basket with my right arm on top. He explained that the quarterback needed a clear window to help prevent a fumble. I mostly learned how to block my first year. Coach was emphatic about keeping your legs moving whether you were blocking or running the ball. Even with limited carries, I listened to all the lessons he told Carson (our starting running back) and the other guys. He would always preach that running the ball was about patience, timing, and knowing when to explode through the hole. He would constantly jump in their face boot camp style, telling them if they got to the hole before the blockers got there, there was no point in running the ball. At our age group, 115 pounds was the maximum weight to play a skilled position. On a good day, I weighed 109. With that being the case, most of the teams we played would petition for me to weigh in before the game. More often than not on Saturday mornings before each game, Coach Green and I would run until I made weight. Ex-military, he could run all day smiling, which was helpful in the mile I would have to run in order to play my position. After a few weeks, we just started leaving the pads out of my pants until after I hit the scale. It only saved me two pounds, but it definitely made weigh-in easier. I actually made exact weight two times without a pregame workout. Wyco had nine baseball fields and two football fields. So if need be, we had plenty of running room.

    Most of the season I spent blocking for Carson, especially after my first touchdown running the wrong direction. Even after my mistake, Coach Green didn't give up on me. Maybe one out of ten plays the coach would call a play for me. When the quarterback handed me the ball, I would run for about seven yards before a huddle would form around me. I was so strong that the other kids couldn't get me to the ground. Being a "coach's kid," I did what he preached from day one, and I would never stop moving my legs. After being wrapped up, I could drag the other team about a yard or two before the refs would blow the whistle. My favorite part of football was the day after the game. Coach Green would invite the entire team to his house so that we could watch the game film. He was trying to prepare us for the next level by teaching us what to expect. He always kept the trash talk down as he taught us through film how to be better.

Even though I wasn't the most elusive running back in the league, between drills or water breaks, we as young men would always have some sort of competition. Thanks to baseball, I could throw the ball just as far as anyone on our team. As the season progressed, we discovered that I could kick the ball off the tee farther than anyone thanks to recess kickball, which got me promoted to kicker. Seeing my rubber band leg, Coach Green taught me how to punt the ball too. Kicking it was the easy part. Catching it from the scared center with his head between his legs trying to throw the ball twelve yards upside down and stand up before the defender pommels him was the hard part. The time Coach Green spent with me in practice paid off. When Coach found out about the punt-pass-and-kick contest, he urged your grandmother to let me participate. With the completion being on game day, we would already be there anyway, so she let me participate. Just as Coach expected, I blew the competition away in the kick and the pass. Not doing too bad in the punt category. I was the overall yard's winner of the contest, earning me a first-place trophy as well as more recognition for our team.

In class, Mrs. Crew had a reward system called Crew Bucks. It was simply fake money with her picture on it. She kept a classroom store where you could spend your Crew bucks on Fridays. The stories of Mrs. Crew being mean or evil were distant memories. Especially after I told your grandmother about the class store. She explained that Mrs. Crew bought the stuff for the store out of her own salary. Even though most of the stuff was school related and wasn't cool, it was pretty awesome to have a teacher care so much about her students that she took her own money, double investing in our future.

The five-pack of Hubba Bubba was the prize to be had. It was my favorite thing to buy anytime I had five Crew bucks. They were simple to earn. One of the ways to obtain Crew bucks was to behave in line in the hallways on the way to and from recess.

One day, I decided to use my newly acquired joking skills on the playground, which had some of my classmates ready to fight. Not just one but four other boys in my class as well. When recess was over, I ran to be first in line, knowing the safest place in line was next to the teacher. Wanting blood for my jokes, the five guys I was using for my material lined up right behind me. As I was leading the line with the five people who wanted to beat me up standing in line directly behind me, I thought we would never get to class. When we stopped for the restroom, I refused to leave the line. With the five of them ready to jump me, I thought it was best. Since they couldn't get me in the restroom, they decided to trip or punch me anytime Mrs. Crew wasn't looking all the way back to class. The tripping didn't break me, but when I got hit, I turned around and returned the energy, hitting Dean.

Of course I was the one who got caught, prompting Mrs. Crew to take three Crew bucks from me. She said, "I don't believe you hit him without him hitting you, and that is the only reason you are not heading to the principal." With the tension in the line, it was the longest walk from the restroom across from the cafeteria in the basement of the school to our third-floor classroom. When we got to our class, Mrs. Crew told me to remain in the hall and told the rest of the class to take their seats. Socially awkward, the one lesson that I valued was no snitching. When she asked me, "What was the behavior in the hall about?" I refused to answer. As she tried to pry the information out of me, I lost my respect, forgetting who I was talking to. Stopping in midsentence, she said, "Wait right there!" She went into the teacher's classroom next door for less than a minute. They both came out of the classroom with an extralarge wooden ruler. Right there in the hallway, Mrs. Crew spanked me with that ruler. After she was finished, she sent me to the office. When the secretary asked me why I was in the office, I kept it short and sweet, saying, "Mrs. Crew told me to come here." I guess while I was sitting in the office, Mrs. Crew was on the phone with your grandmother. About fifteen minutes later, Mrs. Crew called the office over the intercom and requested that I be sent back to class. Almost thirty minutes exactly had passed when the office called our classroom over the intercom.

"Can you please send Christopher Drake to the office."

I didn't know how, but I knew that I was in trouble. When I got to the office and saw your grandmother, I literally started shaking in my boots. The principal volunteered her office for privacy. When your grandmother shut her office door still holding my wrist, I knew what time it was. After punishing me, she went back to work. My empathetic principal let me sit in the nurse's office until the bell rang rather than returning me to class crying. The bright side was I got to leave school a little before Dean and the other four, so I walked home with my head high, thinking that this day was over, only to walk in the door to Ester armed with a belt, spanking me again for the mischief at school. Apparently Mrs. Crew called the house first in search of your grandmother.

The next morning in class, I tried to sneak to my seat. The three butt whoopings I took the day before made me not want any problems in class. I was hoping that all of them had moved on. As I entered the class, Dean was waiting. He walked right up to me, saying, "Your mine at recess!" Being knowledgeable about Mrs. Crew's schedules, I knew that we would only have second recess today because we had art today, which took up morning recess. As the day went on, it seemed to be only Dean wanted retributions for my mouth yesterday. Second recess was at 2:00 p.m. Depending on the day, we could be allowed to play anywhere from ten to thirty minutes. Playing the odds, I faked sick, going to the nurse's office on the way to recess. I had outsmarted him again. I could ride my fake illness until three, getting me dismissed from the office again. I calculated it as a five-minute head start. Living in the city, I could already run, but football taught me how to carry something as I was running. As soon as the bell rang, I grabbed my book bag and took off. There were only seven houses between the school and my grandfather's. Knowing the neighborhood dogs very well, I cut through the Ward's yard. They lived next to the school. I knew that if anyone was following me, those dogs would be a deterrent to my exact path. Making it to the street, I thought I was home-free. Less than a minute later, I heard "THERE HE IS!" It was Dean and the other four running after me. Like the athlete I had been training to be, I took off, making it to the house and up the stairs. I stopped on the porch, being arrogant, watching them running after me. As they reached the stairs, I ran in the house full of adrenaline. Locking the door behind me, I squatted behind the front door, trying to breathe. As I stared at the multiple volumes of the Encyclopedia Britannicas on the bookshelf across from my seat, I remembered seeing my grandfather's car in the street while I was running. In my excitement, it slipped my mind that he was working overtime, which meant that he wasn't working his normal shift. The plant had to give them eight hours off between sixteen-hour shifts, which meant he was asleep. I didn't realize that my adrenaline caused me to slam the door. It jolted him out of his sleep. He came to me in his jeans and T-shirt, saying, "Chris, what's wrong?" I explained that there were five boys who had chased me home from school because I was talking trash the day before. He looked through the small window on the door to see my dismay. Before I knew it, my grandfather had unlocked the door and picked me up and set me on the front porch. With five against one, you don't have to wonder who won, but I did learn that I don't have a glass jaw. With the score settled, school went back to normal.

    The skilled players on the team got to talking about what was next after football. Hearing that basketball was the next season, I wanted to play, especially if my new friends were playing. I told everyone that I had only played in my neighbor Cole's backyard but was still encouraged to try out. I don't know if it was for comic relief or if I was really a part of their crew. We were in the playoffs, which kept us practicing into November. Putting a hold on all basketball conversation, Coach Green was an amazing coach leading us all the way to the championship game. My first season I learned that peewee football wasn't always fair. The championship game turned into 15 against 11 with the refs seeming to side with our opponent, creating an unfair advantage. After the game, a lot of parents voiced their opinions on race playing a factor. Coach Green dismissed all of it,

I COULD'VE BEEN

saying, "I got out coached, we got out played!" It was our only loss of the season, which had some parents ready to fight. I had never seen so much anger or hurt.

Four days after football ended, basketball practice began. The first practice was at a church off Leavenworth Road. When your grandmother pulled into the unlit empty parking lot, I felt like I had been set up as a joke. With ten minutes left before the official scheduled practice time, more familiar cars started to join us in the parking lot. When we entered the gym, Coach Long, whose son played on the football team, had to lower the rims from the raptors. The gym was set for volleyball. With the help of the groundskeeper, it looked like a basketball gym in no time. Coach Long started us with layups to evaluate our skills. I couldn't dribble the ball without looking at it, but I had no problem putting it in the hoop. I spent more time chasing the ball around the opposite direction of the hoop than I did putting it in the hoop. My lack of ball control made it impossible to get the ball anywhere close to the hoop. Entertained, this wasn't Coach Long's first rodeo. He said, "The next practice I will bring some special goggles that will help those who have trouble trusting the ball." When we started the next practice, he remembered the box of goggles. They were specially designed to keep you from being able to look down. There was a hard plastic that protruded forward, so no matter how far you tilted your head, your vision was blinded, and you couldn't see the ball. Coach Long lined us up for the dribbling drills. He explained that the ball was designed to return to the air when it bounced. We just needed to trust that it would return to our hand. It didn't happen overnight. Even after we got the basics, we had to learn to control it while running as well. I ran faster than I could dribble. My first season of basketball was just like baseball and football. I started having no clue of how to play, but by the end of the season, I was better than average. I got to play because no one on our team was an all-star. Our last games of the season, we played against a team that had a very vocal parent. One of the kids' fathers paced up and down the sideline, talking serious trash to everyone on the court that opposed his son's team. Today just happened to be the day we played against his son Patrick. Most of the game we played a 2-1-2 zone until Coach Long realized that Patrick was a real shooter. When we switched to man-to-man, I guarded him. He was lightning quick, which gave me a challenge. I could keep up with him dribbling, but without the ball, I was his shadow chasing him. I didn't really stop him from doing whatever he wanted. My hard work during the game earned his father's respect. After the game, he made sure to find me to talk a little more trash. He complimented my hustle before he introduced me to his son. He made sure we exchanged numbers. He was talking about a team he was trying to put together, but with the season over, he was just getting a head start on next year.

Coach Long started recruiting for his baseball team halfway through basketball season. He was a very business-savvy man who owned a barbershop. His CA taught him that he could write off sponsoring the teams. With his son playing, he decided that he would coach baseball as well. Enjoying my new friends, your grandmother decided that instead of returning to the city league, I could join his team and play at Wyco. Taking after my grandfather, I was the tallest on the team. It was the first team that I had been on that was actually for my age. With my stature and natural strength, Coach Long decided that he was going to teach me how to be a pitcher. He figured if nothing else, I could intimidate the other team standing on the mound.

With growth and maturity all around me, third grade was coming to an end. One lesson that I definitely valued: don't believe everything you hear. The monster everyone told me Mrs. Crew was wasn't true. Despite being spanked by her, I learned that she was a sweet old lady who just wanted to teach us to follow the rules. With daily practice, following Mrs. Crew's rules became a breeze. On the last day of school, I hugged her and said, "Before I started the third grade, I was told you were a witch that kept kids in your basement. After being in your class this year, I know they were all lies. So far you are one of my favorite teachers." To which she laughed and embraced me the same.

With Wyco having leagues from T-ball to 13–14, you could play games any day of the week, which allowed me to spend most weekends in the garden. On the weekends, I had my country life in Missouri feeding rabbits and hauling poop. During the week I had my city life in Kansas working with Coach Long on consistently throwing the ball over the plate. With six coaches, Coach Long focused on me. He would let the other five orchestrate practice while he would grab a catcher glove and catcher's gear and spend almost the entire practice working with me on the pitching motion and my release point. Coach Long, intrigued by my size, showed up to one of our practices with a radar gun and discovered that I was throwing the ball eighty miles per hour at nine years old. After that discovery, he saw another opportunity to benefit from my arm. He knew that I had experience playing catcher last year. His new focus became how fast I could throw to all the bases from a squatting position. He thought we would have an advantage if no one could steal a base against our team. I preferred being behind the plate. It was more comfortable for me. I didn't have to worry about hitting a kid with my curveball. Whenever I did adorn the mound, I was greeted with theme music. "Wild Thing" by the Troggs was sung by every parent on the team until a parent thought to bring their boom box. They sang or played it the entire duration of my warmup. Your grandma would constantly yell, "You can't hit what you can't see!" I didn't know if that was a good or a bad thing. Your grandmother staying involved kept the score book for our team. After every game, she gave me my numbers/statistics.

With less time in the garden and more time at Wyco, there was a hitting instructor selling batting classes. Every time he saw your grandmother, he would flirt with her. Even though she told him clearly where I could hear her that she was committed to Bill, it didn't stop his advances. Because he kept trying your grandmother personally, she gave in professionally and bought me ten classes to improve my batting average. He gave her a money-back guarantee. Without question, the batting classes worked. My reputation was all-or-nothing, either homerun or strikeout. At the end of my second season, I was selected to participate in the nine-year-old all-star game. Our team as a whole was good. We just played the best team in the tournament our first game, ending our season early.

With baseball over and football a month away, home in the room we shared, my grandfather called down the stairs to your grandmother that she had a phone call. Having our own phone line, it hit me as a little weird. As I watched *Quantum Leap*, your grandmother ran to retrieve the call. The episode was so good I didn't notice until it went off that she had not returned. Changing the channel to find *Mash 4077*, I watched almost the entire thirty-minute show before she returned. When she returned to the room, she sat on my bed next to me, which was unusual. She joined in watching television with me until the show ended. She asked me to turn off the television for a second. She said, "There is something I want to talk to you about." She told me my father was in Kansas City, and he wanted to come spend some time with me. She explained that he would come to my grandfather's house to get me, but she wanted nothing to do with him at all. In fact, once I agreed to meet him, she wanted to know the time he planned to pick me up so that she could be somewhere else.

When he picked me up at my grandfather's house, he was driving a T-bird two-door coupe, which was cool. I was just so consumed with his absence, wondering what was better than me to keep him from being a part of my life. I quietly sat there listening to this stranger talk as he drove me across town. We arrived at a beautiful park on the Missouri side of town. My father by title popped the trunk and grabbed two kites. It was perfect weather for flying kites. As we sat in the grass constructing the kites together, he apologized for his decisions that kept him from being a part of my life. It was no secret to me. I knew where my father had been. He would write me sending me pictures with a card for my birthday. I would read the letters, forgetting them faster than I read them. I looked at the stranger in the pictures that I didn't recognize as my father, and just like the shift in the wind that broke our kites, he was gone. I never saw him again. I heard he earned himself a *lifetime* vacation with the State of Missouri.

My experience running the garden was mature enough to handle it all. While Bill was juggling longer trips to make better money, in the evenings after your grandmother was off work, she would take me to Mrs. Grey's house. I would compete with myself on how fast I could do everything. Knowing that watering the garden took the longest, it was always the first place I headed. It just so happened

I COULD'VE BEEN

that the water faucet was right next to where Bill would have the pallets of rabbit feed delivered. After starting the water, I would put a fifty-pound bag on each shoulder, running to the cages. Dropping them sitting up, ready to open, I would race back to grab two more before I tended to the rabbits. I could have every trough full in twenty minutes. With my growing agility, I could fill both five-gallon buckets in a minute each. With every trip down the hill to the compost, I would spend ten minutes pulling weeds on a part of the garden that wasn't being watered. Rotating between weeds and cleaning under the cages, I would change the connection for the water every twenty minutes. With only three total, I should have only taken an hour each day. Whenever we got back in the car, it was always an hour and a half or two hours at most.

With the beginning of football season on my mind, I timed myself every day. After almost three weeks of the same routine, I beat my record. I couldn't figure out how we were getting in the car after sixty minutes, but bored with the same task, I didn't question it. With the forecast of rain being correct, I got a week off the garden. Bill got his brother to feed the rabbits so that your grandmother wouldn't have to spend an hour in the car to and fro. When I returned to the garden a week later, I couldn't figure out why the water was on. After feeding the rabbits, I headed downhill with two full buckets of poop. As I started downhill, I saw that part of the garden was flooded. Looking around at the damage instead of watching my step, I lost my footing and fell. One of the buckets landed sitting upright. The other bucket connected by stick was slung into the air and covered what the mud missed. I was so upset I turned the water off and didn't clean under any more cages. When I went to your grandmother saturated from head to toe, she laughed, saying, "You're not riding in my car like that." After lining her car with garbage bags, she allowed me to ride with her, but she insisted that the windows stay down. Two weeks later, Bill got the water bill, and he was livid. He knew exactly what happened and who did it. When he saw me, he didn't even acknowledge your grandmother. Getting straight in my face, he squared off with me chest to chest before unloading on my chest with a punch that knocked the wind out of me. Before he could hit me again, your grandmother screamed, "CHRIS, GET IN THE CAR, WE ARE LEAVING!" Bill was so enraged that he chased me to the car. He hit me two more times like I was a grown man before your grandmother came around the car to get him off me. On the ride home, your grandmother explained that the water bill was seven hundred dollars.

Still growing, two months from starting the fourth grade, I was the tallest kid in my class. Wearing a size 10 shoe, my shoe size matching my age for the last two years. The first three days of school, my teacher was the lady Mrs. Crew got to witness my ruler spanking. For some reason, the school swapped her and Mrs. Bailey three days into the school year. Mrs. Bailey was a very popular fifth-grade teacher. When I was informed that she would be my fourth-grade teacher, I was very excited. Mrs. Bailey was the Big Momma of the school. Very stern with common sense over nonsense, she ran a very tight ship, but she was as sweet as could be. She herself had four children, which helped her handle all our different personalities well. After last year, the State of Kansas stopped allowing your teacher to physically punish you in school. Mrs. Bailey couldn't pull a Mrs. Crew. She did carry a smaller ruler and would tell you to hold out your hands if you deserved it. Her morality was equal to Mrs. Crew. Turning her class to a powerful learning environment.

Football practice started simultaneously with school. Your grandmother found time to be more involved and worked closely with Coach Long during baseball season to understand the financial aspects of coaching a team. Coach Long answered whatever questions your grandmother could think to ask. She learned his knowledge of write-offs, fund-raisers, and tax ID numbers. Two weeks into practice, she approached Coach Green with incorporating our football team. She explained that we needed a board of directors, and she would voluntarily be our treasury. She set up fund-raisers and organized car washes and helped Coach Green double our team from seventeen players to thirty-five players. The fact that we finished second last year helped as well. Your grandmother was relentless. She used her networking skills to find us a sponsor. Country Care saw her efforts and donated a healthy donation to the cause. Since we were incorporated, it was really just a friendly business write-off between companies. Their name was what we wore on the front of our jerseys. With the proceeds we made from the car washes and candy sales, Coach Green was able to afford to help us all get matching cleats. I guess he heard the heckling last year. On top of that, he teamed up with varsity sports and got us all matching jackets and bags. By the time the season started, we were a well-oiled machine that looked good on and off the field. After learning how the offense worked, defense seemed to be so natural. Coach taught me that the most important part of playing defensive end was to get their hands off me. He also taught me that leverage made me stronger, and I only needed strength if I did have speed to get by them. He also taught me to keep my head on a swivel. He said if you get through unblocked, look for a pull block. He also taught me how to defeat it. He explained that a rip move would make me too small for most linemen to make the block. On our offensive side, it was more like the dog-and-pony show from last year, bigger, still having to weigh in before every game. Again, no kid on the field could tackle me.

Three games into the season, I chipped a bone in my right thumb. Expressing my pain to your grandmother, she took me to our family physician. While x-raying my hand, the doctor became concerned with my breathing. Before he revealed the results of the x-ray, he counseled your grandmother on having me tested for asthma. After listening to my chest with his stethoscope, he recommended a breathing machine, sending me home. This machine with saline concerned your grandmother. I tried the breathing treatments, but they didn't seem to do much. Sitting still for twenty minutes with the noise of the machine was not ideal for my age. With the x-ray confirmed, I had to be fitted for a cast anyway, so the test was performed on my next office visit. On the field, Coach Green switched me from fullback to center. He taught me to play the position left-handed. With my size, it was a natural transition. Checking in weekly with the doctor my next office visit, Dr. Ross walked in the room with an inhaler. He told your grandmother that it was confirmed that I had asthma.

"I recommended that he cease and desist any and all athletic activities," he said.

Refusing his opinion your grandmother accepted the inhaler, telling me the decision was mine on whether I played or not. I laughed and said, "It's been two years, I'm fine, so I say we keep playing." He told your grandmother that I would need to wear this soft cast for three months, which meant that my running back days were over this year. Your grandmother could see all over my face that I wasn't happy. She reminded me that I was still starting and playing. Every Sunday we watched the chiefs together. I loved Christian Okoye, but I saw myself more as Barry Word. With the NFL's Pepsi commercial, your grandmother borrowed the Pepsi slogan and made it ours. Our version was "Mental toughness got to have it." Realizing that she gave me strength, she went to Varsity Sports and had it put on a T-shirt, which I started wearing anytime I played football.

During our games, we were always heckled a lot. Our team looked like we were all too old for our division. Combined with the fact that we only lost one game last year, yet to lose this year. We finally got an opportunity at a rematch from the championship game last year. It rained all week until game day. Jacob and I were on opposite ends of the defensive line. There was a kid who kept running his mouth with inappropriate things during every play. Jacob and I were switching sides like any good defensive line with six-foot-four Dylan playing nose guard between us. I heard the things the kid was saying, but I was ignorant in handling racism. I thought at the time saying "boy" from one kid to another was okay. Jacob, on the other hand, being a little older, took offense. We broke the huddle waiting for them to do the same. As they lined up, Jacob and Dylan were still huddling on a solution to shut his mouth. Lining up for the play, as the quarterback hiked the ball, both Jacob and Dylan grabbed the kid by the back of his helmet, and together they used their four hundred pounds to power-slam him into the mud. All you could hear was what sounded like a baseball bat hitting a football helmet and a kid screaming. The game was stopped for ten minutes as the coaches tried to get that kid's face mask out of the mud. While waiting for the comedy to subside, Jacob informed the rest of us what he and Dylan did. It wasn't the last time we played that team, but it was the last time I heard "boy" on the football field for a very long time. Whoever taught him about bigotry forgot to tell him not to say that to someone twice his size. We only lost one game, and we won the league championship. Again Coach Green encouraged me to enter the punt, pass, and kick contest. Even with a soft cast on, my total distance catapulted me to the victory in my division. Trophies were becoming an addiction, and competition was the path to my addiction.

    School was my happy place for a great majority. I transferred my respect for your grandmother to my teachers. I was learning daily how my actions would determine if I was heard when trying to speak in class. Normally I would steer clear of answering questions. There was something about Mrs. Bailey that brought me out of my shell. Whenever she would ask questions, I wouldn't wave my hand or hop in my seat. I would hold my hand straight up in the air as high as I could and wouldn't bring it down between questions. Knowing the answer was never a problem. I would get so excited that I would really create a scene waving my hand back and forth, hopping in my chair, doing everything I could to be seen. Mrs. Bailey would call on everyone but me. She explained that if she would call on me while I was acting like that, she would be setting the standard for all the little boys to start acting crazy. With your grandma a phone call away, I pressed my luck without crossing the lines. Flirting in class seemed to be the only thing that would get me in trouble. I would always get caught passing the notes. Mrs. Bailey tried to discourage me from passing notes by making me stand at my desk and read the note aloud for the entire class to know what the secret was. Mrs. Bailey and grandma Ester were so much alike. Both women had the biggest hearts in the world. Ester gave to the church like Mrs. Bailey gave to the classroom. I could drive both of them mad; however, they both saw fit in me to allow me to be their helper. I would stay after school to help Mrs. Bailey just as much as me and Grandma Ester were going to church.

    Still afraid to sleep at night, my dreams were so vivid. So real I felt like I could touch them among other things. I didn't understand what was happening in my sleep. Trying to avoid it, I would run up and down the basement stairs. Every time after about twenty minutes, Ester would come to the basement stairs in her robe. She would crack the door open, saying, "Boy, if you don't stop what you are doing, I will make sure you can't sit for a week. If I don't need sleep, you don't need to sit." I still tried to run the stairs at night. I just tried to do it quietly. Every three or four days, I would be startled by Ester threatening my backside. After a few weeks, it became something that your grandmother had to address. As we sat on our bed playing cards on the TV tray, she asked me, "What will make you more comfortable to try to sleep?" I couldn't explain my problems. My only solution was a tent for my bed. It arrived as a fitted sheet with a tent top. It also had two sticks that were connected together by an elastic cord. Inside the tent, there were loops sewn in to hold the bendable poles, which crossed in the middle of the tent. The part that I loved the most was that it zipped closed, giving me privacy. It helped me a lot. I could get comfortable rest without the worry of what my body did while I tried to sleep. I still had a desire to work out at night with all my extra energy. I felt like it helped with the negative dreams.

Basketball season showed me how far I had come. In my second year with better than average dribbling skills. As promised, Patrick's father, Raheem, was involved in coaching a team. With the bond between Patrick and me, as well as the bond between his mother and your grandmother, it was not rocket science. Raheem, being outspoken, would run off the scary or soft parents. What I admired about him was he always told the truth. He wasn't the type to look at kids with no talent and lie to their parents. He would just flat-out tell you that your kid sucked. Our team had respect instead of fear. We consisted of nine players. Basically he built a team for his son to be the all-star. I was just his supporting role. I was more like Patrick's Pippen. He averaged thirty points a game but was capable of fifty. Being on the same team as him made me want to be more like him. I picked up my scoring and started averaging fifteen to twenty points a game, which was good enough for me as long as we won. Teamed with my rival from last year, our new rival was another father/coach, son/player team. AP was coaching his son, who was also named Christopher. We both went by Chris, so when we played against each other, it was confusing. Chris, like Patrick, was a scoring machine. He was capable of scoring forty points. In our game, I had the luxury of guarding him. Chris was little and fast. Guarding him was like Shaq trying to guard Allen Iverson. He ran circles around me. The only advantage I had was that I could block his shot or I could lean on him and wear him down like ankle weights. He kept me so twisted up that when I got tired, I would purposely foul him. After our game, Raheem and AP got together, realizing all the talent between the two teams. Their conversation quickly turned to the idea of basketball being something that we needed to do all year round. Little league basketball was literally six weeks. With our team being so talented, it was nothing for us to show up while our opponent stayed at home. AP expressed that his team was having the same problem. Our season ended in February, which merged our teams to continue practicing. Coach AP's wife was the fitness instructor who hosted her classes in the community center at Eisenhower Middle School. She had the inside track on when the gym was available. It seemed like most all our practices were after her aerobics class. Every practice the coaches told us their efforts to petition for a summer league at Kensington Park. The talk of a summer league grew momentum quick. We never stopped practicing and couldn't wait for competition. Patrick and I began practicing so much I was constantly at his house. Raheem bought an adjustable basketball goal. It had a plastic base that said sand would be enough weight to hold the goal steady. We spent nearly all our free time in their driveway playing 21, horse, or one-on-one. Just as fast as the summer league hype caught a buzz, it died.

 I fell in love with basketball so much that I went home and begged my grandfather to buy me a goal. I could go across the street to play if Cole was home, but I wanted my own. After looking at the prices, he refused to pay $200 for something he could recreate for $30. He went to the hardware store and brought a sheet of plywood. Followed by a trip to Varsity Sports to purchase a rim. Less than a week later, I had a basketball goal in front of the shed in his backyard. It was on a four-by-four. He cut the sheet of plywood in half, which was way bigger than a normal backboard. Using some of the biggest nails I had ever seen, he connected the plywood to the post before adding the rim. When he put it in the ground. It was not even close to ten feet, which was regulation. It didn't matter to me. I had a place to practice my jumper. It sat in front of my grandfather's toolshed, which looked like a miniature barn. There was a swing set directly to the right of the shed. I called it a twisted ankle waiting to happen. The swing hedged the post six inches with the forty-five-degree framework sticking out. The backyard was bordered with a chain-link fence, which kept the ball from rolling down the hill into the street. The concrete walkway and the stairs to the back porch with its handrail were only excuses to the kids in the neighborhood with no heart. Even with the obstacles, I was happy to have my own basketball hoop. Just like any hood when you get something new, everyone wants to have their chance to try to tear it up. So there was always someone ringing the doorbell to play basketball.

Every day I would find something to do in the backyard. As I was outside playing basketball, there was a lady that parked on the side of my grandfather's house. As kids, we saw everything but only told what we were asked. The lady got out of her car, and instead of going to the front door, she came to the backyard. Yelling "Hello" from the bottom of the hill, we stopped our game to acknowledge our elder. She introduced herself as Sister Franklin. She said that she worked for Turner House, which was insignificant, but the next words out of her mouth stole all our attention. She said, "Do any of you want a job making ten dollars an hour?" She told us that Turner House was a government-funded art program that would provide art supplies, lunch, and a check on the first and the fifteenth of the month. Intrigued I said, "Wait just a min." Immediately I ran, opening the screen door to the back porch, opening the back door. I ran downstairs. I knew that your grandmother would never believe me by myself. She was in our room reading a romance novel. I said, "Momma can I have a job?" grabbing her by the wrist, anticipating her answer.

She said, "Boy, you are too young to have a job." Before she could finish her sentence, I was pulling her up from her bed, begging her to follow me. "Hold on, Chris, let me put some shoes on," she said as she could feel my excitement. When we got back out-

I COULD'VE BEEN

side, Ms. Franklin was still there. Your grandmother opened the gate and walked down the stairs as I followed with the basketball under my arm. Eavesdropping in adult conversation, I heard Ms. Franklin say that her program was off Fifth and Quindaro, but she was having problems recruiting kids in that neighborhood. She told your grandmother that the funding was being processed, but the program would start the fifteenth of June until the end of the summer. As they exchanged numbers, I was so excited. I knew it was just a matter of time before I had a job.

All my sporting activities had led your grandmother to buying in bulk. She was constantly saying, "When you know better, do better." She obtained a Sam's club card for team snacks and team drinks during football season while she was the treasury. From football to basketball, she saw an opportunity in our neighborhood. There were two stores in the neighborhood, Mr. Young's and Fast Fred's, which were ten blocks away from each other. With my grandfather being directly in the middle, your grandmother allowed me to start selling sodas and penny candy. With a slow start, I ate more Twizzlers than I sold. With fourth grade ending and baseball teams forming, things picked up for my store. Word of mouth started the doorbell to ringing constantly. My grandfather, being the ingenious person he was, decided that if he couldn't sleep because the doorbell would not stop ringing, he was going to make money as well. Knowing how to coexist, my grandfather never imposed on my business. He instead saw another angle. While reading the newspaper, he found a private distributor of ice shavers and different flavors. After three or four trips across town, he found an ice shaver with fifteen flavors, starting a snow cone business for my aunt Boo-Boo. He would shave the ice and mount it in cups before storing it in the freezer. When you purchased it, you could tell Boo-Boo what flavor you wanted from the list of flavors posted in the glass window next to the door. For fifty cents, you could get a snow cone or soda. With the addition of snow cones to the house, your grandmother took the gloves off and let me have purchasing power for my candy store. Trying to stay competitive, I turned into a full-fledged candy store. You could get Twizzlers, Snickers, Kit-Kats, Reese's cups, bubble gum, Sugar Daddys, Chic-

O-Sticks, chips, and sodas. If it was something that I didn't carry that you would ask for, I would hunt for it at Sam's to try and keep my customers happy.

Every day I would ask your grandmother if I was playing at Wyco again. She didn't have the heart to tell me that their prices this year were ridiculous. Not wanting to let me down, she decided to coach a team in the city league. The city was not giving uniforms this year, so your grandmother used her connections with Varsity Sports and was able to get us tops with numbers on the back. She got in contact with the coordinators of the city league, expressing her interest for participating in their league, and just like that, your grandma had a team. Unlike Wyco, where all the parents had cars, we were back at Klamm Park. Committed, your grandmother would drive her Chevy hatchback all around the neighborhood to pick up most of our team for practice.

School out for the summer. Being past the age of dress-up with Boo-Boo, my size granted me freedom to roam the neighborhood to play. Walking past the school, I saw Mrs. Bailey's car. She was there to pack up her classroom for the summer. Trying all the doors to the school, I found access. Fearful of being caught by the wrong person, I decided to go downstairs to the bottom floor first. Mr. Washington, our big teddy bear custodian, was mopping the floor as if school was still in. I could smell the cleaning chemicals he used that kept Chelsea smelling like a hospital. When he noticed me, he engaged in a conversation, inquiring of my plans for the summer. I told him that the only thing I knew was that I wanted to play baseball. During our conversation, I saw that Mr. Perez's classroom light was on. I had never been in his second-grade class. I knew that he had a small petting zoo with reptiles and rodents. His big personality was the source of the rumors. Allegedly he was a homosexual. I had no clue what that meant, but I heard other kids through the school year call him a fag or gay. When I asked your grandmother what a fag was, she said, "A cigarette in England." Trying to be understood, I said, "No, gay," to which she replied, "Happy." After a few other derogatory slangs, she understood and taught me the correct label. She cautioned me from judgment using one of her favorite sayings,

"Don't believe everything you hear." She asked me if I had any proof, which I did not, so I left it at that.

I did have curiosity for why he was still at the school. Most teachers were packed up and ready for summer break on the last day of school. Passing by his classroom, I made my way to Mrs. Bailey's class. The rest of the week I helped packed her classroom together. On Friday when we finished, I thanked Mrs. Bailey for being my teacher and told her that I was sad that she would not be my teacher next year. She gave me the biggest smile and said, "Christopher, I'm not teaching fourth grade next year, I'm going back to fifth grade again, and I already picked you to be in my class." I was elated and enthusiastic for fifth grade.

On Monday I went to the school knowing that Mrs. Bailey would not be there. I found Mr. Washington in his office. He told me that everyone had left for the summer except Mr. Perez. I could see his light on. Hanging with Mr. Washington as long as I could, I followed him into the cafeteria. Bored with watching him work, I went to Mr. Perez's room. Nervously standing in the hall, I poked only my head in. He was sitting at his desk focused on something on his computer. Looking around his classroom, I saw three other computers set up like workstations. Ten feet away from me, I saw a snake in an aquarium, forgetting he was there, I walked straight up to its glass entrapment. Standing in front of this snake, I didn't know what to think. Every snake I had seen before had been murdered by my grandfather. Realizing that he had company, Mr. Perez said, "Hello." Realizing that, I did not speak. I got nervous. Gathering my confidence, I introduced myself, saying, "My name is Chris, I'm going to be a fifth grader in Mrs. Bailey's class next year. I was just trying to see if any teachers needed any help packing up for the summer."

Looking around his classroom, he said, "I'll be here all summer. Someone has to feed the animals."

Curious, I asked, "What are you doing?" He explained that he was writing a play that he would be producing next school year. I immediately asked if I could participate. Mr. Perez told me that there would be auditions and I could audition, but he couldn't promise me anything. Standing over his shoulder, I had a full view of his classroom. He really had a small petting zoo with over ten classroom pets. I spent the rest of the week watching the animals while he wrote his play. Every day he greeted me with a warm hello, like he was so thankful to have someone in the class with him even though we rarely spoke once he started working.

Trying to find peace, the first thing Saturday morning, my grandfather rolled the pool from the side of the shed and put it in its normal spot. Summer was in full effect, and we were too noisy in the house. With the businesses we had, there were so many kids that would come but wouldn't leave. So Ester insisted that the pool be put out immediately. With the years of putting the pool down, there was no grass in the backyard. Trying to spruce up the yard, my grandfather planted sunflowers along the fence line after he cut down the weeping willow tree. Right next to both gate entrances, he planted roses. Young with no excuses, it didn't stop us from playing basketball. With baseball season underway, it wasn't a priority. My focus was more on logistics, making sure everyone was at my grandfather's house on practice days by six, when your grandmother arrived. She would give more than half the team a ride. Being one of the biggest kids on the team, I got shotgun privileges. Your grandmother could fit eight in her hatchback cheval. It amazed me so much that I would always say, "We almost have the whole team." Your grandmother's response anytime she heard *almost* or *close* was "Close only counts in horseshoes and hand grenades." Every now and then she would let someone small ride in the front seat with me. Mostly if we were trying to get home from the park and she didn't want to leave a child alone or let them walk. The rumors of her love and dedication had spread through the hood, gaining interest from a lot of parents. One of them was a single mom raising four sons who all played baseball. It was her requirement of them. Her oldest had an arm that was a gift from God. Scooter was the first kid I met who threw the ball harder than me. Playing in the eleven-to-twelve-year-old division, the mound was back a little farther, which diminished the heat off my throw. With only fourteen players on the team, your grandmother taught me to play all the infield positions just in case someone couldn't make a game. With your grandmother doing everything

I COULD'VE BEEN

by herself, Scooter's mom decided to help coach as well. We were the only team in the city with women coaches.

My candy store was on autopilot. There was always someone at the house. My Turner house project was 8:00 a.m.–4:00 p.m. three days a week. With the money I was making, your grandmother decided that I needed to give back. She had a coworker whose elderly mother was on a fixed income. She was ninety-one and couldn't manage the yard. Your grandmother made me take some of my profits from the store to purchase a lawn mower. Every other week I would cut this lady's acre plot with my walk-behind lawn mower for ten dollars. I thought that your grandmother was crazy. She kept promising that my blessing would come back. Your grandmother told any and everybody that I cut grass. With her as my manager, we were able to schedule five yards around our schedules. I made profit on the lawn mower before baseball season ended. She never let me charge more than twenty dollars a yard, but some of my customers would sneak me an extra five when she wasn't looking.

At Turner house, my artwork was being praised by Ms. Franklin. She inspired me to challenge perceptions with my paintings. My first painting was titled *Stereotypes*. It depicted an inner-city corner with Caucasian drug-dealers and users. I followed it with *Stereotypes II*. Which depicted black men in business suits on a busy street. My third painting was entitled *Black Jesus*. It depicted my version of our Heavenly Father with tears flowing down his face. To me, my paintings were just average, but Ms. Franklin would glorify each and every one of them. Her encouragement gave me confidence to try my hand at drawing. I talked your grandmother into buying me a Disney calendar to practice. After drawing half the calendar, I shared my drawings with Ms. Franklin, who was in disbelief. I was able to magnify the pictures from the calendar to exact replicas that were five times larger than the original. Seeing my gifts, Ms. Franklin started showing me preferential treatment. She nicknamed me TAG, which she never explained to the other kids, but she confided in me that it meant "talented and gifted." Ms. Franklin pushed my paintings hard and got them put on display in a kids museum. She tried to explain the magnitude of my accomplishments being on display, but as a young man, it meant nothing to me because it was still baseball season.

Baseball practice was hard because our team was divided by rumors. Your grandma was tired of the gossip. The animosity that was going on between our team was driving her crazy. She stopped practice, putting all fourteen of us in the wooden bleachers. Determined to prove her point to us that you can't believe everything you hear, she wrote down, "It stinks when you slide and get dirt in your pants, good thing they made Shout to get it out." She instructed the first person to read it. Then she instructed that we whisper the message from one person to the next until all fourteen had received the message. By the time it got to me, whom she had strategically placed last, what I was told made no sense. It didn't even make a sentence. Your grandmother asked me to stand up and share with everyone what the message was, handing me the paper. Her point was if the message can't make it correctly in five minutes through fourteen sets of ears, how was it supposed to be accurate days later. She preached her motto, "Close only count in horseshoes and hand grenades." To drive home her point of being absolute without someone in between, everyone on the team got her message, and from that day forward, we were a team.

Scooter and I made the all-star team, but it wasn't nearly as fancy as Wyco's the year before. Humble was molded on me. My grandfather could care less about sports, so I knew better than boast my accomplishments. When I tried to share my accomplishments with Bill, he quickly dismissed it, giving me a reality check, saying, "The rabbits need to be fed, under the cages needs to be cleaned, and we will start harvesting in two weeks." He never thought it was possible for me to make a living with sports. He told me that he bought another empty lot down the hill next to the garden earlier in the summer while I was busy playing baseball, and he wanted to spend the next two weeks getting the ground ready for next year. I didn't understand how Bill had intentions to add more to the garden. The last three years it had basically been just me and him with a little help from your grandma and Hazel. He was too proud to ask for help and too conservative to pay someone to help even though he had plenty of money. This year's harvest was the biggest we'd produced so far. It took us seven days straight from sunup to sundown. As I was missing playing like a kid to work, I dreaded his plans for next summer. When we finished the harvest, Bill and your grandmother gave so much of my hard work away. I'm sure they were selling it, but I never saw a dime. What wasn't sold or given away was preserved in mason jars or stored in the kitchen pantry. There was no junk food in Mrs. Grey's house. If you wanted a snack, your options were all fresh out the garden.

Missing my junk food, I was ready for my life without daily trips to Missouri. The success of my candy store was bringing in a profit of one hundred to three hundred a week, depending on what time of the month it was. When I wasn't able to be home, whoever answered the door ran my business, just like I would for Boo-Boo when she wasn't able to be home. With the fifth grade and football just weeks away, your grandmother informed me that I would be buying my own shoes. Having my shoe size match my age for the last three years, I was already in an 11. Needing football cleats and school shoes on top of clothes and school supplies, I was proud to have money to be able to help. We went to the Indian Springs mall for clothes. While shopping, your grandmother told me that she was taking a second job. "The sports you play are expensive, but I know you love it. I love watching you play, and I'm willing to do whatever it takes!" She told me that she might miss some practices, but she would never miss a game.

When school started, my confidence was through the roof. Everyone knew me and Boo-Boo from our businesses and home. Our popularity kept us in knowledge of the neighborhood, so I couldn't wait to get to school to see if the rumors were true. The last few weeks all anyone could talk about was how Bird, one of my fifth-grade classmates, was in jail for murder. I looked for him for two weeks before I believed the rumors true. Your grandmother used the rumors to keep me closer to her. Less than a month into school, Mr. Perez started auditions for his play. After some pleading with your grandma, she let me audition. I was cast as one of the three lead actors in the play. After learning the stage directions to understand the craft, we spent every day after school running lines.

My teacher Mrs. Bailey had one rule that I started off the year breaking: *No homework in class*. She called it homework for a reason, but every afternoon we would have quiet time the last twenty minutes of class. While she sat at her desk behind us grading papers, I would sit at my desk trying to finish as much of my homework as possible. With Mrs. Bailey knowing my personality, anytime I was too quiet, she would get up from her desk and sneak up on me. When she would catch me, she would take my sheet and give me another, but after she realized that I would do it as many times as I had to, she started leaving me alone. With play practice until five and football practice at six, I couldn't afford to waste time.

On the football field, I was way past the weight limit to play any running back position. Coach Henderson started me at center from day one. On defense, I was at home playing defensive end for my second season straight. I was on every special team, so I never left the field. I would kick the ball off to play defense. When we stopped them and they punted, my job was to rush the punter. When we got the ball back, I was the captain of the line and made sure my guards knew who to block. If we didn't get a first-down, I was the punter trying to pin the other team as deep as possible. With your grandmother having a second job, her absence was felt during the week. There was always a parent waiting with me after practice until she could get there. Most of the time it was because they wanted to turn in money for one of our fund-raisers. It was amazing to watch your grandmother juggle all her responsibilities without whining or excuses. With me being such a big part of my team, on game days I would wake up two hours before your grandmother's alarm. Most of the time I would wake from a dream of the game that we were scheduled to play. After being scared awake, my anxiety wouldn't let me go back to sleep. I was afraid that I would oversleep and miss the game, even though your grandmother would never let that happen. Sleeping period gave me anxiety. I tried to push myself every day to the point of exhaustion that I couldn't help but pass out. Everything outside of the sport I was playing gave me anxiety. Even without a doctor's diagnosis, my family secretly knew about my anxiety. My nervousness constantly kept me sweating in the strangest places. Every evening when I would get home from practice, I couldn't even take my shoes off in the house until I got to the back porch. If I took my shoes off in the car, Ester wouldn't permit me to pass through the front of the house. Your grandmother blamed the smell of my feet on the quality of shoes I wore, when it was all preteen anxiety.

My final season of peewee football, we went undefeated. Every year we got better as a whole, even after setting the bar so high our first season, making it all the way to the peewee superbowl. For the third year in a row, I won the pass, punt, and kick contest. After two years of practice, the league was prepared for the competition this year. It was the first time they had a microphone on the field to announce the progress of the athletes for everyone in the stands to follow. Before we started, the league president announced the winner would automatically qualify for the regional tournament with a chance to compete at Arrowhead Stadium for the finals. Hearing all my dreams come true with the mention of Arrowhead Stadium, I passed, punted, and kicked my butt off. No one was even close to me. I defended my title for the third year straight. Bored with the formality of trophies, all I cared to ask was when the regional tournament would be. No one on the field could give me an answer. When it came time for the presentation of trophies, I didn't care to accept it; it wasn't the prize that I wanted. Your grandmother had to give me an attitude adjustment. The fact that we were in public on a football field meant nothing. She reminded me who I represented, starting with herself first, then my coach, then my team. By the time she finished, I humbly went to accept the trophy without any more questions. The end of the season was sad for me. I could never play peewee football again. I knew that I would never see most of these people again, and I knew better than to expect them to call me.

At the end of my first quarter in the fifth grade, I brought home three Cs. School was on the back burner to football and television. I could not fit in socially if I didn't watch the hot new television show that all my classmates were talking about. It was the conversation anytime we were on recess. You could hear multiple kids saying, "No you didn't." Even playing kickball, the references to Homey D. Clown were made every time the ball was kicked over the fence. Seeing myself as a young comedian, I would watch *In Living Color* instead of doing my homework. Your grandmother threatened to take everything that I loved away. The first thing she threatened since football was over was my participation in the school play. She continued with threats of me not being able to play basketball at all. To prove that she meant business, your grandmother sent me to school with a weekly progress report which I was required to have Mrs. Bailey sign. If I didn't get a signature on Friday, I had to sit out of anything happening over the weekend, like I had a forty-eight-hour punishment. Seeing my consequences for cruising the fifth grade, I did a 180 in class. My homework grades starting going up followed by my test grades. When basketball season started, I was back to straight As.

At the start of basketball season, our team was solid. With Patrick and I having a better understanding of how the other person's mind worked, we again dominated everyone in the league again except AP's team. When we played each other, the entire gym was filled like an NBA final. All the teams that selectively miss when they played us would be the teams with a courtside view to watch. AP was a brilliant coach with NBA philosophy. In addition to his son, Chris, he added a new shooting guard to his team. The kid's jumper was lights out, but his handles were just average, so Chris was their point guard. Chris would mix the defense up, dribbling through the defenders like Pistol Pete before passing the ball to James, who would Steve Kerr us every time. He wasn't fast, he wasn't flashy, but he had a good jumper. The games were so good for peewee, having both Patrick and Chris, who would average 30; having James or me that could put up 20. The only thing that Coach AP didn't anticipate was our new secret weapon, Blake. Blake was just as good as Patrick or me. If he was on any other team, he would have been their leading scorer. On our team, he was a humble role player, believing as we all did that no one player was greater than the team. His basketball IQ was through the roof, which made him a great teammate to have. After the game, it didn't take long for AP to convince Raheem to

I COULD'VE BEEN

permanently join forces with him. AP was pushing the AAU circuit since the summer league failed. He had several tournaments lined up with our actual season over. Together we had the best eleven-to-twelve-year-old team in the city. The best part of AAU basketball was that the season was all year except during school ball, which we were all too young to play yet. With all the talent we had from Wyandotte County, we were still told that there was still a team better than ours. I had not heard of the Running Rebels, but their legend was growing like the rabbits. Every game we whooped a team off the court, two more people would bring up the Running Rebels.

When I signed up for the school play, I didn't anticipate it taking the entire school year. I enjoyed it so much that I didn't care, but after six months of practice, I was ready for the game. With school three months from over, play practice picked up. We would run lines with Mr. Perez until six o'clock five days a week. After we were gone, Mr. Perez stayed late every night and created every set. Being an elementary school play hindered nothing about his creativity. Not only did he create every backdrop or skin, he also made every costume in the play. He accepted help with makeup, but he still gave the directors approval on everything. After months of long practices, it was time for dress rehearsal. The thought had not occurred to me that we would be performing this for a lot of people. When he gave us contracts, it said the date he expected to perform, but through practice, we all lost sight of the date. The closer it came to our curtain call, the more nervous I grew. As a final surprise, Mr. Perez told us that we would be performing it twice the same day. Once during school for our classmates and once the same evening for our parents and the rest of the school district. The only catch was that Mr. Perez's flamboyant personality didn't do anything small. The production was over three hours with two intervals of fifteen to twenty minutes with twelve scene changes. The day of the play, everyone in the play got dismissed to the gym after morning roll call. It was supposed to start early enough to be finished by lunch. When the lights went down and the camera came on, we all went into action so naturally. Eight months of practice made it so easy. Being the oldest lead actor, if my fellow leads missed their cue, I was responsible for getting them back on script. We told Mr. Perez's version of the *Wizard of Oz* with a time travel history twist. We went through the pyramids, we went through the renaissance, we touched on slavery and its oppression with how song was the strength that kept most spirits going, all to get back to current day life with the explanation that life is a journey, seek wisdom in everything you do and you will always be home no matter where you were. The success of the play made me crave center stage on and off the stage. My thirst for acceptance, my thirst for success had turned me into a little monster that I didn't quite understand. I couldn't accept being second. I knew that there would always be someone better, but I would spend all my extra time practicing whatever I could. Preparing to prove myself whenever a challenge arose. With Chelsea days soon behind me, I felt like the king of the school. Everyone loved me except maybe Dean. Which convinced me that I was on the right path.

Completing my euphoria, your grandmother got a phone call from a baseball coach. He was a baseball coach who was switching from Wyco to 3&2 stadiums because it was more affordable, and he wanted me to be a part of his team this summer. The stadiums had two fields that sat down one of the steepest inclines ever. The pure majesty of the baseball fields made me want to play for his team. The most exciting part was that my talents got me recruited at twelve.

Smarter than the System

Over the winter, Bill had sold more than ¾ of the rabbits. The compost was nearly full, so we didn't need as many rabbits. Bill left fifty rabbits, but he was still controlling the population, keeping the males and females separate. With his calculations of a pound a rabbit, feeding was back to just one fifty-pound bag a day. Being math strong, I calculated that he had at least seventeen pallets delivered over the year. It was supposed to be a hobby, which turned into a full-fledged investment. The financial burden was solely on Bill. I was free labor, but after the water incident, Bill wouldn't leave me to the garden by myself. His plans after last year's harvest were completely changed this spring. He wasn't interested in farming the new lot addition. After taking the winter to contemplate his vision, he decided that it was already hard to stop the thieves from robbing the garden at night with a clear view from the house. To plant something that could not be clearly seen from the house was begging to be robbed. He said, "I'm not putting up a fence, so we will only plant the land we did last year." Bill always preached how we had to rotate the crops to give the ground time to replenish the minerals. Sitting on the tire rails that created a wall to keep the hill from collapsing, he reached in his back pocket and pulled out a restaurant napkin. On the napkin was a new legend for the garden. He had it scaled to rows and feet. Starting our fourth year, he knew exactly how many seeds he could plant in each row. He also knew how far to space each of the different crops. Holding on to the napkin because I did not want to make a mistake, I knew he had every detail in his head. His rough draft of predictions on a restaurant napkin came to life and were 100 percent accurate right before my eyes. When I tried to tell Bill how he impressed me with his precise knowledge. He said, "If I tell you a rooster can pull a wagon, hitch it up!" as if he was too tough to simply say thank you, forming my first quote, "*Words are words what I love are verbs.*"

My bat on the baseball field garnered me a respect from my new teammates. Last year, no more than three players played together on the same team, so we were all getting to know each other. Coach Price played me the same as Coach Long. primarily as a catcher that would pitch every eighth game. He would also respect that I didn't want to be behind the plate every game, letting me play second base and left field. His son Devin also played catcher. Everything he did was part of a strategy. He coached me how to block the base on a steal attempt. He had me and Devin constantly working on throwing the runner out on a steal attempt. When he worked with me in left field, he was enamored by my strength. Holding me to the expectation that no one was to turn a double when I was in the field. We had a lot of talent despite our record. We finished the season in third. With it being our first year together, it took all season before we started to jell. When we did, we won ten games straight. It was my worst season as far as record, but with so much potential, I couldn't wait for next year. Coach Price promised to coach next year, saying, "We will start practicing at the end of March to be ready for 13–14." Our new age division.

While I was busy playing baseball. Your grandma was formulating a plan to change the middle school I was scheduled to attend based on our address. Your grandmother kept sharing her concerns with all the mothers of my teammates. Eventually crossing the ears of Ms. Lewis. Her son, Cheeks, was on our peewee football team the last two years. When I was recruited, my mom told Coach Price about Cheeks, and we played baseball together as well. Ms. Lewis was a single mother with a big heart who happened to live in the Eisenhower attendance zone. Your grandmother was familiar with the school because we practiced at the community center. Eisenhower was on Seventy-Second Street between Parallel and Leavenworth Road. With my grandfather's house on Twenty-Fourth and Wood, it was

I COULD'VE BEEN

forty-eight blocks away. The district zoned Eisenhower to pick up kids from the inner city. The zone was from Fifth and Quindaro up to Thirteenth and Quindaro to all kids who lived north of Quindaro. Your grandmother was relentless as always. After doing her homework, she found a permissible reason to change schools for me. It was a babysitter's transfer. By law I was not to be left alone for too long without supervision until the age of thirteen. Playing between the lines, my mother convinced Ms. Lewis to sign a note saying that her older daughter was my babysitter. It was a joke to me because Tee-Tee was only two years older than me. I really was infatuated with her and didn't want to claim her as my babysitter. I knew that if I ever said that out loud, she would never consider dating me. It was just a way to attend Eisenhower instead of Northwest. The graduation percentage of kids going to Northwest Middle School was less than 12 percent. Your grandmother explained to me that statistically I had a better chance of dying than I did graduating Northwest to make it to high school. I wanted to graduate, and I didn't want to die, so babysitter's transfer it was.

My aunts went through Northwest, and they seemed to be doing fine. They did seem to be boy crazy, but I thought it was normal. When they got out of school last year, they would get home and watch music videos on BET or MTV. With Boo-Boo and me being the youngest in the house, we watched whatever was on the television. Even if it was singing, "Don't trust a big butt and a smile," which seemed to be on BET every day for almost a year. My favorite songs were "Iesha" by ABC and "Motownphilly" by Boyz II Men. The sound touched my soul like jazz music. Boo-Boo's favorite was anything Tevin Campbell. "Round and Round" was her absolute favorite song. Every time it came on, she would break out in dance.

My new adventures of being bused to Eisenhower were fun. Minus the fact I had a female bully at my bus stop. When I got to school, I felt like the Fresh Prince of Bel-Air without the mansion. Your grandmother using their rules to be smarter than their system, I was definitely in the minority. The population of the school was 80 percent Caucasian, 15 percent African American, and 5 percent other. The only problems I had with my transfer was bus related. The little bus came to pick up my bus stop. Once I found out my bully's name was the title of my favorite ABC song, I tried to befriend her through song. Every morning while waiting on the bus, I would sing to her. When the bus would pull up, she would shove me out the way to get on the bus before me. My third week of school we arrived at school as the other buses were unloading. A kid whom I had been hanging out with at lunch asked, "Are you slow?" pointing to the bus I got off. I knew the jokes from elementary school even though I never rode the bus. I looked him directly in the eye and said "My bus got here the same time yours did" without missing a beat.

Middle school was nothing like elementary. Transitioning from season to season with sports taught me how to transition from class to class. I got to pick two classes called electives to go with my five core classes. PE, social studies, math, reading, and English. Your grandmother, watching me turn into a little monster, was trying her best to keep me grounded. She had one rule when it came to my electives: in order for me to play sports in school, I had to participate in choir. Being the ruler of my domain, it was the first elective I selected. It was really crazy how I seemed to have teachers back to back in elementary. Now my elementary school music teacher was my music teacher at Eisenhower. Two teachers had me for multiple years. Ms. Nap was the first teacher to teach me in two schools. Knowing what to expect from her made adjusting to middle school choir easy. The hardest part was staying under the radar of the upperclassmen that were bullies spending their second or third year in the eighth grade.

Football practice started the first day of school. My Wyco reputation preceded me, and my middle school coach, Coach Foster, already had expectations of me. When he saw my size, the first question he asked me was, "Who blocked for you to run the ball?" My response was "Anyone." Realizing that I was serious, he gave me a shot at fullback. Seeing my understanding for the position, he changed his mind from leaning toward me playing center, on offense. On defense he kept me at defensive end. Now at my third year in the same position, I was a beast on defense. Most schools would run the ball opposite the side I was on. Coach Foster saw all my gifts and tried to embellish them. Coach Green had taught me how to long snap, but Coach Foster wanted me to be the best long snapper. I explained to him that I didn't like being upside down, so Coach Foster worked on building my confidence, erasing my fear. He earned my trust, which allowed me to listen, turning me into a great long snapper. Our season was only a seven-week season. Coach Foster, seeing that I was athletic and that I was coachable, asked me to come out for the wrestling team. He was the head coach and thought I would be great at it. The respect he had for me over the season made me try. I went to practice for three days. On the fourth, I transitioned to the team manager. Wrestling season taught me a lot. Sitting on the sidelines, I found time to do my homework, so when I got home with nothing to do, I spent my evenings at home watching music videos. Halfway through wrestling season, a new group named Kris Kross came out with a new hot song, "Jump." With my name being Chris, I emulated everything about them. I started growing my hair so that I could have braids like them. The fact that they were close to my age made me believe that I could be Kris Kross. I always felt like I was about to "Warm It Up." Your grandmother never said anything about me wearing my clothes backward.

The school bus would drop us off with thirty minutes before class started. Most mornings would lead me to the cafeteria to be watched by a teacher even though I wasn't a breakfast eater. I made it more than halfway through the school year without incident. My behavior was good, keeping my name out of the office. Trying to fit in, I decided to sit by people I knew. It was a mistake. I got in trouble with Dean Bean again. I was much bigger and stronger than I was in the third grade, so I will never understand why Dean would dare challenge me to a game of open chest, but he did. Part of me wanted revenge from the mobbing three years ago, which made me agree to play. Knowing from third grade I could take his punch, I let him go first. He hit me as hard as he could without making a scene. There was a teacher who was monitoring us, but most mornings they didn't pay attention unless the stoplight turned to yellow. His punch was solid but did nothing to stop the buzz in the lunchroom. Our stoplight turned yellow. Looking around, the monitor cautioned us to lower our voices to avoid a red light. I waited as the light went green. It was my turn now. Knowing the volume of voices would rise again any second, I waited. Just as the buzz started again, I hit Dean so hard that the sound sensor stoplight turned to red. Instantly the teacher monitoring the lunch room asked everyone to put our heads down and be quiet. We were warned at the beginning of the school year that if we hit red, we would lose our speaking privileges. The entire cafeteria remained with our heads down until we were dismissed for class. Dean continued to lay there. I was in fifth-period math class when I got called to the office.

The sixth-grade principal invited me into her office and asked me to have a seat. Unbeknownst to me, your grandmother had already been called. The principal asked me, "Did you hit Dean in the cafeteria this morning?"

I responded, "We were playing open chest, and he hit me first."

She sat there quietly for a minute thinking. When she spoke again, she told me that Dean was sent to the hospital. What seemed to be simultaneously, your grandmother arrived. The principal had told her what Dean said when she called her. When your grandmother sat down, her face looked like she was trying to break my butt mentally. With her look of disdain, your grandmother started telling the principal her plans to correct my behavior. As the principal suggested an out-of-school suspension, your grandmother scared her with saying what her intentions for me were if I was not in school, threating to send me to Bill's to clean under the rabbit cages. My principal thought that your grandmother was being too hard on me. After a lecture on how other parents trust that their kids will return from school the same way they left the house in the morning, she decided to spare me of a week in Missouri. I ended up with in-school suspension and spent a week in the detention hall. Of course, your grandmother still tore my butt up. ISS was in the wood shop classroom in the basement of the school. The teacher's only instruction was to remain quiet the entire day. His class was an elective, and he only taught a few days a week.

School basketball hadn't started yet, so our team was practicing with AP under AAU bylaws. We had a few weeks before school ball as wrestling season was finishing up. AP was always looking to improve,

I COULD'VE BEEN

so they found a tournament for us to play in. The tournament was in Liberty, Missouri. We had been practicing since school started without competition. The tournament was just what all of us needed to get us ready for school ball. With timing being everything, tryouts started the Monday after the tournament.

School basketball broke our team up again. It was back to Patrick and Blake and I at Eisenhower and Chris and James at Arrowhead. School ball wasn't just our team playing against each other. The Running Rebels were split up between schools as well. Our seventh-grade team had two athletes from my peewee football team that played for the Running Rebels. I looked up to both of them. The skill level in Kansas City basketball was insane in the sixth grade. It was rumored that two kids in the eighth grade could dunk. Every grade played separate; we just all practiced together, playing on different days of the week. While we were very good, we would still get embarrassed in practice because the older team's basketball IQ was still superior to ours. Our sixth-grade season was over as fast as it started.

My first year at Eisenhower was amazing. I was able to express myself freely without judgment. I finally had enough hair to have extensions added, so your grandmother braided my hair like Kris Kross. As I walked the halls to class, my popularity grew. Most all the school knew who the kid with the braids was. Going to school with upper middle class made me forget that I was sharing a room in Grandpa's basement. The fact that everyone in the school talked to me made me forget that color existed. In my reality, we were all just people. Your grandmother tried to influence my interest, saying, "The only thing to come in my house white is the bread, and even it has a brown crust around it." Which really just confused me because we live in my grandfather's house, and I was more into sports than anything. Your grandmother never once said anything negative about anyone because of the color of their skin. I had never heard her refer to another man as handsome other than me, but I heard her on the phone referring to AP as handsome, and he was Caucasian. Your grandma persuasion was too late. I had already had my second crush. She was a Caucasian young lady with long flowing locks of gold hair.

When I told your grandmother her name, she dismissed it, knowing my schedule was too busy for what she considered nonsense. I really think she was happy to hear a woman's name since I hadn't spoke of one in a year. My fifth grade crush was from the neighborhood. She was the baby of her family, which made her one of the most mature girls in the hood. She gave me play, but the rumors through the neighborhood was that she had already had sex, which made your grandmother tell me that I could no longer talk to her. After your grandmother said that to me, I quit sharing with her about girls that I might be interested in for fear that she might disapprove. With sports being most important, I didn't really have time for girls except for the summer. Arya never picked up on the fact that I liked her. Maybe she did, but being polite, she never spoke on it, knowing it could never happen. We were from two different worlds. With middle school offering so many new lessons and growth, I found a new crush during track season. She was a beautiful upperclassman named Tamika.

    When the announcement was made for track season, I didn't have a clue what track was about. I just knew Patrick said he was doing it. Working it out to walk to Patrick's house after practice, I was allowed to participate. I knew the definition of endurance, but track personified it. I had speed for a short distance from football and basketball. I started running the hundred-yard dash, trying to be like Patrick. He was the closest thing I had to a brother, so I admired him. It was like no matter how many times I ran down the track, I would always lose my legs about seventy yards out, and the rest of my team would blow by me like I was never in the race. After about two weeks of coming in dead last, my coaches decided to get me more involved in the field events. I began to experiment in long jump, high jump, discus, shot put, and something that really got my attention, the softball throw. Coach Foster coached shot put and discus, so he hand-selected me to be in this new event. I was decent at high jump, but my behind got in my way. There really weren't any twelve-year-olds that could clear six feet. I could clear five feet, ten inches, so I won a couple of medals for second and third. In long jump, I never made it into the medals. Fourth place was my weekly best. The kids who would have blown past me in the hundred-yard dash at the last thirty yards were the kids who kept jumping past me, landing me in fourth. The one event that I was the undisputed king of was the softball throw. Playing baseball for the last three years gave me an unfair advantage. I would easily throw the ball almost twice the distance of my closet competitor. The day after a track meet, my favorite day of school. I fell in love with getting my name called on the morning announcements for first place in the softball throw. It fueled my ego and love of competition.

Track and field was all the athletes' sign that the school year was over. Minus a few tests, track practice was the highlight of the day. Two more track meets were all we had left of sixth grade. During practice every day, a beautiful set of twins would walk home past where we were practicing. They were identical to the point that I really couldn't tell them apart. It was my first encounter with twins. It amazed me that they were both so beautiful. Their skin was golden brown like Jasmine Guy. Their hair was long and flowing, which captivated me. All the women in my grandfather's house with the exception of your grandmother had seen one too many run-ins with a hot comb. Your grandmother had a jerry curl, which I was embarrassed about for years, so to see these beautiful young ladies with their real flowing long hair made me want to know more. They walked the same direction we walked when we were finished with practice. They weren't on the team, so they had a few hours' head start. When we got to Patrick's house, we had an hour before baseball, so we couldn't search for them. With just a few days of school left, I gathered the courage and asked one of the twins for her number. Believing that it was a fake, I called the number as soon as I got to Patrick's house. I could not believe it when their father answered the phone. Without fear or hesitation, I asked to speak to one of his daughters. As polite as he could, he said, "She is busy at the moment. Would you like to leave a message?" Declining the message, I hung up. When I got off the phone, I celebrated like I scored a touchdown even though I didn't even talk to her.

When school let out for the summer, the bond between Patrick and I cemented itself. Just like my other friend Cheeks last year, I got

Patrick on Coach Price's team this year. With us both still playing basketball for Coach AP, who was officially declaring us an AAU team, we often spent so much time together that I started calling his mother Momma. I definitely admired her. She worked full time at the post office. She was also a part of their union. Her heart was so big that she opened her home to foster kids, trying to give them a better life. On her days off, she would always take us to Kansas City Community College to walk the trail. More often than not, we would practice at Eisenhower for baseball and Turner recreation center for basketball. With Patrick's proximity to both, I tended to just stay at his house all the time. It wasn't unlikely for us to have both practices in the same day. With the addition of Patrick to our baseball team, I was no longer needed as a pitcher. I was able to concentrate full time as a catcher, which increased my skills at the position. My bat was gaining acknowledgment after I hit a couple of over-the-fence home runs on the big field at 3&2.

 The hitting classes combined with getting to go to the batting cages which sat at the top of the hill paid off. I preferred to get to the game two hours early so that I could spend forty minutes in the cages. I gained the nickname Baby Bo after one of my favorite athletes, Bo Jackson. Everyone in the league knew that I played multiple sports and was good at them. Coach Price got on the board of directors for the league, which kept him in the office before and after our games. Sometimes he would have to let us coach ourselves so that he could be a part of a board meeting. Hosting the eleven-to-twelve-year-old state tournament was 3&2 with this year, 3&2 was hosting the eleven-to-twelve-year-old state tournament and there seemed to be a lot of last minute decisions. Your grandmother never missed a game. She was the scorekeeper for our games. She always sat high enough in the stands to see the pitch over the umpire's shoulder. Whenever she saw a pitch that she felt the umpire called wrong, she was very boisterous with her opinion. I'm just thankful I never saw her drink any alcohol. She said she quit the night after she got pregnant with me. As passionate as she could be expressing her opinion if she was a drinker, she would have gotten tossed out the park plenty of times. Your grandmother's voice made quick friends with the people who were running the park. When the state tournament started, your grandmother volunteered to be the official scorekeeper for the state tournament. I use the word *volunteered* lightly. The league paid her twenty-five dollars a game. Back and forth all season between baseball and basketball, after we got blew out of our age division's state tournament, I still made the all-star game. We had five people from our team in the all-star game. Playing for Coach Price made the park my third home. I had access to everything but their concession stand. I would brag to my friends that I had a key to the park like the mayor had the key to the city.

At home, my candy store was growing. I wasn't able to keep it stocked, being so committed to my athletics. Whoever opened the door was still selling it for me. If I didn't take inventory before I went to bed, I would run out of something. A trip to Sam's had to be scheduled around multiple schedules, forcing me to purchase my estimated sales for the week whenever I went. My business philosophy came from my grandfather. He would always say, "It's better to have it and not need it than to need it and not have it." Most mornings the doorbell would start ringing at 10:00 a.m. and would ring just about every seven or ten minutes all day and all evening long. At twelve years old, I would profit a few hundred a week, which made me feel rich because I always had more money than all my friends. Grandma raising me to be humble kept me from parading my success with my candy store. Every time I amassed too much cash, she would make me set aside the money to restock before taking me to the Fun Factory, the movies, or shopping at Indian Springs. I liked to spend my money on clothes and shoes. Having the funds to buy my own clothes, I was well dressed all the time. If we spent too long in the mall, we would eat at Big Al's, which was one of my favorite places to eat.

After years of persistence Coach, AP's vision for summer basketball was heard. For the first time ever in Wyandotte County, there was a summer basketball league established at Kensington recreation center. Kensington was on Twenty-Ninth and State Avenue, which is only a few miles from home. Coach AP always wanting to push us to be better. He signed us up to play up one age division. Which meant we were the youngest team in our division. There was a division for our age. Coach just felt like we wouldn't get better blowing out kids our age. We heard that the Running Rebels were in the league; we just had not seen them. Knowing our schedules would soon cross, Coach AP told us to be two hours early for the next game.

When we walked in, the Running Rebels were playing. The scoreboard read 66 to 12 in the third quarter. Watching this team play was amazing and intimidating. Sitting in the stands, watching their full-court press with a fifty-point lead made their coach, Ivan Edwards, seem like an asshole. Six feet tall and built like Mr. T, he stood on the sidelines with his arms crossed, not saying a word as his team seemed to coach themselves into running up the score. Every five minutes the players would make their own substations. Bringing in a fresh five guys onto the court. It was the first team I saw as competition. All fifteen players on their team played equal minutes. It was the first time I ever saw the scoreboard turn over. The message was sent. They murdered their opponent, beating them by one hundred points. A couple of weeks later, we faced the Running Rebels. We didn't win, but we made sure that we didn't lose by one hundred points. Once Coach Edwards found out that we were younger, he had a mutual respect for Coach AP.

After the game, the coaches shared their respects, exchanging numbers. Coach AP was about collaborations. Coach Edwards was looking to expand his brand, being dominant to Kansas City Basketball. Coach Edwards and Coach AP merged at the end of the summer. Now just about every talented kid playing basketball in Kansas City played for the name Running Rebels. Having so many kids, Coach Edwards ran ten to fifteen practices a week, spending every day in the gym. We were practicing wherever we could. A lot of our practices were at Bell Recreation or Bethany Community Center. Coach Edwards had us all captivated. His mission was to teach every player on our team how to dribble like a point guard, shoot like a shooting guard, and rebound like a center. Most of our practices were right after our older team. It was amazing to walk into the gym with Kansas City legends. Coach Edwards, being the brilliant coach he was, had collected the top fifteen players from all over the city.

They were scheduled to attend schools like Pembroke, Raytown, Washington High school, even a kid from Central High School. Every game they played they would dominate their opponent. Mercy was not something that Coach Edwards coached. One of his favorite coaching points was "Don't play down to the team you are playing!" Coach Edwards gave us confidence in ourselves. He could also break us when we scrimmaged our older team. Coach Edwards's primary focus was getting a sponsor so that we could travel to compete.

With everything going full speed, I didn't work the garden at all. My activities kept me so busy. With no scheduled games, basketball practice was my only commitment. Since we didn't practice on Saturdays, I convinced your grandmother to spend the rest of our summer skating on Saturday mornings. With several weeks' absence, when we returned to Wyandotte Skateland, they were extremely short-staffed. Your grandmother raised me to help people and expect nothing in return, so I didn't even ask to work the skate rental counter. I just jumped back there and started collecting tickets and passing out skates. I handled it so well that the manager offered me free food and free admission. He had an employee quit and offered to compensate me for helping. He tried to offer me the job until I informed him that I was twelve. He couldn't believe my size. After a couple of weeks without him finding a new employee, your grandmother took a copy of my birth certificate and changed the year, making me thirteen. State law said that any child of age thirteen or older could be employed. I only worked Saturdays because of my schedule. I was so happy to have another job.

When I did make it to Missouri, the garden was done. Bill had managed everything without me. He didn't have to say he missed me. He announced to everyone at dinner that he would not be taking on the responsibility of the garden full time next summer. "Mama, I'm moving out," he said. He had acquired too much stuff for his tiny room. He bought a house in Kansas City to be closer to your grandmother and work. He had been driving for the same company for years, earning his seniority to be home more didn't want to be trapped in his room at his mother's house.

Bill was very humble. His house had only the barest of needs. He lived like Hakeem from *Coming to America* once he got to Queens. Home maybe four nights a week, Bill got a dog that he said was mine even though I lived with my grandpa. He was hoping that the dog would make me feel more at home. It was a beautiful golden Shar-Pei. I named him Sharp. As a puppy, he was so adorable. As he grew, so did his aggression. Bill knew that once school and football started, I would only able to see him on the weekends. I got two and a half solid weeks with sharp before I was scheduled to attend the Derrick Smith football camp. It was the first time I had to be away from your grandmother for an entire week. She dropped me off like the brochure said. They had staff to help us get to our dorm room for the week. I cried like a baby for, the first two hours. When my roommate showed up, I forgot all about being away from your grandmother. The next morning, we started drills at 8:00 a.m. We did combine drills all morning. After lunch we got to have fun and compete a little, playing seven on seven. The last two days we had a flag football tournament. The week passed so fast I was disappointed when it ended. It was a great opportunity, and there was a slew of college and professional coaches at the camp boosting my scholarship potential.

When I did get back to Sharp, he didn't look like a puppy anymore. Almost double in size, he had a mean personality, and his little butt bit me. When I picked him up by the skin on his neck, he didn't like it and tried it again. I didn't consider him my puppy anymore. What Bill thought would make me want to come around more became something that kept me away. Sharp was mean and aggressive with the ability to jump the fence. My last time in Bill's backyard, Sharp had found a way to get on top of the car port. When I stepped into the yard, he jumped down on me, scaring the shit out of me, making me refuse to have dealings with him.

Dream a Little Like Dr. King

I started the seventh grade on the chubby side of healthy. On my downtime after camp, I laid into my profits a little heavy at the candy store. Knowing how active I was, your grandmother never taught me to be concerned with calories or diet. Football wasn't as easy as it was before. The leg I broke in second grade was starting to give me ligament issues. Our family physician sent me to a specialist who recommended a knee brace specifically made for me. The price of the special brace was over four hundred dollars after insurance. Your grandmother immediately said we could not afford it. Knowing my pain, I used my earnings from the store and paid cash at the end of my fitting. Four days later, I had my new knee brace. Between my weight and the brace, I was a lot slower. Returning to my familiar positions, I just needed to polish my technique. I really gained a defensive edge from camp. They had an emphasis on combining techniques, which kept me leading the team in tackles. Our season created a bond on the field and in the classroom. Everyone loved me, while I just loved hearing my name on the announcements.

Having such a happy-go-lucky attitude caught the attention of my English teacher Mrs. Martin. She tested me in class for a few weeks before she pulled me to the side and asked me if I would be interested in saying the "I Have a Dream" speech. Doing what I've always done, I agreed before I knew all the details. Having to stay after school to practice for forty-five minutes every day, the speech got me out of practice, and I got to skip the part of practice I hated. Stretching was pointless to me, so I was defiantly happy to get out of it. When school was dismissed, I would hang out around her class until everyone else left. Mrs. Martin's class being the last two hours of my school day, I would try to extend class as long as I could to make the class take longer to clear out. Every day she would give me one-on-one coaching with memory requirements that started to help me commit the speech to memory like it was a play on the field.

Football season flew by, after adjusting to my knee brace, I continued to make a name for myself on both sides of the ball. Sixth-grade football was separate from seventh and eighth, who played together. Our seventh-grade schedule added a school named Sumner Academy on our list. Sumner was a college preparatory school that you had to be invited to attend. It was unique because you could leave your middle school at the seventh grade. Sumner was an eight through twelfth grade school that provided the structure to take AB classes, which could give you college credits in high school. We played the Sumner Academy Saber's our last game of the season. They had a thoroughbred named Tyler Lewis who had been running track all his life. On the football field, his speed was no different. Tyler would break for sixty-yard runs regularly. We had Sumner backed up with the ball on their twenty-yard line until they ran a sweep away from me. Instantly, like a stallion, Tyler was in the wind running past our defense. Seeing the play develop, I started taking an angle of pursuit behind our defense like we worked on in camp. My angle was perfect. Even though I wasn't as fast as Tyler, I was on his heels. After running for sixty yards, he started to lose steam. I never quit on the play. I caught him at the seventh yard line with a shoestring tackle. After getting up from my dive to tackle him, I was called to the end-zone sideline by the coach, who was standing, watching. He asked me, "Son, what's your name?"

I answered, "Christopher Drake."

He said, "My name is Coach Russell, I'm head coach of varsity football at Sumner Academy."

After football ended, I was still committed to stay after school to practice the speech. I didn't even try to be the wrestling team manager. When Mrs. Martin and I finished our practice, I would walk to Patrick's house. I often thought about the twins on my walk.

Every day when school let out, I would spend an hour with Mrs. Martin then walk to Patrick's house and spend some time trying to call the twins. They knew that I couldn't tell them apart, and they began to use me as their entertainment. The fact that their voices also sounded exactly alike made it very hard to distinguish who was who. One minute I would be talking on the phone to Tina, the next I was talking to Tara. They only pulled this prank on the phone. I kept asking to take Tina out on a date. Her father wouldn't have it, so they kept stringing me along. I was persuaded to buy their attention with jewelry. She told me that if I got her some jewelry that I could come to their house. I had never brought jewelry before and had no clue where to get it. I did the next best thing. I started collecting whatever discarded jewelry I could find. After a couple of months, I had acquired a bag of crap that at one point might have been nice. Now with kinks and missing stones, it was all garbage. With Christmas break near, I knew that it would be a few months before I would have time to attempt to see Tina, so I kept collecting any discarded jewelry.

After Christmas break, basketball started immediately. After tryouts I had to let the coach know that I would be late to practice for a couple of weeks. "I'm practicing the 'I Have a Dream' speech preparing for the assembly in two weeks," I said. Gaining his approval, I missed the first hour of basketball every day. Our seventh-grade team had talent, more than half the eighth grade talent left to attend Sumner. Some seventh graders got to play eighth-grade basketball as well. Playing with the eighth graders wasn't fun at all. The only seventh grader they would pass the ball to was Patrick, who wasn't going to pass up a shot.

January 16, 1992, I was asked by Mrs. Martin to wear a suit. My grandfather and his wife were so involved in the church that wasn't a problem. I was ready and had mastered the speech. I expected that I would only be in front of the school when I signed up. Boy, was I wrong. I had the privilege of delivering the speech for an all-school assembly. Eisenhower's gym was the only gymnasium big enough for every middle school in the district to attend. Mrs. Martin pulled me out of class early for some last-minute coaching. She said, "I know that you are going to be nervous when you get to the podium, but just remember we've been practicing for five months." She encouraged me, reminding me that I would be fine, just treat it like practice. I took my seat on the stage with a program on my chair, looking over the program while the crowd got seated. I realized that there were several dedications before I had to go. It took about an hour to seat all the different schools. As the schools were filling the packed gymnasium, in came news reporters who set up in the middle aisle, twenty feet from the stage. They probably wanted to get closer, but the floor was marked for the small dance routine at the end of the program. I had not heard Mrs. Martin talk about anything or anyone else performing while we were practicing. Everything was just a little overwhelming.

As the head principle of Eisenhower addressed every middle school in the district, a calm settled on the gym. As the program started, my anxiety rose. Going through narratives and poems, choir selections, orchestra selections, I started enjoying the show so much that I forgot I was a part of it. When the MC introduced me, I looked around for someone else. It took me a second to realize she had said it was my turn. I stood up nervously, making my way to the podium. After clearing my throat, I stepped forward and adjusted the microphone. Standing there as I looked around the entire gymnasium, I was petrified. Once I opened my mouth and said, "I say to you today, my friends, so even though we have the difficulties of today and tomorrow. I still have a dream. It is a dream deeply rooted in the American dream," my five months of practice took over. Like a trained assassin, I killed it. I said the entire speech verbatim. I never looked in the camera. I looked straight ahead at Mrs. Martin the entire time, just like practice. After the assembly, Mrs. Martin came straight to me. Her hug was full of elation and gratitude. She said, "Christopher Drake, that was amazing. The pause you gave in the beginning was so powerful." Accepting her praise, I tried to explain that it may have seemed planned, but I was really trying to get my nerves together, realizing that it was easily a few thousand people all watching me. After the assembly, I felt like the mayor of Eisenhower.

Vowing that I would be as nonconfrontational as possible as long as a possibility for communication existed.

Seventh-grade students were starting to get their acceptance letters to Sumner. Most would come to school bragging that they were moving on because they were smart enough to go to Sumner. Their acceptance was based on our CBTS test scores. Since the third grade I had always tested three to four grades ahead. Every day when I got home, I asked, "Did I get anything in the mail?" and Ester would reply "No, what bills are you paying?" I was so busy with athletics that I quit looking for my letter, but it seemed like every day someone else would announce their acceptance to the acclaimed Sumner Academy. Not getting an acceptance letter made me question my intelligence. All my friends already had their letters. The one thing that kept me from losing my mind was that Patrick had not gotten a letter either. When I asked him if he wanted to go to Sumner, he said, "Not really. All of my friends are going to Washington." I knew Washington wasn't something that would make your grandmother happy. My grandfather's house was in the Wyandotte High School zoning area. I knew that your grandmother would never let me attend Wyandotte. To her it was worse than Eastside High School. My aunts Nora and Leah scared her with their horror stories of gangs, guns, and fights in school. With the uncertainty of which high school I would attend, it was hard trying to stay focused in school. My desire to stay on the basketball team was my only motivation.

My basketball coach for school basketball was old school compared to our AAU coaches. He believed in the traditional lineup. With my size and height, I played power forward, which put me close to the basket. Our AAU coaches taught everyone to play point guard. School taught us places to run on the floor to start our offensive play. Our defense was so good in AAU that we seldom used plays. When we did, they never had people standing under the basket because that was where one of us was trying to go. Now being told by my school coach to run to the low box confused me. Trying to fit his system, I started watching the NBA, studying my position, looking for a role model for how to play the position. Dennis Rodman was amazing with rebounding and angles, but he was wild. Karl Malone and Charles Barkley also dominated the position, so I tried to play like them. Shooting all those shots in my backyard gave me a good jumper, so I didn't like being under the rim. It was a little too close for me. Anytime I got the ball, I was afraid that I was going to hit the bottom of the rim as I tried to score. Being a team player, I did as the coach said for school. I knew that as soon as it was over, we would be back to *run-and-gun* Running Rebel basketball.

It was almost track season, and I still haven't gotten a letter of acceptance from Sumner. To prevent my disappointment, I had given up. I mentioned to your grandma that school was almost over, and the letters for Sumner seemed to have slowed down. With her dreams of better for me, she took it upon herself to call Sumner and ask why I hadn't received an acceptance letter. A week later I got an envelope in the mail. It was finally official, getting my acceptance letter validating me. Proudly I was again chosen among the elite, scheduled to attend Sumner Academy. I was more excited that your grandmother could quit stressing about my future high school. I was so excited feeling validated as more than just an athlete. I took my letter of acceptance to school with me in my back left pocket just in case anyone tried to question me in my word, especially since there was less than a month of school. So consumed with my new legacy of being a *Sumner Academy Sabre*, track season flew by.

Physically I was still a little chubby, despite all the games or all the practices. My knees were hurting constantly, like I was growing but it wasn't happening fast enough. My weight kept me grounded on the track team, and I wasn't even looked at to participate in the jumping events. The softball throw was only for sixth graders. This year it was just shot put and discus. Coach Foster knew that I had natural strength and could qualify in the shot put purely off muscle. He focused on teaching me technique. He gave me the choice of the spin or glide. The spin technique was not easy for me. I couldn't keep my size 13 feet in the little circle whenever I would spin. Coach Foster did it perfectly every time, which made me try harder to master it. At thirteen, I was five inches taller than my coach. He would always accept my failures because of my height, so I never really applied myself. At the competitions, I would use the glide technique.

I COULD'VE BEEN

I never finished lower than third, but Coach Foster had first-place dreams. The discus used the same circle at most schools with almost the same technique. I tried to gain full understanding of the discipline, I just couldn't throw as far. I did a 450-degree spin/hop combo that allowed me to soar the discus like a bird. In the seventh grade I had no competition, but I couldn't compete with too many of the eight graders at the meets. Still, my favorite part was the day after the meets, hearing my name on the announcements. With the school year winding down, I started trying to capture as many memories as I could because I knew that I would not see more than half of these people next year, starting my new adventures as a Sabre.

Our AAU basketball teams were preparing to go to Vegas for the national tournament, so practice was in full swing as school was ending. Coach Edwards didn't believe in luck; he believed in hard work, skill, and preparation. After combining teams and growing, we had enough players for two thirteen-year-old teams. It took a great deal of planning and coordinating by every coach, wife, and parent that cared to help. Coach AP, Coach Edwards, and Mrs. Edwards made it happen. Practicing four or five times a week, it was convenient for me to spend the night at Patrick's house. Staying at Patrick's put me in close proximity of the twins, putting Tina on my mind. I still had the crown royal bag of jewelry. I found the bag like I found the jewelry. Calling their house, I told Tina that I had some jewelry for her. She told me how to get to her house. It was literally two minutes from Patrick's house the whole time. As I walked up, I saw her standing on the porch. She looked confused as to why I had a crown royal bag. She didn't open it in front of me. I stood there and stared at her for a bit before making my way back to Patrick's house. A couple of days later, I called and asked to speak to Tina. When she came to the phone, I asked if she liked the jewelry. She said, "You didn't give me any jewelry, you gave it to my sister." She said it was all junk. "Listen, since you can't tell the difference between us, I don't want to talk to you anymore." The voices of my friends and the names they called the twins ran through my mind. I was tired of the games being played. It was easy to let go. Patrick had found a club for thirteen and up next to a movie theater in Shawnee Mission.

We started asking to go to the movies with full intent to go to the teenage club lest than twenty-five feet from the docile movie theater that we pretended to frequent. The club was just for teenagers. It cost ten dollars at the door and closed at 11:30 p.m. At first it was only a Friday thing. As our confidence grew, so did our attendance. Our parents busy with life couldn't check up on us with everything. Their go-to question was, "Do you have homework?" In order to play for Coach Edwards, you had to be intelligent or talented. My social circle of teammates was both. Meeting our coach's expectations and dominating our opponents gave our parents trust in our competence. Watching the fifteen-year-olds make out was the closest I had ever been to being kissed.

Our baseball season was underway, and both Patrick and I informed Coach Price of our commitments to our AAU basketball team when practices started at the end of April. With the national tournament a month away, basketball was our priority, practicing five times a week. Sometimes we missed baseball completely because we were so invested. Most of the time on the baseball field, we were just exhausted bodies in uniform. We played our hardest, but the fatigue from all the practices, for both sports plus the games, wore us down. It seemed that all our games this year were scheduled at the other property that was owned by 3&2 Stadiums. It was called Linedotte off Sixty-Third and Leavenworth Road. Our team loved playing at the Linedotte ball park. Our games couldn't be interrupted by a board meeting. The park was nowhere near as beautiful as 3&2 Stadium. It was a real hole in the wall. Once the game started, it didn't matter. The field was slightly larger than most thirteen-to-fourteen-year-old fields, which prevented me from hitting traditional home runs. I actually think Coach Price preferred the bigger diamond because I could clear all four bases as they chased down the ball rolling to the fence. My athletic abilities caught the attention of the umpires who seemed to regularly work our games. Playing catcher, I was constantly talking to the umpires. Both of them knew the rules like they wrote the book and had passion and integrity behind all their calls. The way they umpired made them a league favorite. Just about every game our team would hope the Starr brothers were umpiring the game.

I COULD'VE BEEN

Three months' shy of fourteen our AAU teams were Vegas bound. The first thing that caught everyone's attention when we stepped out the airport was the humidity. In August, the heat in Kansas City was capable of getting over a hundred degrees. Sometimes we would have to practice football with just helmets because the humidity was so bad that kids around the state were dying. In Vegas, in June as soon as that humidity and heat hit us, it took our breath away. Our coaches rented vans to get us around. Your grandmother couldn't make it to Vegas. She took a third job on the weekends a couple of months before the trip to make sure that she could afford to send me. When she started, she didn't request the time off and was committed to work. Not used to one-hundred-degrees-plus temperature, our coaches tried their best to keep us out of the sun. Our rooms were booked at the Circus-Circus, which was abundant with distractions for kids. When we weren't practicing or playing, we spent our time in the game room of the hotel. With almost thirty teammates, it was hard for me to keep track. I don't have a clue how the coaches did it. Our first game in the tournament, we got to play on a UNLV court that was already adorned with the name Running Rebels, which filled me with pride, making me more of a Jerry Tarkanian fan. The amount of players we had split our team into two teams, team A and team B. Both teams played well, especially having all the other distractions. Only playing one game a day, we had a lot of free time in the hotel. One of our teammates was sexually active and found a young lady in the game room who was as well. While Coach AP gathered players interested in walking down the strip, more than half the team had piled into a room with the young lady they had met. I was informed of my teammates' intentions. Never having any contact with a woman except holding hands, I wasn't interested. I wanted my first time to be private and special. I decided that walking down the strip seeing the sites with coach was more my speed. As we walked down the strip, I was mind blown. Prostitution was legal, and as the sunlight faded, more and more people just seemed to come out of nowhere. They were handing out flyers. Even though we were told not to accept them, I took a few so that I could see what was on them. It was pictures of naked women with stars or hearts to cover their explicit parts. I couldn't believe my eyes as I marveled at the card stock fliers. Being a kid that likes to push the envelope just a little, I held on to the cards up until I saw our hotel in site.

    The first thing I did after our walk was to go to my room. Coach's room required him to take a different elevator, leaving me and a few teammates to ride up by ourselves. Trying to go our separate ways as we got to our floor, we were greeted by Rabbit. He was one of our teammates who had tons of energy. We could see the excitement all over his face. He couldn't wait to say, "Y'ALL MISSED IT. SHE LET EVERYONE SMASH!" I was in disbelief with her and my teammates. We still had time before curfew. I needed to hear it from someone other than Rabbit. Instead of getting off the elevator with the rest of my teammates, I stayed on riding it downstairs to the game room. When the elevator doors opened, another one of my teammates was standing in my way. He was smiling from ear to ear. I asked him to walk with me so that we could talk in private. Once we got around the corner, I asked if what Rabbit said was true. Smiling bigger than ever, he said, "Smell my fingers." I was repulsed as he put them toward my face. The odor that filled the air was pungent. He went on to say that at one point, it was fifteen guys in the room at the same time with the one girl. Shaking my head, we went our separate ways. Honestly, I was a little jealous because I was still a virgin. I decided to look for someone that I could possibly be with in private. I walked into the game room, seeing this beautiful angel. She looked Latina by nationality. Forgetting everything, I started playing the game right next to her. After about three minutes of acting like I really wanted to play the game, I introduced myself. She smiled and said, "My name is Faith." Far prettier than all my previous crushes, I was mesmerized talking to her, until the coaches came to sweep for curfew. I asked if I would see her tomorrow as she told me that her family was leaving first thing in the morning. Having enjoyed my time as much as I enjoyed hers, she stopped a cocktail server, asking for a pen and a napkin to give me her number. I was so on cloud nine. Faith lived in California, and I knew if your grandma had to work three jobs to send me on a trip she couldn't attend that I would never see her again. Her beauty made me hold on to the num-

I COULD'VE BEEN

ber. Both teams finished well in the tournament. Between us we lost three games. It was our first loss as Running Rebels. Taking second in the national tournament was pretty good for our first attempt. With basketball over, I wanted more than anything to get back to your grandma and my comfort zone.

The first practice after Vegas we were given our commandments: #1 God, #2 Mom and Dad, #3 Basketball, #4 You.

Coach Edwards was already established as a coaching guru with his collection of all the elite athletes in Kansas City. He said something that would resonate with me for the next few years. He said that he knew that we were out of our element, that was why he put us in the tournament. "If you are going to be national champions, you need to get comfortable with being uncomfortable!" Coach Edwards being twice our size moved closer to one of my teammates. He got so up close and personal that I almost peed down my leg. He reminded us that if we were not growing, the world was still spinning, and it was passing us by. His message was that change is necessary for growth. School was just a few weeks away. It was time for me to change to football. Our teammates that didn't play football kept practicing with Coach AP and Coach Edwards until school ball started. Our teammates that did play football could practice but were not required to.

Preceded by Reputation

My grandfather's brother, David, had a daughter named Eva, who was four years older than me and was in her senior year at Sumner. It was nice to have a cousin attending Sumner, someone to show me the ropes. It gave me confidence that if she could do it, so could I. Her father, who preferred to be called Sonny, would come get me on Saturdays or Sundays when I wasn't in the garden or in church and take me fishing or garage selling. The time he gave me meant the world to me. He could turn a simple garage sale into treasure hunting, making me feel like we were pirates out to negotiate the best steal we could. He would pick me up at 4:00 or 5:00 a.m. to start on our mission because it was always a road trip regardless if we were fishing or headed to a garage sale. The love I had for him made me love my cousin Eva like she was my sister. Once she got news that I would be attending Sumner, she told all her friends. She was so excited to have someone in the family attending Sumner with her. One of the luxuries of attending Sumner was that class didn't start until 8:05 a.m., which meant I got to sleep in later than middle school. The first day of school, our phone line rang at 7:00 a.m. It jolted me out of bed. I was too excited to sleep and was lying in the bed, waiting until my 7:15 a.m. alarm. It was my cousin Eva telling your grandmother that she would pick me up for school. Twenty minutes later my cousin was outside blowing her horn. I opened the door to see this car with shoe polish all over the windshields with toilet paper on the antenna. Before I could open the car door, she explained that I had to ride in the back seat because it was senior parade, and she couldn't let her friends see a "rookie" in her car. Hiding in the back seat, Eva headed to the rally point, where she met the rest of her senior class. Everyone's car was decorated with school spirit. Blue and white shoe polish decorated the windows of every vehicle. Once everyone was on full display of their class pride, the caravan of cars took off in a line that stretched over three miles, carefully navigating from Blessed Sacrament on Twenty-Third and parallel down to Eighth and Washington Boulevard. After making the left turn onto Eighth Street, passing Mt. Calvary Missionary Baptist Church, every car in line started blowing their horns to make sure that everyone saw them. We drove straight into Sumner's roundabout parking lot back to the corner. Following the one-way streets. The long barrage of cars made the entire trip around the school. Hiding in the back seat, the horn blowing and yelling made me peek my head to see that the school had been tee-peed. After the seniors found a place to park, they all entered the school from the senior's parking lot and paraded around every hallway of the school, announcing that this was their school, their year, and they were proud of it.

Growing taller over the summer didn't seem to help my fluffiness. I wasn't fat. I had plenty of muscle; it just had insulation. When my fourteenth birthday came, my shoe size again matched my age. I was six feet tall, strong as a mule, just clumsy, learning to manage my size. I could trip over my own feet. The only time it didn't affect me was during the game. I was taller than most everyone that came out for football. My first day of practice was a peewee football reunion. Seventy-five percent of our eighth-grade team had played with or against me at Wyco or in middle school. Seeing that most all of our team had knowledge and experience of the game of football, we as a team were excited with our next five years together. Coach Eliopoulos, our Greek coach, was the shortest person in practice. No one could pronounce his last name correctly, so he asked us to simply call him Coach E. His assistant coach was Italian, who also has a name that no one could pronounce, so we called him Coach K. Their coaching methods were all about respect with understanding through coaching proper technique. They treated us like men, so we handled ourselves accordingly on the field. With Coach E's efforts to hear our voices, showing value to our opinions, we all left our hearts on the field every day. We all loved Coach E so much that we really didn't care what positions we played. Coach K convinced Coach E to try me at tight end. He knew I had hands but saw that my speed wasn't the best. I practiced the position for three weeks before they decided that center would benefit the team the best. I didn't care as long as I was playing. Just like peewee football, I never left the field. Our seven-game season was over so fast. The excitement of my new school hadn't even worn off before the season was over. We had a great season, and Coach Russell was our biggest fan. He saw all the talent that was coming up and didn't miss any of our games. He always watched from a distance like a shadow.

Utopia is the only word I could use to describe my feelings about Sumner. I had always been a little nerd. Being in a school where everyone was supposed to be intelligent gave me comfort to proudly be myself. I was surrounded by geniuses everywhere. Most of them had lineage of intelligence with older or younger siblings to expound ideas with. Being an only child, I had to learn fast because no one except your grandmother cared to make sure I understood. Once I learned the definition of *idiot savant*, I thought it defined 80 percent of students at Sumner. The brain waves flowing through the halls were amazing, but everyone was in their own little world, and nothing outside of it mattered. As a part of Sumner's curriculum, we were required to take a foreign language class as eighth graders. Foreign language classes were not available to anyone else in the district until ninth grade. Your grandmother tried her best to convince me to take French, which I probably would have done, but after my summer encounter with Faith, I decided Spanish was the language for me. Along with a foreign language, Sumner also required a typing class as part of the district curriculum. Your grandmother's position about singing hadn't changed and took two of my four electives because all choir classes were full-year classes.

Every day in the hallway, Eva would bring someone new by my locker to introduce to me. It happened so frequently that I was forgetting names as fast as she threw them at me. My cousin was so proud that someone in our family was at the same school regardless of our age difference. She was my biggest advocate. Daily my popularity grew. It got to the point that girls would walk up to me and say "You're Eva's cousin" and walk way, leaving me confused. Eva picked me up every day for school, which humored me because if it was really important to her, she could have introduced us before school. I always wondered, did she walk by my locker on purpose or conveniently?

Sumner was challenging. Only the top 2 percent of students academically in Wyandotte County were chosen to attend which made everyone in the building feel special. Trying to adjust to my new social popularity as well as Spanish and algebra. I spent too much of my time in the hallways, studying all the extraordinary personalities, causing my grades to decline which placed me on academic probation. Academic probation was when your grades weren't good enough to participate in athletics. You could practice, but you couldn't play in games. My best subject all my life was now killing me. Midquarter progress reports came out two days before Sumner's open house. Bringing home two As, two Bs, two Cs, and a D, your grandma made sure to attend, introducing herself to all seven of my teachers. It was my worst GPA, but I was able to convince your grandmother that it was going to be better next week after the algebra test we took got graded and added.

The week after open house, my algebra teacher gave me a note to take home. He put it in a sealed envelope that read, "To the parents of Christopher Drake." Your grandmother killed me with her glare as she read the letter. The next day she sent me to school with a full-page letter to my teachers inquiring about my behavior and grades. At the bottom of the paper was her phone number and email. Under her contact information, it said, "I'm only twenty minutes away." She was office assistance at Hawthorne Elementary School, which gave me even more pressure. This time with my weekly progress reports I had seven teachers to get signatures from. After a few weeks of embarrassment, I brought all my grades to As in everything except math. His method of teaching didn't register to help me understand. It was his first year teaching at Sumner. Our energies clashed so much I grew very opinionated about what I thought of him as a teacher. I told anyone that would listen that I thought Mr. Bell was the worst teachers ever, who was only failing me because I wouldn't flirt with him. One of his favorite things to say to me was, "I don't care that you are a popular athlete that everyone expects to play." He was more focused on integrity, trying to teach me that athletic privilege wouldn't let me coast through his class. I challenged Mr. Bell every day in class, asking questions in class like, "When will I use x or y in life?" To me, none of it was practical. My misunderstandings made me challenge him, while his frustrations made him challenge me. After eight weeks of me trying Mr. Bell for a realistic example for a reason to use algebra in a practical moment, he requested a conference, sending me home with a note on Friday. Monday immediately at 3:15 p.m. exactly, ten minutes after school was dismissed, your grandmother met with Mr. Bell, while I sat in the hallway on the floor. When she came out of his class, she was frustrated, not allowing me to read her energy. I jumped up, following her from a distance, not sure whose side she was on. After we were outside of other ears, your grandmother said, "I see why you don't like him. He's an asshole! Regardless, you have to pass his class to graduate." She told me she agreed for me to meet with him after school Monday through Friday for tutoring. Staying after school for one-on-one tutoring gave both of us a chance to understand each other, changing my grade along with my perspective of integrity.

My after-school tutoring introduced me to the late bus to get home. Sumner's students came from all over the district, covering every inch of Wyandotte County. The late buses would drop people off at some central locations, which gave all riders a little walk to get home. I got to talking sports with Morgan, who stayed after school for band practice between her athletic seasons. She asked me what my plans were since football was over. My mind was focused on AAU basketball until school season starts in January. Daily she suggested that I become manager for the varsity girls' basketball team, which was her next sport since volleyball was over. Staying after school was a limitless adventure which excited me. I loved having something to do, so I thought about it. She stayed on me every day for weeks. She was very persuasive. I just always followed my own energy. Trusting my gut, I felt like her intentions did not have my best interest at heart. My desire to stay after school made me try wrestling again, expecting a new experience. We sparred one-on-one in three-minute intervals with challenges called out by classmates. I survived two back-to-back challenges with upperclassmen hazing in addition to ten laps around the school hallways. Before we stretched, Coach pulled us in a circle in the middle of the mats. Laying out his expectations for perfection, he encouraged us, giving us one of the most motivational speeches I had ever received. He had me pumped up with excitement. After another hour of sparring, he pulled us into a huddle again for a brief moment before he said, "Forty laps." A lap consisted of us running up one staircase to the third floor, across the hall, down three flights of stairs back across the hall to our original starting point. My cousin's friends who were on the team gave me encouragement through the first ten laps. I tried to maintain their pace but fell behind. Mentally my mind wasn't in it. I kept pushing at my pace, realizing that it wasn't good enough after being lapped. The upperclassmen I started with were passing me. Determined, I picked up my pace, not wanting to quit again. I kept pushing to hear that I had just finished my twentieth. It took me fifty-eight minutes to complete all forty laps. Finishing dead last, I didn't return. The next day I went straight to the gym to inquire about becoming the manager for the varsity girls' basketball team. I had already told Grandma that I would be staying after school, so switching to manager would be my secret until she asked.

Growing up with a house full of women that either lived in or visited my grandfather's house, I thought I had heard or seen it all, especially with Mrs. Stark as a neighbor. When the girls played Ottawa, which was a school in our Huron league, they showed me otherwise. The trip was a seventy-five-minute bus ride both ways, allowing plenty of time for them to make me as uncomfortable as they could. Other than Coach Adams, I was the only male on the bus. On the way to Ottawa, I made the mistake of sitting in the back of the bus. Their conversation started about menstrual cycles and transitioned to sex. With eight women grilling me about my knowledge of the subject, I blushed, shying away from their conversation. My shyness made them even more inquisitive, leading to inquiries as to the size of my package. I entertained the conversation without comment. I was confident about my size below my waist, but I still didn't know exactly how to use it. When the bus stopped at the school, I opened the emergency back door exit to get away from the heat. Excusing myself with, "I have to unload the coolers." One of my cousin's good friends, Rose, was on the team. I had a crush on her. She was beautiful, six feet, two inches, with long beautiful legs. She happened to be one of the tallest players on the team, which intimidated a lot of guys. My only intimidation was her being five years older than me. Knowing that Eva trusted Rose, after the Ottawa trip, I started to sit near her on bus rides, trying to alleviate some of the sexual conversations. If the team started going in on me too hard, she would come to my rescue, saying, "Leave him alone!" calming the female hyenas. Morgan was close friends with Rose. They played three sports together through school. Morgan's brother played on my AAU team. We had been teammates for almost a year. I had seen Morgan drop him off at practice a few times. Riding the after-school bus, we had plenty of normal conversations, which made me trust her more than the rest of the team. With all the time we spent on the bus riding from game to game, we all confided in each other that we were all virgins on a late-night ride from Atchison while everyone else seemed to be sleep. Our little secrets kept us close through the season. Rumors started swirling between the seniors that quickly got back to me. Allegedly my cousin Eva was staying after school to see her boyfriend who was on the basketball team. He would miss the first half hour of practice, using the excuse of needing tutoring to see her (he knew he would never be welcomed at her house). After learning the lessons of the whispering game in baseball, I dismissed anything anyone said to me about her. If they brought their gossip to me, I would say, "It's not my concern, I don't want to hear anything about what my cousin is doing." The rumors of my cousin turned up the heat on me. Rose and Morgan decided that they didn't want to graduate as virgins. It became a competition for them on who could make me more uncomfortable. The rest of the season, they ran a salt-

I COULD'VE BEEN

'n'-pepper back and forth on me, talking to me about sex whenever they thought that no one else was listening.

Halfway through the varsity girls season, eighth-grade boys basketball started. Since there were already six teams practicing, our eighth-grade boys got the pleasure of 6:00 a.m. practices. We had to be committed, wanting to play bad, for the love of the game, to get up at five every morning. For three straight days we were pushed to the limit in tryouts. Drill after drill for over an hour before we ended with conditioning. Our coach preached from day one, "If you can't run, you can't play! I can teach you what I want, but you have to be in shape to execute it!" After school on the third day, there was a list on the wall. All my years of playing had me confident that my name was on the list. When the bell rang, I headed straight to the bulletin board in the hallway heading to the cafeteria. I nervously peeked over the shoulders of a shorter player to see my name. Finding my name on the list, it was certified that I was chosen as one of the sixteen out of the fifty eighth graders that tried out for the team. Just like football, I had either played with or against 75 percent of my team. We had a very talented team with no egos. Everyone had a blue-collar hustle for the ball with no-excuses mentality. No one was too proud to sacrifice their body to obtain the basketball. The gym we played in was a concrete pit. Like ancient Rome, the stands sat high over the court. It was appropriately named the Old Gym. The court was surrounded by brick walls less than two feet from every line on the court on all four sides. Both team benches and the scorer's table were so close to the court if anyone stretched their legs, you thought they were on the court. Seating was limited to only two sides of the court. Directly behind the benches, six feet in the air, was for saber fans, and across the court was the same wall and bleachers for visitors. In pregame warm-ups, I always felt like a gladiator facing life or death. Once the game started, it was just another game. Coach Bennett took us to a pretty good record. There were only seven middle schools to compete with.

During the course of the season, we had a player on the team who was jumping higher than anyone. He claimed that he could dunk on a ten-foot goal. I had lowered Patrick's goal to eight foot and dunked on it but was nowhere near dunking on a ten-foot goal. The last week of practice, the buzz of Bryson being able to dunk got back to Coach King. He didn't normally come to eighth-grade practice, so we were all curious for his purpose in the gym at 7:00 a.m. Coach Bennett stopped practice, giving Bryson the ball. As he handed him the ball, he said, "Go for it." Before anyone knew it, we saw and heard a loud thunder sound as the breakaway rim gave way. Seeming unimpressed by his thunderous dunk, Coach King smirked, turned around, and walked out of the gym. Everyone on the team lost their minds getting us excited for our last game of the season. Bryson's dunk had everyone believing that they could be Like Mike. Half the team was envious; the other half was jealous. I had no time for either. My focus was already on AAU basketball with four weeks to track season.

AAU practice was 6:00 p.m. until Coach Edwards decided that he had challenged all of us to fix our own weaknesses. He only stopped practice when he saw a flaw in our skill or decision-making, teaching us to identify our weaknesses, using them as teaching moments to explain what he called "ignorant or lazy." With years of domination in Kansas City basketball coaching all the top talent, at the end of practice, Coach Edwards announced that we were blessed with three new things. First our new sponsor, Children's Mercy Hospital, changing the name of our team from the Running Rebels to the CMH 76ers. The most significant thing he said to us was that the gym we just practiced in for the first time was ours gifted to us from our new sponsor named Guardian Angels! Never again would we have to wait to practice when we could where we could, eliminating our rec center hop scotch, alleviating concerns of which gym practice was at (eliminating JFK, Bell, Bethany, Turner house, Eisenhower rec, or Kensington). We hit the ground running in our new home like we had a lot to make up for with our school ball break practicing three or four times a week. Coach had found a local tournament for us to compete in to qualify us for the National AAU tournament in Florida.

Monday to Friday until 5:30 p.m. I had track practice. By 6:30 p.m. I was at basketball practice on Monday and Wednesdays and

Thursdays. Those four weeks flew by so fast, focused in the next practice. When we hoisted the championship trophy at the William Jewel Tournament qualifying us for the National Championship, nothing changed. We just added fund-raisers to trying to earn the money to go to Florida. As school let out, if we weren't playing in a weekend tournament, we would skip practice on Thursday to practicing on Saturdays. Saturday practices weren't really practice. We would scrimmage the whole time. Five on five no substitutions, game point 12. Trusting Patrick, who kept practicing after football started since his mother wouldn't let him play, he practiced with the older team up until school ball started. He told everyone that practice was at 11:00 a.m. Which was true for him. The rest of our fourteen-year-old teams' practice time was actually at 1:00 p.m. With our entire team dressed and ready for practice at 10:45 a.m. our seventeen-to-eighteen-year-old team looked at us like lunch meat with six players ranked in the top twenty in either Kansas or Missouri. Once Coach saw us strapped up, ready to go, he decided not to waste the opportunity. All of our teams always competed in tournaments one age group up to challenge our basketball IQ. Our teams were the best in the city, not finding much competition, so Coach Edwards was excited to humble us with our older team challenging us to scrimmage. After he addressed us, Coach Edwards took a seat. He never ever sat down. He always paced the gym from the moment he got there until the time he left. Both teams huddled separately at opposite free throw lines. Facing five players who averaged forty points a game in school ball, our focus was their two giants. Will, at the height of six feet, six inches, along with AR, who was six feet, seven inches. AR, the number 1 ranked player in the nation, who attracted pro scouts at every game he played. AR generally only practiced on Saturdays because he attended school in Wichita, which was three hours away. Finishing their starting five with KT, who averaged forty points at Washington High School along with TNT, who both played at Raytown High School, combining for seventy points a game, earning the only true senior on our AAU team a full ride scholarship to the University of Nebraska.

We were coached to always play man to man, breaking down our opponent's weakness, making them play to their own weaknesses. We decided that since we were outsized that we would run a 2-1-2 zone, which wasn't our game. Our older team didn't think twice playing us man to man. Down the court, back and forth we could score, but it was clear that we were outmatched. Their shooting guard, KT, was six feet, one inch, which was six inches taller than 75 percent of the players on our team. He was one of the shortest on their team. Anytime they would steal the ball, they would slow it down to let us back into our zone, toying with us, asserting their dominance. I ended up on the bottom right box, being one of the taller kids on the court, almost six foot tall. When the ball came to my side, it was my responsibility from the free-throw line to the baseline. I got caught going through the motions, running out with my hands up but returning to my starting position with my hands down. KT saw it, setting me up. He swung the ball to my side as I ran out to defend Will. He was ranked fifth out of the top one hundred in the nation for his age division, number 1 in the state of Missouri, playing school ball for Pembroke Hill. Will immediately threw a cross court pass back to KT. Heading back to the box, which was my starting position. I saw it like slow motion with the ball floating toward the hoop. Perceiving that it was too high for me to jump for it, I squatted to box out. The next thing I knew Will was flying through the air over my head like Vince Carter snatching the ball out of the air. He jumped straight over me without even touching me. Coach didn't allow us to celebrate stuff like that, so practice continued like it never happened. After practice, my teammates made sure I knew that they were happy it was me and not them. It was just something else to keep me humble. I could barely touch the rim. Being dunked on embarrassed me more than anything ever in life. It taught me how much I hated to be embarrassed as I swore on my life that it would never happen again.

    The number of athletes that came out for track was insane. Unlike the other teams that practiced by separate divisions, everyone out for track started practice stretching together. It was easily over a hundred and twenty kids on the team from eighth graders to

I COULD'VE BEEN

seniors. Separated by sexual orientation, there were four divisions with eight teams. Eighth grade boys/girls, freshman boys/girls, JV boys/girls, and varsity boys/girls. All the teams were loaded with athletes. Our varsity team had multiple competitors with state-wide reputations. The team motto was "Go hard or Go home!" inspired by the seniors. Everyone proudly paid fifteen dollars for a team shirt. Some teammates bought more than one even though they were all the same. Morgan was in the top four in the state for shot put, while Rose medaled second in the hurdles at state last year predicted to break the state record this year in the 110 hurdles and 100-yard dash, which kept us around each all the time. They both continued to secretly flirt with me even though I never took them serious. They didn't want their classmates to know that they were trying to seduce a *rookie*. Morgan and I practiced together five days a week on our shot put techniques. Her only event as a returning senior trying to better her nonmetaling finish at state last year. At six feet, three inches, 220 pounds, she was able to toss 8 pounds 8 ounces, forty feet consistently. Seeing my gift, she took it upon herself to help me with my technique, which added an extra five feet to my tosses, averaging me the same distance as her, making me number 1 on our eighth-grade team competing every meet for a metal position. After weeks of helping me with my technique, Morgan asked me to ask your grandmother to braid her hair. Once a month since school started, my cousin Eva got her hair braided by your grandmother. With her hair freshly braided, it became a daily conversation of Morgan's, which crossed Rose's ears, making her join the hair braiding agenda wanting her hair braided too. They both asked me for the number to the house to contact your grandmother. I conveniently never gave it to them out of fear for their motives. We never seemed to have a pen when it was on their minds. My rookie track season ended way before I presented it to your grandmother. They both qualified for sub-state competition. When I did bring it up, your grandmother said, "Eva already gave Rose our number. We talked about it, I'm going to try to braid her hair next Wednesday after your basketball practice. Give Morgan our number so we can figure out our schedules." We only had one number, the house phone, which also made me accessible.

With school almost finished and my first year at Sumner in the books, the one class I didn't know if I would pass was my typing class. In order to pass the class, we had to take a typing test with the keyboard covered. I felt so much pressure to keep up with the assignments. I never committed to trusting the classroom lessons. Everyone else seemed to be picking it up except me. With the work getting increasingly harder, I hated going to computer class. It wasn't a teacher-interactive class. It felt like the only time I talked to the teacher was for her to show me another C or D that I earned. When she called me up to her desk telling me that I was needed in the office, I almost pissed my pants. Normally the office called you down over the classroom PA system. With no call at all to the classroom, I thought I was getting kicked out of Sumner. It was the longest trip down one flight of stairs ever. I knew that I had not done anything wrong. I just never seemed to win when I got sent to the office. I entered the office to the secretary greeting me, asking me my name. After answering, she said, "The counselor is waiting to see you down the hall," scaring me even more. I had convinced myself that I wasn't Sumner material struggling in three classes.

When I got to her office the door was open, poking my head in, I announced myself as she invited me in, asking me to shut the door. I took a seat across the desk from her. She took a deep breath, looking me squarely in the eyes.

"I'm sorry to be the one telling you this, but Bill passed away this morning. He had a heart attack. I'm sorry that your mother isn't here to tell you, but you can imagine how much this is affecting her."

Not knowing what emotions to have, my mind spiraled with different emotions. My first response was denial, thinking that she wasn't telling me the truth. Quickly that lost rationality, realizing that she knew his name. Immediately I turned to anger, questioning who in the world was this woman that had the audacity to tell me that the man that defined my definition of a man was dead. He was my father who taught me everything I knew about working hard with integrity, proving to me every year that God would reward hard work through the yields of *our garden*. My role model, my daddy, the only man on earth that I feared, my molder of perfection beating into me for years that mistakes are a lack of respect. Realizing that she wasn't smiling or laughing, it took weight. I broke down into a ball of tears as she came around her desk to hug me. After I collected myself, I sat in the vice principal's office heartbroken until we were dismissed at the end of the day. I caught a ride home with Eva since her father forbade her from staying after school anymore. I was home for about an hour when your grandmother arrived. I felt her energy, sensing her pain, as she opened the basement door. When she opened the door to our room an hour and a half earlier than usual, I saw her pain written all over her. I hugged her as we cried together. Between tears, she told me that Sumner was freezing my grades, passing me to the ninth grade. There were only several days of school left, making the counselor think that Bill's death would affect my test grades. In death, he saved me because there was no way in hell I was going to pass my algebra final with Mr. Bell or typing final, which was 50 percent of my grade.

Bill's wake was cold and disenchanting. His mother being distraught that her baby boy was dead arranged to have the seating at the funeral home divided with a white ribbon down the middle of the room, separating the families like a wedding. The glares that came from their side of the room looked like they thought your grandmother had something to do with Bill's death. Neither side of the funeral home filled up. The trucking company with almost all of its sixty employees showed up to show their love. They took up a collection, presenting your grandmother with a large ziplock bag with over five thousand dollars in it, which created more tension in the room. When the wake ended, Mrs. Grey went to the altar, taking the urn with Bill's ashes, storming out the funeral home. It upset your grandmother because Bill was her husband. The money your grandmother spent on the urn didn't matter with the ziplock of cash. Mrs. Grey was upset that Bill left his life insurance to your grandmother even though they were married for years. My last memories of Mrs. Grey were her showing her emotional rage in grief, directing it toward your grandmother. After the animosity combined with theatrical performance, your grandma wanted nothing to do with the life insurance benefits. The day after the wake, she found a lawyer. Mrs. Grey was *pissed* by the notion that she didn't have control of the money. She tried to hire a lawyer to amend the life insurance policy since they got a divorce three months before Bill died. The letters from her lawyer stopped after three weeks because legally there was nothing they could do. Your grandmother had her lawyer set up two separate trust funds for Hazel and me. We couldn't touch the money until we were eighteen without a serious need. Any needs had to be requested in writing by Hazel or me with detail of the necessity combined with three different prices for anything deemed a necessity. Authorized by three signatures—lawyer, guardian, and beneficiary—it could take two or three months to get a check from the lawyer.

Transition to Drake

Baseball practice officially started in March, giving us two chances to knock off the dust adjusting back to throwing a baseball. After it rained out every practice Coach Price scheduled in April, the timing of Bill's death kept me from rejoining the team until a week before our first game. We were rained out six out of our first eight games. The weather was so bad that Coach Price started scheduling practices indoors. When the rain finally cleared, we were playing three or four times a week to catch up the season with only a few weeks before the leagues were scheduled to end, determining which teams qualified for the state tournament. Only the top three in each league qualified. Our team played eight games in ten days, having three double headers.

Almost every game we played the Starr brothers were our umpires. They seemed to umpire all the thirteen-to-fourteen-year-old games. They were the most consistent, unbiased umpires in the league. You could tell that the Starr brothers Kaleb and Karl were related despite their efforts at individualism. Wearing the same exact uniform didn't help. Kaleb was twenty pounds heavier than Karl. In practice our jokes about Kaleb were never about his Coke bottle glasses. My teammates would always joke on the fact that he had a jerry curl, which I had to stay out of for fear that they would say something about your grandmother's. Karl didn't get any passes looking like a five-foot miniature version of Snoop Dogg. He couldn't have weighed one hundred pounds. His hair was the focus of all jokes. His perm looked like he kept a beautician on call. When we would pass him in the parking lot of the stadium, someone from our team would start an impromptu Snoop song.

Your grandmother kept the score for every game I played in after she stopped coaching. Everyone in the park knew who she was, either her from keeping score or as Chris's mom. She was always talking to plenty of umpires between innings as the official scorekeeper. Seeing her talking to Kaleb between innings wasn't unusual although it seemed to be happening more frequently. After most games, the Starr brothers would be in the parking lot talking about the game they called. Kaleb called me over, starting with small talk about the game while I was waiting for your grandmother. He said, "Chris, I think your mother is beautiful, and I would like to take her on a date." A week later they went on a date. Three weeks after their date, your grandmother was moving us into a new place, joining households. Naomi was his oldest daughter choosing to live on her own. Aubree, his second daughter, was the same age as me, being his only daughter to move into a duplex with us. His youngest daughter, Megan, who wasn't in school yet, still lived with her mom. The duplex they chose together gave both Aubree and me our own rooms. Outside of being a part-time umpire, Kaleb kept two other jobs, working a factory job Monday through Friday from 6:00 a.m. until 2:30 p.m. He worked at Venture in the evenings from 5:00 p.m. to 11:00 p.m. Venture was Walmart's major competitor in Kansas City. His manager at Venture was on the board at 3&2. Having insight to his umpire schedule, she made sure that if he wasn't umpiring, he was at Venture. He worked seven days a week in the summer. When it wasn't baseball season, he worked forty hours on both jobs. I trusted your grandmother's decision, reserving my concerns for how fast they were moving.

Kaleb's schedule made it feel like only three of us lived in our house. When he was home, you could smell him long before you saw him. Both adults smoked cigarettes in the house. Kaleb smoked marijuana as well, which made the house reek. Being an athlete, I didn't care for Kaleb's drug use. My integrity for all my disciplines made me stay away from anyone that sold drugs or used them. Living on Twenty-Fourth and Wood, I knew kids my age who claimed they had smoked pot already. Your grandmother's respect in the neighborhood made them stay far away from me with that. My new reality embarrassed me. Both my "parents" had curls leading to a lot of

"Soul Glo" jokes. Anyone that asked me if there were two spots on the couch immediately became my enemy, so only my close friends could come over. I acted a fool whenever I opened the door to my safe haven greeted by the stench of marijuana throughout our home. Showing me his love for your grandmother, he was willing to compromise, agreeing to only smoke pot in the garage. I could still smell it when I passed the garage door, enraging me slightly, making your grandmother invest in ways to alter any smells.

Our duplex was off Seventy-Third and State Avenue. Living off a busy pass-through street, we never used the front door. Our corner driveway behind our duplex was triple wide minus the entryway, allowing our neighbors to park three cars next to each other on their end of the cement slab. In our two-level duplex, Aubree chose the downstairs room away from the rest of us. Like Kaleb, it really seemed like she wasn't there either. She was totally the opposite of me. I generally maintained a 3.0 or better, while she didn't care if she brought home five Fs with two Ds. My room was always clean, while her room always looked like a tornado hit it. She would only come out her room when she was forced to join the rest of us for dinner or family game night. Kaleb's reputation at 3&2 opened doors for me that I would have never imagined. He was solidified as some of the glue to 3&2 by the Board of Commissioners, who all knew his new relationship status. Your grandmother would go watch him umpire when I wasn't playing or didn't have basketball practice. I would always tag along, never wanting to stay in the house. Whenever we went to the park, she would stop by the office to say hello to Tim, the league treasure. Tim could easily get overwhelmed, asking everyone who crossed his path to help him preserve the image of the park he loved. He asked your grandmother if she would be interested in working the batting cages. The person who was supposed to work it didn't show up. She told Tim that she had no interest in sitting at the top of the hill in the hundred-degree temperatures, but I would do it.

Tim desperately needed help, quickly accepting your grandmother's negotiation, asking the groundskeeper, Kyle, to take me up to the cages to show me the ropes. Kyle unlocked the fenced cages followed by the change office immediately to the right of the entrance. He showed me where the key was to collect the money. He made me count the sixty-dollar bank in front of him for verification. It was twenty dollars of quarters, twenty dollars in fives with twenty ones. I was instructed that if I ran out of quarters to go collect them from the boxes outside the cages. Marc quickly explained that if someone paid for the hour to remove the box that collected the quarters leaving two. It was fifty cents for two minutes with five seconds between pitches, giving twenty-four attempts as long as the machine didn't run out of balls. He explained that my major focus was whoever was walking in the gate to the cages, my second priority was to collect the rubber baseballs to replenish the machines. I was also told that the sodas and waters were counted, so nothing was free. If I wanted something to drink, I was to send someone to the concession stand, where anything I wanted was free while I was working. I did exactly as I was told.

As the sun started to fade, I picked up every ball and returned them to the pitching machines. I cleared the boxes, collecting the money, locked the office to the cages. then locked the cage themselves before I scurried down the hill to give Tim the metal box with today's collection in it from the cages. Your grandma taught me integrity at a young age. On my third job with two different businesses that I was responsible for, I left the batting cages looking better than kids four years older. With Tim's recommendation, they offered me the job. I was paid forty dollars for less than four hours of work. After the second game started, the cages didn't get any business, allowing me to clean up the cages volunteering the rest of my evening working in the concession stand. Kaleb saw my happiness with the forty dollars from the cages and told me that I could make thirty dollars a game as umpire with a two-game minimum a night. I did the math quickly, understanding the opportunity. I took home the umpire handbook, studying it with any free time. A week later I took the test, passing with a 98 percent. Tim knew the schedule of all the teams, scheduling me around my games. With one of the best umpires in the city living in my house, we bonded over testing each other's knowledge of the rule book. In no time I memorized the umpire's handbook of professional baseball. I could correct Kaleb

I COULD'VE BEEN

on the rules and quote them exactly. "8.02 the pitcher shall not…" Tim was amazing, juggling my AAU basket practices, baseball games, along with my umpiring schedule. With Coach Price on the board of directors, he knew my baseball practice schedule as well, maximizing all my free time. If I wasn't working with Kaleb, I was working with Karl, who shared whatever insight he could to make me better. Overnight I went from playing the game to defining fairness between craftsmen working to improve themselves regardless of their talent level. Redefining my definition of love as sacrifices made. The bond with baseball built a relationship between me and Kaleb. I saw that smoking weed didn't make him stupid, maybe lazy at times, but with three jobs, who was I to judge.

Kaleb was always home from his first job by 3:30 p.m. Baseball games didn't start until 6:15 p.m. We would always get to the baseball park early about 5:30 p.m. We showed up to the park as neither field was lined ready for competition. Tim was on the phone cussing out the groundskeeper, who refused to come do the fields. Your grandmother had mentioned to Tim previously, bragging about me having a grass cutting business. When he saw me, he asked if I had ever lined a field before. I said, "Never personally, but I had watched Kyle do it plenty of times."

He said, "If you could line the fields today, you can make a hundred dollars."

I took off. Game time was less than an hour away with two fields to remove first and third base and run a chalk line to the fence. Thank God it had not rained in a week, so the lines were still visible from the weekend games. I raced to the shed at the end of the fields, grabbing the lime spreader. After drawing out the batter's boxes along with the catcher's box, I walked as fast as I could and as straight as I could follow the preexisting lines all the way to the fence. With ten minutes to spare, I informed Tim that we were ready to play ball on both fields. He thanked me as I went on to my field to start my two games. After the games, I stopped in the office. Tim asked, "Would you be interested in being the groundskeeper for the rest of the season?" He told me that I only had to cut the fields when needed, normally twice a week. He explained that I would need to hook up the mesh chain to the riding lawnmower and drag the fields on game days before lining them. After he told me that it paid fifty dollar a field a day for just lining the fields, and it was also fifty dollars when I had to cut the grass, it wasn't hard for me to commit.

In total 3&2 was four fields, two on Parallel and two on Leavenworth Road, so on a good day, I would make four hundred dollars cutting, dragging, and lining all four fields along with sixty dollars for umpiring my two games in the evening. My first week performing both duties, my check was fifteen hundred dollars. It was the first work check I had ever seen over three hundred dollars. Your grandma's grass cutting karma had paid off full circle, able to make two hundred dollars almost every day with something that took me thirty minutes a field, averaging two hours a day unless the grass needed to be cut. The first thing I bought myself with my new wealth was a pager. With my schedule packed, your grandmother couldn't object. I was the only one of my friends that had one. I was so excited I wrote my number down in five rows, filling the college rule paper. To ensure that people could read my number, I took the time cutting out each number on the paper instead of tearing it, passing out my beeper number to anyone that would take it. I also bought myself a Gameboy, which was the biggest conversation among all my friends.

As summer was coming to an end, our AAU coaches took us to the AAU showcase tournament, where all the top teams in the nation were scheduled to compete. Our coaches chartered two buses to take our three teams. They were beautiful bus looked amazing with two restrooms, reclining seats, along with a monitor on the back of every seat. An hour into the bus ride, almost everyone on the bus was complaining of how hot it was. The vents were cold; the air just didn't seem to be blowing out of them. To keep us distracted, we watched movie after movie for the entire ride as long as our chaperones approved. With four stops for gas combined two stops for food, twelve hours into our ride passing through Cincinnati, one of the jingles from one of your grandmother's favorite shows kept repeating in my head: "I'm living on the air in Cincinnati, Cincinnati WKRP… Just maybe think me once in a while, I'm at WKRP and Cincinnati." A few hours later we made it to our hotel in Columbus, Ohio. While

Mrs. Edwards went inside, Coach Edwards announced that after dropping off our bags, we would meet back at the bus in three hours to go practice. The hotel looked like it should have been in foreclosure. The pool was closed with yellow caution tape around the iron gate, filled with old bedroom furniture. We didn't travel this far for a pool. We came to execute everything most of us had been taught for years. Stretching our legs, dribbling our basketballs as we waited. Mrs. Edwards returned, passing out room keys along with room assignments. After a short practice, Coach called it a night, setting a 9:30 p.m. curfew, announcing a 10:00 a.m. game time for one of our teams, with a noon game time for another, while our older team was scheduled to play at three. Our older team's talent always packed the gym, with five prospects for McDonald All American recognition.

Our first game was at a school under construction. It was securely locked combined with a chain locked around the door handles. Coach Edwards was upset, venting to our chaperones with us. Coach Edwards used the cell phone that he shared with Mrs. Edwards to call the tournament director. I listened from a distance as he explained over the phone his frustrations.

"We paid good money to compete, as well as chartering two buses, as well hotels expenses."

During his phone call, two officials showed up locked outside the gym with us, waiting for the building to be opened. Coach Edwards, whose voice was already intimidating, raised his voice, expressing his disappointment, catching everyone's attention.

"This is supposed to be the national showcase tournament!"

Twenty minutes later, the tournament representative showed up with keys to open the gym. It was almost 10:30 a.m. when the score clock was turned on with a twenty-minute running clock for warm-ups. Still with no opponent, Coach told us to warm up anyway. After the score clock buzzer sounded, the officials waited ten more minutes before the game was declared a forfeit. As we were starting to pack up, eight players along with their coach arrived rushing into the gym. Since it was the first day of the tournament, Coach Edwards withdrew the official forfeit, allowing us to play the game. It took fifteen more minutes before we had an official scorekeeper with someone to run the clock. Doing what we were trained to do, we beat them by twenty-five points, applying a man-to-man full court press the entire game. Coach Edwards was trying to send the message that our three teams from Kansas City were here to play. Looking up in the stands between quarters. It was the first time we played for a crowd of less than fifty people as we hurried from one gym to another for our other team's game. The next day we played a team from Atlanta who, like us, had a team in every age division. The gym looked like an airplane hangar with three courts side by side. The courts were so close it was hard not to watch the next court for fear of a loose ball. The entire game the lead went back and forth. As the buzzer sounded, they hit a game-winning three-pointer, giving us our first defeat in almost a year. The last game we had, a team within thirty points of us was the game we lost last year at the national tournament. The next game we played a team from Ohio. Coach Edwards never let us make excuses, but we got homeschooled. The refs made the game so lopsided that Coach Edwards lost his temper. Which was a little amusing because part of his coaching was how to play dirty as well. He would always say, "It's not cheating if you don't get caught!" Seeing him lose his temper, we played in anger, which lost us the game. Ohio was rough, devastation was everywhere, and the gyms we were playing in were all on their last legs. Their community was flooded with house after house run-down and boarded up looking like a war zone. It was the first time I had ever seen anything like it, even spending a lot of time in Kansas City, Missouri. After we were knocked out the tournament, I definitely came back humble, counting my blessings. The bus ride home was less than fun. It was the first time any of us had faced two losses or being knocked out any tournament. In Kansas City, the only team that could beat us was our older team. When we got about one hundred miles from Kansas, Coach Edwards told us that we played up a division.

"I didn't think your age group would be a challenge," he said. Which lifted the heavy hearts we were carrying. We got back from Ohio on Saturday, and football camp started on Monday. It wasn't mandatory, but it didn't look good to miss it either.

I COULD'VE BEEN

The first day we huddled prepractice for Coach Russell to give us a rundown of what was to come over the next week, ending our week with a blue-and-silver game. After his rundown, he asked if anyone had any questions. I raised my hand. He called on me. "Drake, what's your question?" Never being the only Chris or Christopher in the room, Drake made perfect sense. Life had given me three first names. While your grandmother was pregnant with me, she was told she was having a girl, so she was prepared to name me Olivia. When I came out a boy, there was no name picked for me, and not wanting to name me junior, she settled on transposing my father's first and middle names. It really amazed me that the varsity coach remembered my name. I wasn't the only freshman that he knew on first and last name basis. We still had two weeks before school or football when camp ended. State law would allow us to practice until the week before classes. That's how the CAMP idea came about.

For the first time in a long time, I had two weeks in the wind. No practices, no games, with only a few yards to cut. Our schedules were wide open, opting for your grandmother to make some pocket change braiding hair. She braided Rose's hair first, which started Morgan to calling daily until she was able to catch your grandmother. When Morgan finally caught your grandmother, she pushed the urgency to get her hair braided quickly, saying that she was scheduled to report for school in less than a week. With your grandmother always trying to help, she agreed to braid Morgan's hair during her workweek. It normally took three or four hours, so she pressed for Morgan to have the hair and be at our house ready to start at 5:00 p.m.

Morgan being punctual got to the house by 4:50 p.m. Your grandmother was late getting home, starting to braid Morgan's hair after six. At 10:00 p.m. your grandmother still had a quarter of Morgan's hair to braid. As I lay in my room playing my Nintendo, I realized that it was almost midnight. I went to check their progress again. Your grandmother said, "I have three braids to finish, and I'm going to bed. I have to be up at 6:00 a.m. for work." When your grandmother finished with Morgan's hair, she came into my room telling me good night. Wanting to see the final outcome, I went into the living room to see Morgan's hair. Your grandma was so exhausted she announced that she was going to bed. Morgan told her she would leave in a minute.

She said, "I want to hang out and talk to Chris about school for a little bit." Your grandma needing her sleep quickly left us alone. All the talk on the varsity girls' basketball bus was in my face again. This time without being able to run. I tried to escape to my room, but she followed me, shutting my door behind her. Feeling that she was no harm to me, I didn't complain. As she sat on my bed next to me, she asked, "Are you still a virgin?"

I replied, "Yes."

She grabbed my crotch with both hands. Now excited and filled with blood, curiosity had me. As she started to remove my shorts, I didn't say anything. Morgan was intimidating off height alone, never mind the fact that I was saw her bench press more than I could at the beginning of track season. She stood up and motioned me to lay down. A little curious, a little afraid, I did as she asked. She removed her pants and got on top of me. She placed me inside of her as I kept my mouth shut, letting her have her way with me. In my excitement, I lost it inside of her almost immediately. I was afraid that I got her pregnant. I wasn't ready to be a father, especially without a diploma. I refused to admit losing my virginity. I just knew that my mom was going to get a call from my cousin Eva telling her that Morgan was pregnant. She was heading to a HBCU somewhere in the South. I stressed about being a father for two months until the excitement of my birthday.

Freshman year it was required that we take an American government class. There was only one teacher that taught the class, Coach Russell. Every day as he would take roll call, he would use everyone else's first name in the class until he got to me. Every morning just like clockwork, he called me Drake, to which I would respond, "Here." It wasn't just the football team anymore. Everyone in the class called me by my last name. Before his class, the only people at Sumner to call me Drake was my crew. I played basketball with two of them for three-plus years now. We called ourselves the 98 Bad Boyz. It was our middle school crew of Don, James, Chris, and me with the addition of Bryan. Bryan and Don wrestled together, while James, Chris and I played basketball together. Together the five of us represented every sport in the school, including golf. As Don and I started freshman football, Bryan and James started cross country. In the spring Bryan, James, and I would go out for track, while Don played baseball, and Chris was on the golf team. We were all top athletes in the sports we played.

Our freshman season started with a fresh new look. Coach Simmons was the Western civilization teacher. He had a knack for people and an unbelievable football IQ. While he was our coach, he was also our friend. With a school full of talent, Coach Simmons was able to lead us to an undefeated season. It was the first time in school history that the freshman team played a league schedule. One by one we defeated Turner, Atchison, Ottawa, Bonner, Ward, and both Blue Valley and Blue Valley North. The last three games of the season we averaged forty points a game. Coach Russell kept close eye on our team. For the last two games of the JV season, Coach Russell suited me to play. Devin got suited out one game before me, but Coach saw us both as being man among boys. Thriving at defensives end, the varsity team was my biggest supporters. Nothing changed on the field except the ages of the people I was playing against, which basketball had made me used too. At the end of the season, my popularity was through the roof. The class of '98 was well respected in the school.

When I lived in the basement of my grandfather's house, I had so many dreams that seem to be so real that I could touch them. They never seemed like dreams, feeling like I could touch my visions. When I was really young, I would dream that I was standing in front of a urinal every time before I wet the bed. The dreams were always so vivid that I grew fearful of sleeping. When I would dream, I always wake up in the moment of chaos. My dreams were so vivid, so real. What I had dreamed about before now seemed to be happening right in front of my eyes, like I was living déjà vu. Fearful of the chaos which woke me from my dreams, I would be on eggshells in real life, fearful of the conclusion. My maturity seemed to bring more premonitions. Dreaming realistic dreams seem to be a nightly thing.

Not knowing who to talk to about it, I became introverted. Outside of sports, I felt like no one would understand. Not wanting to end up in the mental hospital, it took me some time to even talk to the one person I knew I could confide in, your grandma. She encouraged me, saying, "It's your Native American heritage." Early in life I knew that I was black and Native American. The Native American side just wasn't discussed a lot. I never got the chance to meet my great-grandmother or to learn anything about her culture or her other than she chose the name Olivia to call herself. My dreams scared me so bad that I got anxiety whenever it came time to go to bed, struggling to sleep unless I was dead tired.

The school of geniuses that I had the privilege of attending gave all of us a place to share our individuality. I found two friends outside my crew freshman year. Both shared their interest, stimulating my mind more than any teacher in the school. Seth, who was the best saxophone player in the school, taught me how to code programs on our TI 82 calculators. We were required to purchase the hundred-dollar calculator for geometry class. We both got them before most of our class. The programs he made would ask you questions The outcomes varied based on your answers. It captivated me so much I insisted that he teach me everything he could. Between athletic seasons, with no reason to stay after school, I created one. I begged Seth to stay after school to teach me. It took some convincing, but twenty dollars a week goes a long way to a freshman. On my fourth day after school, I finished my first program with still twenty-five minutes before the late busses. Roaming the school, I headed to the locker room to see if any of our basketball coaches were in their offices. As I entered the locker room, the only thing I could hear was a buzzing sound echoing off the concrete walls. Searching for the source, I found another freshman who was cutting hair on the JV side of the locker room. With one head almost finished, he still had two other people sitting there patiently waiting. With my business experience, I knew he was selling his service.

"Excuse me, I'm curious, what do you charge?"

Turning the clippers off, he paused just long enough to look up at me, saying, "Three dollars." Before he was back to finishing the head in front of him, I took a seat next two the other two while he finished his current head. When the clippers cut off, I learned his name was Nick, as he sterilized his clippers with alcohol and dusted the bench seat of hair.

I asked, "can you cut my hair?"

He said, "Not today because I have to catch the late bus. You can be my first head tomorrow."

True to his word, the next day I got a three-dollar fade in the school locker room that was barbershop quality. Once a week I would let Nick cut my hair as I studied his technique, watching him cut his other customers' hair. The convenience of the locker room made it a no-brainer to me. I used word of mouth skills to help Nick's business grow, making him an extra fifty-plus bucks a week. As appreciation, he taught me his technique on how to cut hair. When basketball season started, he was banned from cutting hair in the locker room. His loyal customers started going to his house. The first time he cut my hair at his house, I learned that he was an introvert also, embarrassed by his perception of his socioeconomic views compared to the rest of the school. His real passion was model cars, being too young to own an actual car. He opened up to me, sharing his passions by showing me his collection. I learned that he didn't just construct them and paint them; he was teaching himself how to motorize them, including hydraulics to make his model cars ride on three wheels, replicating what he saw living on Quindaro. He was just learning how to motorize them after years of constructing and painting them. With the level of trust our relationship had, he shared every new advancement with me on my weekly appointment. When he suggested that we use my head as his billboard promoting his talent, I went with it. We started with a Nike swoosh on the side of my head the week of freshman tryouts. Each week we brainstormed together for something new, pushing his gifts to evolve based on our scheduled opponent.

Our freshman basketball team practiced before school, like the eighth-grade team out of shivery to our female freshman, waking up at 5:00 a.m. for another year, proving our dedication to the game we loved. The week of tryouts wasn't really tryouts. We knew who was going to make the team. Everyone from the eighth-grade team was there except Bryson. His leaping ability earned him a varsity tryout to play for Coach King. Bryson gave the entire freshman team hope. We all wanted the opportunity to be on the varsity team. Everyone on the freshman team stepped up their game. Our varsity team was mostly juniors, which made it even more of a realistic goal. There were only two seniors on the team, so the nucleus would be back next year. Coach Edwards's oldest son was a junior on the varsity team. His basketball IQ made him the team captain, mentor, and role model for our school. Sixty-five percent of the kids out for school basketball played for one of Coach Edwards's teams at some point in their careers. Our coach for freshman year was coach Hughes. He was ex-Sumner alumni that played overseas after college basketball until he injured his knee. After he ended his career in the D league, he started coaching.

With two gyms for eight teams, we would practice anytime we could. Saturday mornings the gym was always available. Saturday practices sucked. Coach Hughes saw it as the perfect time for extra conditioning drills, preaching, "They won't beat us because you're tired." Sixty seconds was the time to beat doing sweet sixteens, eight trips back and forth the width of the court. Suicides were his second favorite, eight touches the length of the court in different intervals, touching every line, returning to the baseline until our touches completed the court. My change of direction was great keeping me from finishing last. My motivation became the thought that if my teammates could do it, so could I. Coach Hughes had talked enough trash through weeks of practice to get Coach King to schedule a Saturday practice for the varsity during down time for Christmas break. We started our practicing in two different gyms. Our freshman team was confused practicing in the new gym, while the varsity practiced in the old gym. Thirty minutes into practice, the varsity team joined us in the new gym, halting our practice. Coach Hughes pulled us to a sideline huddle to prepare us for the challenge in our face. We scrimmaged our varsity, leaving everything on the court. Our loss wasn't a defeat, earning the respect of Coach King. Our varsity team did everything they could to break our spirits. It was the first time that

I COULD'VE BEEN

I played against a team that cheated on purpose. Our varsity team played dirty, holding our shorts or stepping on our shoes, preventing us from moving, slowing us down tremendously. Practice stopped shortly after Pete punched me in the nuts. I dropped like deadweight, giving a four-on-five advantage as they easily scored, while I was laying on the court in agony. Coach King grimaced as the only witness to the attack. He joked with me in his gym class for weeks after the on slaughter. Coach Hughes was so impressed with our efforts against our varsity team that he used his connections to get a small Division 2 school that was traveling through Kansas City to come to Sumner to scrimmage us. Their team was three to seven years older than us. Once the game started, age didn't matter. Coach Hughes was so happy with our performance that after the scrimmage, we only conditioned for ten minutes instead of running for the usual thirty. Playing the Division 2 school gave our team a real confidence, turning our season around, playing kids our age. We finished our season 7-4. At the end of our season, we had five freshmen that were also suiting up for the JV team, four of whom played with me for Coach Edwards.

My school work seemed to be a lot easier this year. My only problem areas as far as grades were English and Spanish, forcing me to stay after school daily for extra help. Reading *The Birds* bored me, so I bought the Cliff Notes version from the bookstore. Apparently my teacher Ms. Nelson bought it too, failing me three quizzes straight, making me have to apply myself to reading the actual book, using time after school to read in my English teacher's classroom to avoid the hallway distractions. Sumner's hallways were predesignated for each grade's lockers, assigned alphabetical by last name. On my way to Spanish tutoring, I would pass Isabella. She was black and Latina. Isabella didn't play any sports but rode the late bus every day. We didn't ride the same bus. Her beauty just made me notice her all the time. While I was sitting on the stoop in front of the school, she passed me with my Spanish book in my arms. She said that she could teach it so that I would understand it easier. Offering her help to me, she sat with me on the hallway floor by her locker after school to tutor me, giving me clarity to the classroom lesson. We only spent twenty to twenty-five minutes a day, when the late bus bell was forty-five minutes after school let out. The way she explained it slowed it down, helping me comprehend. If I didn't understand, I wasn't embarrassed to speak up. Some days after we finished, I would go to Ms. Nelson's classroom until 3:50 p.m., when the bell rang for the late bus. During the school day, Sumner gave the entire school a twenty-minute snack break every day after second period. Our snack bar was above the cafeteria next to the gym. During games it doubled as our concession stand. In the forum next to the snack bar were six vending machines selling soda, juice, or PowerAde. Isabella used her free hallway tutoring asking me for a dollar every morning, telling me she was hungry, batting her eyes at me with her sad face. As retribution, I gave it to her, cutting the five dollars a day your grandmother gave me for lunch. I never paid for school lunch. I would go to the gym and play 21 to win my lunch gambling on my basketball skills. We weren't supposed to gamble at school, so we never played for money. I could win three lunches in one game while everyone else was in the cafeteria eating. After I earned my free lunch, there was never a line. I just had to eat in ten minutes or less. I was so competitive that some days I would miss eating, sweating my clothes out, going to sixth period looking a hot mess. I can't tell you how many times I went back to class with my khakis looking like I poured water in my crotch or my button-down shirts looking like I took a shower in it. Your grandmother insisted that I dress business casual for school. School was my business, and she wanted me to take it seriously. Which I did for the most part. I had to maintain my grades to play sports. I took basketball extremely serious, never making excuses while playing in dress shoes.

 Track as a freshman was great. I was officially competing on my third junior varsity team. Coach Break and Coach Shine, our varsity coaches, loved me. Both head coaches knew that I was athletic since they both worked overtime during every athletic season watching me from a distance all school year. They would let me try any event I wanted in practice. I wanted to compete in my comfort zone of shot put and discus, but I was fascinated by the high jump. I spent more time working on it than I did shot put or discus. Every day I would follow Sophia to watch her practice. I admired her precise technique more than anything. Watching her fly through the air was poetic, always with perfect form with a gazelle-like leap. She high jumped like she had been trained by an Olympic coach. I worked every day to replicate what I saw her do. Repeating her technique, I was able to clear six feet, two inches, which was third on the JV team. Coach Break would joke that if he could cut my feet off, I could clear six feet, six inches, which would tie me as the best on the varsity team. Every week before a varsity meet, we would have a showdown in practice. The top four got to compete with six people jumping for the spots. Six feet, three inches was the mark to hit, which kept me just short. My long jump distance was similar to my high jump efforts, short of varsity averaging between fourth to sixth every week, making me fight practicing harder than my opponents. I could practice long jump by myself after practice was over, staying late while everyone else left. I would take fifteen to twenty more attempts than any of my other teammates. Seeing my desire to compete, coach Break decided to put me on the four-by-eight heavy man relay. It was a relay for athletes who only competed in field events. Every time I ran the first lap in sixty-five to seventy-five seconds, the second lap my legs turned to jelly depending on how many practices I had in the week. My first relay split was 2:30. Every meet my split time got worse. After my fourth relay, coach pulled me to focus on my other four events.

 The most important track meet to me was our meet at Shawnee Mission North. With the graduation rate of Wyandotte County, Patrick's mother chose to transfer him to SMN halfway through his freshman year. Patrick's new school opened up new opportunities with a whole new side of town. After my events, the first thing I did was find Patrick. walking around the track meet, I met a young lady named Mary who kept smiling at me, which made me notice her in the crowd of four hundred at the meet. We exchanged numbers, talking on the phone for a few weeks, never discussing age until I asked her on a date to the movies. She told me that she was twelve, about to turn thirteen, which confused me, wondering how she got to the meet. She was way too young to date. Not wanting to be an asshole, I kept our friendship to her but changed gears, treating her like a little sister. Mary realizing that we were not going to happen spent her time trying to play matchmaker for me, treating me like *The Dating Game*. Mary told me she was working on hooking me up with her old babysitter, Monica. She told me that it had been a while since she talked to her since she lived too far away to babysit regularly. Checking my pager after basketball practice, Mary's number was on it. Calling her as soon as I got home, she was excited because she talked to Monica, giving me her number. Mary told me that she gave Monica my pager number as well. Fearless or stupid, I called Monica the next day when I got home from track practice. A man answered the phone, informing me that she wasn't home. A few hours later, my pager buzzed with her number across the screen. Calling it back instantly, I again found the courage to say, "Hello, may I speak to Monica," to the sweetest voice on the other end of the phone saying, "This is her." After an hour of conversation, I don't know who was more enchanted. Me by her sweet, honest, innocent personality, or her by my charm. My grandfather's house taught me a lot about charm listening to my aunties. Wanting to meet my new enchantress more than ever, we talked almost every evening around our schedules, making me need a plan. My biggest obstacle was that she lived in Grandview. Now that school was out for the summer, my schedule was really packed, either I was at basketball practice, driver's education classes, or umpiring.

At the end of my baseball season last year, I knew that I wouldn't play it again. Instead of playing spending money, I wanted to make it instead. I started my season umpiring nine-to-ten baseball. Every week it seemed like I was umpiring kids older and older. It really hit me how I was good as an umpire when I got my first thirteen-to-fourteen games at fifteen. I handled myself so well. No one ever questioned my calls or my age. My size at six foot two, weighing 220 made everyone assume that I was older. With the lack of available quality umpires, Kaleb was able to get me in on umpiring Legion baseball. The pay was great, sixty dollars a game. Legion baseball started at fifteen, which meant that I would be umpiring the kids my age or older. He cautioned that if I didn't act like a professional that the players wouldn't respect me. Loving challenges, this made me start studying the rules of baseball even harder with all the seasons between. My knowledge improved with almost the entire handbook committed to my eidetic memory. One of the best parts about knowing the rules completely is that the game doesn't change, only the players' ages do. Not one for boring, I made umpiring fun, especially when I was behind the plate. Doing what felt natural, I called *"Sttrrrikkkeee"* when the pitch passed perfectly through the strike zone. I got such a positive energy from the crowd that I couldn't just point any more with my right hand. Every single good pitch that came across the plate was met with long passionate strike call. If you struck out, I added "Punch out," which seemed to engage the crowd more with the game. My knowledge of the rules and craftsmanship had half the league telling Tim that they wanted me as their umpire, making me a hot commodity. When I got news that our park was hosting the eleven-to-twelve state tournament, I didn't think that I would be considered to umpire based off my age. The board had received so much positive feedback about me that they voted unanimously to include me in the scheduling. Before the tournament started, I was counseled again about my professionalism. I was reminded that I was in control of the game, and I needed to keep it. The teams playing were from all over the state, having never played with me, so they only knew what I told them. Feeling the magnitude of the situation, I kept my conversations behind the plate with the catchers from being personal. The whole week of the tournament, I never lost control of a game, so no one ever questioned my age. The highlight of my summer was being able to call the plate the semifinal game for eleven-to-twelve state tournament. We used four umpires like the pros did for the semifinal and final round of the tournament. For the finals, I umpired first and third base just three years older than the players competing.

At baseball's end, I was exhausted. Last year I might have played two games a week with Coach Price. This year I umpired twelve games a week. If we would work four games Saturday and Sunday, I could umpire up to eighteen games a week. Needless to say, I was happy to only have AAU basketball for a few weeks before football started. With only a month before school starting, my break wouldn't last long. Football camp was right around the corner. Without school to fill my day, I'd spend most of my mornings playing basketball in the driveway or talking to Monica if she wasn't busy working at Topsy's. I had been pleading for weeks with your grandmother to let me plan a date with her. Since your grandmother would have to drive me, she put it off as long as she could. Tired of me bugging her daily, your grandmother agreed to talk to Monica's mother. I called Monica, saying, "Can my mom talk to your mom?" They hit it off well over the phone, so your grandmother confirmed my date plans with Monica's mother. With school and football underway, I planned our first date on a Saturday to the haunted houses. When we arrived in Grandview, I didn't know what to expect. I still had not seen a picture. The only thing I had to base whether or not I wanted to meet her was her description of herself and her moral character. I knew I spent three months talking to this young lady, and I enjoyed every minute of it. I climbed the stairs to the stoop, ringing the doorbell, as your grandmother stood down the stairs behind me. The man of the house answered the door. It was her mother's boyfriend. I was taller than him, which helped me keep my confidence. As much time as I spent to get to this moment, I couldn't run now. Introducing myself, he did the same, telling me his name was Seth. He invited me and my mother in, introducing us to the whole family. While he and Sarah (Monica's mother) talked to Grandma, they let Monica give me a tour of the house. The tour of the house left us in the basement, where for the first time I got to stare in the face of who I'd spent the last few months talking to. Monica was beautiful, with beautiful long golden-brown hair. she was also very petite without a blemish on any skin I saw. To me, everything was perfect about her. I knew through our conversations that Monica had braces. It was something that bothered her, making her insecure. She was always worried about having food stuck in them. Your grandma called from upstairs announcing that it was time to go to the haunted houses. As we made our way outside, I couldn't take my eyes off her. In the back seat together, I held her hand as we rode to the West Bottoms. Haunted houses being a big attraction in Kansas City with over a dozen to choose from, I bought us a two-package deal. We stood in line with your grandmother behind us even though she had no inter-

I COULD'VE BEEN

est in going in any haunted houses. I was so happy to be spending my time with Monica my anxieties disappeared, keeping my hands dry, allowing me to hold her hand the entire time. As we made our way through the haunted houses, I tried my hardest to stay fearless. It wasn't ten minutes into the second haunted house that a guy jumped out from nowhere with a chain saw. I knew for a fact that I screamed louder than she did. After that I was unamused. My masculinity was challenged, and I lost. The ride home we sat in the dark back seat of your grandmother's car, staring at each other. When we arrived back at her house, I walked her up the stoop and hugged her good night. Neither one of us had kissed anyone before, so our first date hug was perfect. Overjoyed by the evening, I convinced Grandma that the forty-five-minute ride wasn't that bad. Monica and I negotiated with our parents for us to get together the following Saturday. With the distance between us, the weekends were the most convenient time for us to see each other. With formalities out of the way, your grandma dropped me off, promising to be back in a few hours. Sara and Seth were in love like they just had a honeymoon. Consumed in each other, they gave us two options. We were told we could hang out in the living room with them, or we could go in the basement to play on the computer. The living room with them lasted about thirty minutes until we relocated to the basement. We hit the bottom step, and as soon as we were out of sight, I pulled her to me for the kiss I'd been dying to get. Locking lips, we imitated what we had seen on television. She pulled away, covering her mouth with her hand, explaining her discomfort because of her braces. I told her that I could not tell she had them while we kissed, which changed her confidence, making her become the aggressor. As our first intimate experience together, kissing was everything. We could kiss for twenty minutes straight before separating from our lip-lock. In the basement, there was only one chair that we could move to the computer. With Monica sitting on my lap, we tried to play games on their computer, kissing between every lost game. I would die intentionally just to kiss her. It didn't take long before my crotch was bulging with her in my lap, increasing the intensity of our lip-locks, which always seemed to be right at the time to go home. Inspired by my emotions,

I started writing poetry, trying to articulate my feelings. Trying to express my love, I proudly read to Monica, "What would be today if we didn't grow, learn a couple things that we didn't know, if knowledge is power mine will show because I will stop some but my love won't." She didn't understand my poetry. She did understand how to read my unspoken language, which stimulated me to even try to express myself.

After a great summer working making good money, your grandma told me she needed help to get me ready for school again. She could have done it, making something out of nothing again. Seeing the checks I was bringing home weekly, she knew she didn't have to. I saved almost every dime, so it was only right I took the responsibility of buying my shoes. It was hard to find me shoes that cost less than a hundred dollars wearing a size 15 shoe. With my shoe size matching my age for the last five years, it's grown increasingly harder to find shoes that I liked. The stores in Indian Springs didn't carry my size regularly. Your grandmother had to take me to Overland Park to Just 4 Feet. Finding an abundance to choose from in my size. I bought three pairs of basketball shoes along with two pairs of casual shoes, spending $543. Your grandma believed that perception was reality. Determined to have me represent her well, she only bought me khakis and button-down shirts for school. I spent more on four pairs of shoes than she did for clothes for two weeks. Clothes were never an issue. I had every color khaki that she could find. Indian Springs being less than ten minutes from the house still had a Sears despite half the stores closed or closing.

JV football was good for me. As a team, we sucked, according to our record. We had plenty of talent. We just couldn't seem to put together a complete game. We managed a 2–7 record, which was more than disappointing considering our undefeated freshman year. My sixteenth birthday was four games into the season, which overshadowed our football season for me. My grandmother, your Gigi, brought my uncle a plane ticket to fly to Arkansas to drive one of her old cars up to me for my birthday. My grandmother had told me her intentions a few months back, but with the distractions of life, it slipped my mind. When my uncle showed up two days before my birthday, handing me the keys to my Pontiac J6000. It got very real, very quick. Gigi new that I had taken driver's education over the summer and already had my license. I jumped in the car full of excitement and drove straight to Grandpa's house. My grandma had instructed that I let him check it out first before it was all mine. He took his time checking everything before he said, "Let's go for a ride." After a couple of trips around the neighborhood, it was all mine. The last three games of my sophomore year, Coach Russell played me on defense on the varsity football team, ending my season on a high note. Being one of the few sophomores who dressed out for varsity changed a lot of things in my life. Especially now that I owned my first car, able to drive myself to my commitments. No more being dropped off by Mom gave me my first scene of freedom to my life. All my practices combined with school, I spent limited time at home. When I was home, I rarely saw my stepsister, Aubree. We were still total opposites. She was so introverted that she stayed in her room all the time. Her room was a mess all the time. You could never see her floor. The chaos on her floor made it hard to distinguish her bed from the dirty clothes. She only came out of her room for family meals or chores. Aubree didn't care to go to school. Being bullied by her classmates, she was flunking every class. Your grandma didn't play about school, so she quickly made a trip to Turner to address the bullying. After it stopped, she added punishments at home to motivate Aubree to fix her grades herself.

School was exciting with basketball tryouts underway. It was really just an extension of our AAU basketball team again. Coach Edwards's oldest son was finally a senior. His maturity made it feel like he was a senior for the three years he started varsity as the captain of our team. I was more excited about not having to wake up at 5:00 a.m. than I was worried about not making the team. We had a very talented varsity team that had been playing together for years. Still the same team that played dirty even in practice. With daily practices I couldn't even count how many times I was elbowed or kneed in my crotch or had my shoelaces stepped on if they came untied. They would step on laces, providing a head start. I didn't understand the point of their shenanigans in practice. Early in my career I was taught that you play how you practice, encouraging me to give my all. My integrity wouldn't let me stoop to their level. Our school pride kept our fans loyal. Our senior class created unique cheers every game to show the support our basketball team had from the student body. My favorite was "Take your hat, your coat and leave!" This was the reverberation from our bleachers during any home victory, giving us a reason to leave it all on the court. Every practice was a lesson, only losing two seniors to graduation. Coach King padded his imprint only keeping eight players for a fifteen-man roster, five seniors, two juniors along with Bryson, allowing seven players from the JV squad to suit up for the varsity games the entire season. every sophomore played sparingly, mostly to give the starters a break, preparing us mentally for the varsity stage. When we made a mistake, Coach King would explode on the sidelines, like Jerry Tarkanian throwing clip boards, cups, or slamming chairs, immediately sending in a replacement. Even though our seniors wouldn't verbally coach us, they did every day in practice when they bullied us as underclassman trying prove their dominance instead of sharing their knowledge with us as their predecessors. The bone-crushing picks set by my own teammates in practice expanded my peripheral vision to almost 180 degrees, learning to anticipate the pick. Sensing the energy around me opened up a new dimension to my basketball IQ. Our varsity team won 5A Substate, qualifying for the state tournament. The first game was tough; we barely won. The second game we got down by twenty-five, pissing Coach King off, pulling all the upperclassmen to put the sophomores in the game. Every senior on our team was my role model. All of them were amazingly talented, so it was a shock to see Coach pull them to put us in the game, playing how we were trained. We reduced the defecate even though we lost. Coach king was always preparing for the future.

With a few months of independence under my belt, I convinced your grandma to let me drive to Grandview to see Monica. Monica's parents wouldn't let us go anywhere in my car, so we were confined to the basement. Playing games on the computer with her on my lap got my blood flowing, forming a bulge in my pants. With all the phone conversations, I knew she was a virgin. Feeling like my first sexual experience was unwanted, I wanted a new experience with Monica. As the kissing got hot and heavy, I put my hands down her pants. Kissing on the back of her neck, pressing the right buttons, I was almost able to get her pants down before Seth hit the stairs. He came down the stairs periodically, trying to check on us. Hearing the stairs squeak as soon as he hit the first stair gave us twelve steps to be presentable as we gathered ourselves quickly, counting down silently each stair he walked down. As soon as the coast was clear, we got back to where we started. Kissing led to touching, which led me to begging, "Let me just put the tip in!" Succumbing to my pressure she let me. In the excitement, I quickly lost control, exploding all over her back. We cleaned up, tried again, still half-dressed in case Seth hit the stairs to do a check on us. The entire ride home I was on cloud nine, taking her virginity. I was in love. No one else existed or was worth my time. When I wasn't at school or practice, I was in Grandview pushing limits, taking risk, each time learning to get dressed faster than sixty-five seconds. When I got home, I didn't want to shower. I wanted to smell the scent of our lust forever.

Everywhere in the Sports Pages

The state of Kansas allowed javelin to be thrown during track season again after being banned from competition for a few years. Being the undefeated king of the softball throw in middle school made me oh so excited to try javelin. The grip was uncomfortable, like trying to throw a curveball with a golf ball. At 6 feet 2 inches, 240, it just didn't feel right in my extralarge hand. Coach Break took an hour a day coaching me to understand. My raw talent alone could help me medal, but we wanted to be champions, averaging 163 feet 3 inches, Coach Break wanted to add 20 more feet to my throw. Competing weekly in three events, my primary focus was javelin. The season started with me placing second at a JV meet in javelin while placing third in shot put. On a good day I might place in discus. My medal counts slowly continued to climb. All season long I placed in at least two out of my three events at JV meets, sometimes placing in varsity meets as well. As a sophomore, I was beating juniors and seniors regularly. Seeing my name in the *Kansan*, our Wyandotte County newspaper, weekly as well as hearing it on the announcements made me compete harder, keeping copies of the school newsletter to take home to your grandmother. I bonded with Dominic, who was a freshman blessed with great speed that allowed him to compete at the JV level. His sister was a senior well-known through the city as a gifted sprinter as well. Every day after track practice I would take him home, making him my family. His mother embraced me as family, which solidified our friendship, she was the prettiest woman I knew in Wyandotte County, which made me want

I COULD'VE BEEN

to be around her, admiring how she moved as a successful single middle class black mother of two. Week after week I couldn't wait to get the Kansas City *Kansan* on Sunday searching for my name in bold black print. Your grandmother started a scrapbook after my third season of athletics. The clippings from the paper became more motivation fueling my ego. I barely missed qualifying for the state tournament placing fourth at the substate regional in javelin. With classroom finals underway, I was happy to miss the state tournament. My grades were slipping. Between umpiring or AAU practice, I was borderline failing three classes, needing the extra time to stay after school with Mr. Bell or Mr. Coffee, who already caught me cheating on an after-school makeup test, borrowing a friend's perfect test, I used my TI 82 to make a program. I programed it to give me five answers at a time with a blank screen between answers, with my calculator sitting on my desk when he left me alone, I raced to finish. Returning faster than I expected, he caught me pressing buttons, moving it to a blank screen. Snatching my calculator, looking for proof, he was dumbfounded with the blank screen. He pressed buttons for a good five minutes before he took my test, ripping it in half. He failed my test even though he couldn't figure out how I was cheating, saying, "Electronics are not permitted during Latin test!" which made me actually have to study for his final. I created flash cards which I carried everywhere using any free time to study. My English final was ten questions about the novel *1984*. Reading was boring to me. Daydreams always overshadowed the words on the paper, losing concentration four words into anything I didn't read aloud. I had so much going on that my patience for reading didn't exist when it was longer than a newspaper article talking about me. For the second time I finished a school year with Cs on my grade card, barely passing advanced algebra, Latin, or English.

    Clear of classes to focus on my second full season of umpiring with my stepfather and uncle was the best summer of my life. Passing the legion test, earning me certification to umpire teams my age or older, my biggest excitement was driving myself to the park for games. Driving myself made everyone assume that I was older. Between my stepfather, uncle, and myself, our knowledge and consistency made us a popular request among legion coaches, giving us statewide popularity through all age divisions or leagues. Despite it only being two umpires per game, Tim was great at rotating us so that we were constantly working with each other. We spent most our summer at Eisenhower, umping fifteen-to-sixteen- or seventeen-to-eighteen-year-old games. Legion rules declared that they play two complete games, no time limit for either game. The rules stated that each game must complete seven innings. If and only if a team were down by ten runs at the completion of the fifth inning could it be called. It was the only grace called, which I was thankful for when games were 14–2 in the second inning. The longest it took me to complete two games was five hours. The games always came down to pitching. Every team had hitters, depending on the quality of the pitching against them, confirming your grandmother saying when I was a pitcher, "You can't hit what you can't see!" I was so solid in my calls that never once all season did I have anyone question my age. I went five weeks straight scheduled to umpire nothing but legion games to end the regular season. As the league prepared for the nine-to-ten state tournament at 3&2, the teams poured in from all over the state. There were nine-to-ten-year-olds telling me that they heard about me in the other leagues in other cities throughout the state. It wasn't just kids from Kansas City telling me stories of my infamous strike call. Our league had two very good teams that lost less than four games combined all season. Both teams felt like it was their championship trophy, especially with the home field advantage.

All records went out the window for the tournament with the structure being a two-loss elimination. When we reached the final four teams, each game required four umpires by state tournament rules. The Starr brothers, Rodney, and I were the four chosen. After eliminating all but two teams, the records went out the window again. To establish the true state champion, you had to win twice. With a 3&2 team versus a team from a Topeka league, I was given the honor of calling first game of the finals behind the plate. Kaleb called the second game. With the teams splitting after the first two games, the state rules required one last game. Our crew of umpires huddled, deciding the positions we would like to work. I told my

I COULD'VE BEEN

uncle Karl that I wanted to call the plate again. Without reservation, he let me. It was an honor to me considering my age with the years of experienced umpires in the group. I called the best game of my life. Between innings, the only person I talked to was your grandmother. She was the official scorekeeper, which kept me neutral to everyone watching. Even though the team from our league lost, they couldn't complain about anything. Heading into the office after the game proud of my season, Tim told me that I was chosen to umpire the all-star game next week. It was a unanimous vote by team coaches for me to call home plate for the thirteen-to-fourteen division league all-star game. I was on "the big field" with the all-stars from the oldest age division at 3&2. A week later it was showtime. Lights, camera, action. The pitching didn't disappoint, elongated strike after strike I put on a show just as well as the players did. When it was over, I was hoarse for three days. Thank God the season was over.

Using some of my profits from umpiring, I bought my own sand-base-secured basketball goal. The extralarge driveway had a corner of our side that was the perfect place for my hoop. Even though football season was next, AAU basketball kept basketball on my mind full-time. Every morning I would get to do sit-ups, push-ups, and squats before picking up my basketball. I had the skills, I just needed to work on my conditioning, running the property line around the duplexes. Our housing division was fifty duplexes that stretched a good mile. Turning the corner to make a full circle made it a little over two miles. Starting on my run, I left out the duplexes first so I could finish the home stretch in the complex. I hadn't even made it halfway to the stop sign before an old red Ford pickup truck came flying by. One of the passengers riding in the back of the truck threw a bottle my direction, yelling, "Nigger!" I stopped in my tracks, thinking that I would have to defend myself. The truck stopped at the stop sign but kept going. Realizing that the threat of violence was gone, I went on with my run. I finished the lap, determined not to let hate stop me. After that, I decided it was best to stay in the duplexes versus running on the main streets. If they would have stopped the truck, it would have been five on one, making me reevaluate risk versus reward. In the duplex behind ours, there were three kids that were always outside playing. Across the street from them were two more. I went and introduced myself to the single mothers of both homes, telling them I would like to entertain their kids for a couple of hours a day playing basketball. Both agreed. As summer was winding down. I would wake up, put on my jump sole tennis shoes before going to get all five of the kids. They were all under seven years of age, giving me confidence to play all five against me. I worked to improve my ball handling skills without hurting any of the children. Five children coming from all angles was definitely a challenge. Three kids were so small that they could chase the ball through my legs if I left them open too long. Coach Edwards had been grooming all of us to be able to handle the rock like we were point guards. The kids just proved that everything we were learning in practice worked. I could go twenty minutes or longer before I lost the ball. My confidence was on the rise as my dribbling skills improved, so was my jumping ability from wearing my jump sole tennis shoes every day.

Football camp started. Coach Russell had ideas for this team since we were rookies. With Bryson as quarterback, being the fastest kid on the field, we ran a wishbone option offensive with plenty of speed in the backfield. Devin played tailback, while I played halfback. Even our fullback, Bryon, who was Rose's cousin, was faster than me in pads. Coach started me in the backfield purely for intimidation, using my size like Christian Akoya, standing six feet, three inches in cleats, weighing between 225 and 240. Most teams found my size intimidating. Anytime I was given the ball, I could easily get five yards straight up the field, on the option I could maintain a good pitch relationship. I just had to run the perfect pitch relation or Bryson would leave me. The teams we played couldn't seem to tackle me to the ground similar to peewee football. The blue-and-silver game was our yearly intersquad scrimmage at the end of camp. During the game I earned my offensive position carrying the ball eleven times for eighty yards averaging over seven yards a carry. While I was a small part of our offensive, I was a big part of our defense, standing out in my seven years straight playing defensive end. My eidetic memory made mastering the techniques that all my

I COULD'VE BEEN

coaches taught me easy, destroying pull blocks or splitting double teams, keeping everything inside of me, knowing that I was the last line of defense. I was so disruptive that other coaches would run away from me. My defensive tenacity kept me in the newspaper weekly. With my popularity rising through the entire city, it would scare me when I tried to introduce myself to someone who would say, "I know who you are!" I didn't play for fans. I played for love. The popularity carried a weight of expectations that I didn't care about. In my mind I felt like the people who would say they knew me were stalkers, only knowing what they heard or read. I led the state in tackles from my defensive end position all season long. Earning my spot to be selected with the honor of First Team All-Kansan Defensive Team as a junior. I was the only player from Sumner to earn the accomplishment, which made me the talk of conversation when talking Sumner football. In light of my accomplishments, your grandma wanted to plan me a party, which I felt was unnecessary. I was just doing what my coaches taught me. It was nice to lead the state in tackles. I only cared about winning. After losing our district finals to Blue Valley and Blue Valley North, I didn't really care about the praise, making it a minor accomplishment to me. Our 2–7 record wasn't anything to celebrate. The Kansan only represented the metro Kansas City, Kansas, side and the metro Kansas City, Missouri, side of Kansas City. With all due respect, it wasn't like I made all-state. My celebration was simple, with a trip to Grandview to go out to eat at Applebee's with Monica.

I begged your grandma to let me sit out of basketball. I knew I could make the team. I was more concerned with Coach King's temperament. My integrity made it hard to want to play for someone who didn't coach cheating but accepted it. Experiencing the physical and mental bullying from a few of last year's seniors, I wanted time to reevaluate my career. I knew through experience that when you worked hard, you didn't have to cheat. All the effort I made cheating for tests were frivolous. Had I spent the same time studying, I wouldn't have had to cheat. I was evolving socially, growing tired of practices. I wanted to know what it felt like to be "normal." I tried to explain to your grandmother how spending the season watching might give me more of an appreciation for all the sports I played.

Your grandma said, "Boy, I have invested too much time with too much energy running you from practice to practice all these years because you wanted to play basketball!" Emphatically she would not accept no for an answer. As a trade, she agreed to let me get a tattoo if I played basketball. The Saturday after tryouts, I made her keep her end of the bargain. We went to a tattoo parlor on Leavenworth Road to get my first ink. Wanting something that explained me without words, I chose the Tasmanian Devil in combination with the words "I Bring the Ruckus" from the Wu-Tang Clan spaced around it. I thought hard about using Tupac's "Me Against the World." It made me feel like I was encouraging a fight when I was looking for peace. Knowing that it would be on my body forever, I didn't want it to create constant confrontation. I was the first and only player on our team with a tattoo.

With only two returning starter from last year's varsity team, Bryson along with David Jr., the rest of us suited up playing more JV than varsity. Coach King already had a vision for our team, which was still primarily an extension of Coach Edwards's AAU basketball team. Having played with most of the team for five years or better, we were already jelled. We just needed polishing. To officially start the season, we played our blue-and-silver game. Pregame warm-ups were all about showing our potential athleticism. I was one of four people on the team who could dunk, just barely scraping the ball over the rim. In all my years of playing sports, every coach I played for corrected privately in practice. Coach Edwards never yelled or raise his voice at us. He would just bring a substitute, making us learn from sitting on the bench. Coach King didn't have a filter coaching whenever he felt fit. I hated being yelled at. I hated being publicly humiliated. With all the respect I had for Coach King, he seemed to always be frustrated with something I would do. He was constantly articulating his disappointment with me, trying to break me down to build me back up to play his style of basketball. Any mistake I made was met with more disappointment than any other player on our team. He crippled my confidence, saying, "I just need you to rebound and play defense!" His yelling put a pressure on me that I didn't like, especially since he couldn't do what he expected me to do. I never tried to be the all-star even though I knew through AAU that no one could stop me from scoring. I just wanted to play how Coach King wanted me to play so that he wouldn't yell at me. Coach King expected me to play perfect basketball all the time. With no one being perfect, I felt his expectations were unreasonable. His yelling slowed me down trying to understand what corrections he wanted me to make, trying to understand his anger to get to his message. By default, I found his approval starting all but one game my junior year. My athletic ability continued to land me in the newspaper despite his constant corrections. I modeled my game the after Charles Barkley with all our physical comparisons. I spent the season chasing rebounds and playing defensive more than trying to score, even though I was lights out from anywhere I shot the basketball. Coach King embarrassed me more than once yelling at me during a game on the sidelines. "I DON'T NEED YOU TO SCORE, I NEED YOU TO REBOUND!" seemed to be my greeting anytime he pulled me out of the game. It was nothing like making a three-pointer and getting chewed out for taking my opportunities to score. I was so shook from his yelling that I would only shoot wide-open shots. I would only risk being yelled at if we were down trying to put my team on my back, asserting my leadership and confidence for clutch situations. Seventy percent of the time I would nail my shot, forcing the opponent to take a timeout. Coach King's verbal assault proved his lack of trust in me, which confused me, intelligent enough to understand that trust was earned through efforts combined with loyalty, consisting of accountability. Trying to earn his trust, I kept my mouth shut whenever he chastised me. I promised to myself that I would never let him yell at me twice for the same mistake. Playing to his expectations, defense became my focus, mastering how to control whoever I was defending. making them go the direction that I wanted them to go. Showing me respect for my defensive efforts, when we played Washington High School, Coach King matched me up with KT. He was the leading scorer in Kansas City, ranked twelfth in the nation. He normally averaged thirty-five points a game. He left our Sumner basketball court frustrated, only scoring eight points against me, proving my defensive mastery. I ended the season being able to tomahawk dunk, keeping my wrist swollen, blackened, and bruised from trying to rip the goal down, proving my leaping superiority. Finishing 10–8, losing more than I cared to, I thanked your grandma for making me go out for the team after realizing the evolution of my game over the season.

The "athletic privilege" Mr. Bell taught against had my life on autopilot, skating through the fourth ranked high school in the nation academically. I couldn't do any wrong as far as my faculty of educators saw it. Reading *The Adventures of Huckleberry Finn* in English class consumed my life, trying to stay academically eligible for track season. School was boring to me as a whole. I spent more time trying to outsmart my teachers. I rarely studied, being bored of lectures and taking notes. I didn't understand the point of listening to lectures when I could spend two hours reading to know what the teacher was boring me to sleep with. Using my athletic grace, I constantly pushed the envelope.

After almost a year straight in the newspaper the *Kansan* for multiple sports, getting out of class was easier than anything. I had teachers I knew didn't care as long as my grades were good. Once or twice a week I would make an excuse to roam the halls. I could get out of at least two classes a day to "go to the nurse, counselor or bathroom." Playing in the hallways crossed my path with Paige. She was a freshman cheerleader who was a rumored Hoover, able to break any man in less than five minutes. Allegedly she was so skilled she could take care of whomever she chose between classes during our five-minute grace between classes without making you late for your next class. The day we locked eyes in the empty hallways, I was infatuated with the way she looked at me lustfully. I quickly pulled my pen from my pocket to write down my pager number as I was heading in her direction. I walked over to her, trying to introduced myself.

"I know who you are," she replied.

Before I could even give her my number she grabbed my wrist, leading me to the stairwell outside the old gym. I had dreams of sex in school, especially with the rumors of my cousin. I never imagined while everyone else was in class there were unoccupied places in the school that we could go. I followed her down the stairs into the old gym boy's locker room. The only class to use the locker room was our swimming class. She knew like I did that there were only two swimming classes a day, leaving the locker room wide open. As we stood in the locker room shower, she placed her lips against mine. Her lips were so soft it melted me to my core. As the rumors clouded my head, I pulled away disgusted. As she stared into my eyes, she slowly dropped to her knees, unzipping my pants without breaking eye contact. With the softest, most sensual embrace ever, she had me shaking out of control in less than five minutes. It never even crossed my mind that I was cheating on Monica. When I got back to class, I had only been gone fifteen minutes, hearing Coach Edwards in my head saying, "It's only a crime if you get caught." Knowing that my teacher didn't have a clue gave me confidence to plan meetings with Paige periodically throughout the week.

Track season started with great expectations. Coach Break's first goal for me was to win the Huron league in javelin as well as placing in the top three in shot put. Coach Edwards didn't waste any time getting us back in the gym for AAU basketball practice either. He was looking into the future and wanted to destroy every team playing in the liberty tournament. Having my own mode of transportation made me thankful, allowing me to get where I needed to be. After school five days a week with track practice until five thirty to six o'clock before heading straight to basketball practice three days a week. Showing up late to six o'clock basketball practice made it obvious that the stragglers were all out for their school's track team. Just about every practice I walked in with Daryl. He lived in Wyandotte County close to Patrick. His mother got him transferred like Patrick out to Shawnee Mission West. Daryl knew that I had my own car. Tempting me with the promise of promiscuous girls that he met in his school district, I started hanging out with Daryl all the time. When he introduced me to his girlfriend, Lauren, it blew my mind that he was still chasing other girls. After a month of hanging with Daryl, meeting new girls almost every time through his introductions, I made a clean break with Monica, wanting to keep her respect for me. We still talked on the phone as friends. I just made it clear that we could date whomever we wanted. Daryl seemed to get at minimum five numbers at each track meet. Every week he bartered to be driven somewhere new. I was more concerned with making the newspaper than getting phone numbers. Daryl was just as talented or gifted as me; he just cared more about women. He was recruited young to run track for an AAU team, running into one of AAU track teammates at one of the first track meets of the season. Daryl told me that his friend gave him the number of this young lady that went to Blue Valley North. Daryl was determined to get to Blue Valley to hook up with this girl his friend was talking about. Trying to persuade me to take him to see Emily, he told me that she had a sister that I could hook up with. Suspicious of any girl wanting to hook up that I had not talked to, I didn't want to make the forty-minute drive. Anytime I saw Daryl, he asked me to take him, getting my pager number after a basketball practice, he would page me on days that we didn't have basketball practice, trying to convince me that we needed to make the drive. Wanting to help a friend, I eventually gave in to his offer of gas money, giving him a ride across town. In our conversation on the way, I told him that I had no expectations of her sister.

When we pulled up to the house, this beautiful six-foot-one girl was standing outside as we circled the cul-de-sac in front of her house. "THAT'S HER!" Daryl said, as I looked for a place to park. The closer I got to her, the more I thought she looked like a black Jessica Rabbit. She was one of the sexiest young ladies I had seen outside of school. I couldn't believe my eyes. Beautiful full lips, long flowing hair, with some of the biggest boobs I had ever seen in my life. She was legs, boobs, and a beautiful face. Knowing that she had a sister made me excited. After she greeted Daryl with a warm hug and kiss, she escorted us in leading us downstairs to her sister, Teagan, who was sitting on the couch. Teagan looked nothing like Emily. In fact, she was completely opposite minus her beautiful face. She was gorgeous. She didn't have the athletic physique I expected. As Teagan and I conversed on the couch, Daryl and Emily disappeared. Thirty minutes later they rejoined us in the common area. Emily's hair was a mess. Still being naive, it never crossed my mind to try to have sex with Teagan while we were alone. On the ride home, Daryl told me that he smashed. I didn't believe him, so he slightly raised the edge of

I COULD'VE BEEN

his shorts, allowing the odor of sex to saturate the air in my car. The whole ride home I pressed Daryl to get Emily to hook me up with one of her friends instead of her sister.

Every practice I asked Daryl for an update. He told me that she was working on it, asking for another ride to see her again, offering more gas money. I sat on the couch downstairs in the common area with Teagan as they disappeared again. As we were preparing to leave, Emily gave me the number of her friend Riley. I talked to her on the phone for a few weeks before I went to visit. She was beautiful. Her forehead was big for my preference, especially for her petite hundred-pound frame. She wasn't allowed to leave her house in my car, which left us sequestered to the basement of her home. On my third visit to Riley's house, I moved in kissing her as we said our goodbyes. There was no magic at all between our kiss, which instantly put her in my friend zone. After avoiding her for a week, blaming my schedule, she was over it, realizing that it wasn't going to work between us. On my fourth visit when we said goodbye, she told me that she understood that I just wanted to be friends, giving me the number of her friend Nina. Knowing that beautiful women associated with other beautiful women, I couldn't wait to talk to Nina, calling her the next day.

The conversation was so easy that time flew when we were on the phone. We got to know each other well through our hour-long conversations. We talked to each other every day. Both our schedules were packed, mine between track practice and AAU basketball, while hers stayed busy with piano practice and debate. Neither one of us pressed the issue of meeting. We just appreciated what we got when time allowed.

My busy schedule allowed junior prom to sneak up on me. Not knowing Nina long, it never crossed my mind to ask her to my prom. Wanting to attend, I didn't know who I should ask to be my date. The week before prom, my procrastination kept me dateless. I still had not asked anyone. James said he wasn't going with Kathrine. He was now single, ready to mingle. I asked him if it was cool to ask Kathrine before I actually asked her. He said, "Sure. we broke up, I'm going with Stacey!" Confused, I left it alone, knowing that they had been together for five years. To me, she was still his girl. I didn't want to miss out on the event or memories, so I asked Kathrine to join me nine days before our prom.

Kathrine told me the color of her dress, as your grandmother rushed to coordinate our colors for pictures. On short notice she found my tie and pocket square along with corsage to match. I was clean as a whistle when I arrived to her house. Her father greeted me, entertaining me, while it took almost an hour before her mother was satisfied with her hair and joined us in the living room to prepare for pictures. Once her camera was ready, she called for Kathrine to make her entrance. The bedroom door opened, allowing the ballroom version of Cinderella to walk into the room. My jaw hit the floor, convinced that James had lost his mind. Her mother captured everything click after click, dressing her wrist with the corsage. We posed for a few pictures before the limo with six of our friends arrived to get us. Time kept photos limited still with another couple to pick up. I figured Kathrine had been with James so long that they would eventually get back together. Being a true friend, I didn't want to be part of the problem, so I maintained my gentleman's nature, focusing my concern on both of us enjoying ourselves. With my beautiful date, the night was fun. We danced after dinner, separately checking on each periodically. As my evening alone progressed, I couldn't get my mind off Nina, so I left the ballroom to try to gather my thoughts. Immediately outside the ballroom, the extralong line for pictures distracted me. I was amazed at the length of the line. I walked the entire line searching for the source, stopping to talk with friends as I passed countless couples patiently waiting over an hour for a picture to capture the memory of the eventful night. Kathrine found me talking to friends close to the front of the line, allowing us to skip most of the wait. After waiting thirty-three minutes for one picture, our night ended as the limo arrived to get us home safely. The ten of us rode back to Wyandotte County together, dropping every one of our friends off before we got back to my car at Kathrine's house. We were dropped off at her house a half hour before midnight. I hugged Kathrine goodbye, racing to my car. I was upset, knowing I missed the opportunity to call Nina. I wanted to call, but it was too late.

I COULD'VE BEEN

Even though we were only a few weeks into our phone conversations, my heart was heavy, like a part of me was missing for the day. I got my first cell phone three days later through Verizon's prepaid option to make sure no long car rides stopped me again.

Coach Break prepared me realistically based off my average throws all seasons. He knew that my best in all my events wasn't good enough to prolong my season with a trip to the state track meet, so my focus was already on my second love, basketball. Preferring to play outside, I kept up with the weather forecast like my job. It amazed me when the meteorologist missed completely, forming my opinion that "it was the only profession that you could be wrong every day and keep your job." Buying a degree from college, trying to use science over our God-given intuition. Trained to kill any competition with my gifts like an assassin, I entertained myself predicting my forecast before watching the news, wondering daily if meteorologists felt like losers when they were wrong. The batting average between news channels was horrible. If it wasn't raining, I would call Jake or his brother Ray, searching for the best playground competition in the city. Most days we headed to the outdoor court on Eighty-Fifth and Antioch. Ray played for our older AAU. At five feet, seven inches, he played more of a shooting guard position, having plenty of talent able to score at will. His younger brother Jake played on the team with me. He didn't play football, so he spent all year practicing with Coach Edwards until school basketball started. Jake dominated the court, making me elevate my game. Our motto was anything you could do, I could do better, feeding off each other for the oohs or ahhs of the onlookers waiting to play. All of us had confidence that everything we learned in AAU practice was right, running any court we played on. It got to the point that we had to start playing against each other on different teams in order to have competition. Our bond kept us together all the time. On the weekends, Jake and I would join Ray attending teenage clubs. With our popularity in the city, it was always a fun night that kept us out way past curfew.

Every year graduation was a little sad. It was that one last week for seniors to say their goodbyes or tell people how they really felt. Knowing that we were a week away from being seniors, our class was full of pride. Not unlike any other class, we wanted a parade at the end of the school year too, coordinating a secret parade to announce that the school was ours. Those who were informed met at the Greater Jerusalem Baptist Church. Decorating our cars with shoe polish, we started our procession with a third of our class, driving our parade two blocks to Sumner, boldly trying to park in the senior parking lot. The security guards saw us coming, refusing our entry into the senior parking lot, forcing us to park in the church parking lot across the street. Entering the school from the back door, we started our hallway parade. As we walked around each hallway of the school, our crowd grew. When we got to the senior hallway, we were met with resistance from the graduating seniors. They formed a barricade, closing the doors to their hallway, refusing to let us pass. The standoff at the entrance of the senior hallway got the attention of the office as the noise grew quickly. The principals came braking up our celebration. It was our school now. Graduation was three days away. I left the parade with an escort to class in the form of Becky. She was an underclass cheerleader that flirted with me all the time. With summer upon us, she wanted to exchange numbers. She lived right behind Patrick. She made sure I saw her speaking to me anytime she saw us playing basketball in his yard. Technically I was single. I liked Nina, but we still had not met. Nina had commitments to a summer camp, so I figured Becky's friendship would be harmless. My first stop anytime school wasn't in was always Patrick's house. Monday the third day of summer, Becky snuck out her house, joining me. We hooked up in basement bedroom in Patrick's house. As she was leaving, she said, "We can do this Monday to Friday before five all summer long." Raised on both sides of the city, my "show me" mentality came out, so I made plans for Wednesday, telling her to wear her cheerleading uniform, even though school was out. Patrick's jaw hit the floor when she came over Wednesday in her uniform, following my orders completely. He couldn't believe it was that easy. Patrick started calling me the Pied Piper, joking that I could have made her hula hoop while we were hooking up. Becky told whom she considered friends about our hookups, making them chase me too. Two weeks into the summer, I was secretly hooking up with one of her teammates who wanted to sleep with me because she didn't like Becky.

From five to ten during the week, there was no point to call my cell phone. Either work or basketball practice consumed my evenings. Before leaving for her third year of summer camp, Nina set my expectations. She explained that she had scheduled activities twelve hours a day, five days a week, with only one phone for campers in the bedroom cabin, making it impractical for someone to answer the phone. She stressed that she would call me every night when the phone was available. She was constantly on my mind unless I was distracted with work, practice, or booty call. Even though I was hooking up with a few chicks, they only crossed my mind when I was horny. Otherwise my thoughts were about Nina. I called Nina whenever she was on my thoughts for longer than five minutes. During the day, the phone would ring forever with no answering machine. In the evenings after seven, someone would answer, placing me on hold until the relayed message made her ears. Matching my efforts, she called me just as much as I called her. After our long days, we could spend three hours on the phone, tying up the only phone access to forty other campers.

After nights of me singing to her to express how she made me feel, covering every popular R&B love ballad as well as any song in the top one hundred, she told me that she had talked to her mother about me, making it a priority for formal introductions as soon as camp was over. She added so much pressure, telling me that they were both corporate lawyers under salary with Sears. Nervous about meeting everyone at the same time, I prepared myself, knowing that I had to use every lesson I learned growing up off Twenty-Fourth and Wood to survive her parents. Being genuine, having integrity, respect without jealousy, and letting my actions speak for me instead of talking about it. Fearless, I couldn't wait to meet the yin to my yang, the compassion for my fury, the humbleness to my arrogance. The first girl to exceed my perceptions of your grandmother's intelligence. I was smitten with the voice on the other end of the phone, eliminating distance or time. The more we talked, the easier it was to remove all others from my life, only making myself available to Nina.

As the summer days passed quickly, we spent the Fourth of July over the phone listening to fireworks exploding over both backgrounds during our conversation. Consumed in my feelings for the mind of the voice over the landline, it was so easy to converse with Nina. When I looked at the clock to see that I had been on the phone almost four hours straight with someone whom I still had not met, I knew I had secretly fallen in love with her. On Thursday two days after she got home from camp, I was invited to her house. She knew that I could get to Emily's house, giving me directions from there. Using landmarks, I navigated to her home. Entering her subdivision, I was immediately in awe of the beautiful houses. When the directions expired, I found myself in a cul-de-sac with four of the nicest houses in the entire subdivision. I parked my car by the car she told me she drove, calling her from my cell phone, not knowing what to expect. My stomach was in knots, my hands and feet were sweating, being nervous about not only meeting her but also her parents. Looking up as I sat in my car, I saw this beautiful brown-skinned girl, barely five feet tall, having long golden-brown hair. Making my way up the stairs, the closer I got to her, the more she took my breath away. Speechless by her beauty, I fought to maintain my excitement. She was the prettiest woman I had ever met in my life, more beautiful than I ever could have imagined, with a smile as bright as the morning sun. With a beautiful strong dimple in her right cheek, her black and Pakistani complexion glistened like gold. She looked like a shorter, thicker Jasmine Guy with a slightly darker completion.

We both were nervous, and it had nothing to do with meeting each other. She told me before I even made the trip that her stepfather, David, could be rude as he was hard to impress. Full of confidence, I was excited to meet him. Nina greeted me with the softest, warmest hug ever before she took my hand, leading me inside. As soon as the door closed behind us, my tour of her home began.

"This is the piano room, that's one living room that we don't really use, that door leads to the basement."

This was the first house I had been in with an atrium having a chandelier hanging twenty feet in the air. The staircase along the right side of the door wrapped with the wall leading to the second

I COULD'VE BEEN

floor. I stood for a second in amazement, forgetting all about meeting her parents. Still holding my hand, she led me into the kitchen, which was adjacent to their second living room, where her mother and stepfather were sitting watching television. Her mother was sitting perfectly to see everything coming or going. Seeing me coming, she said, "Hello, Christopher, I've heard a lot about you. My name is Sarah, and this is my husband, David."

Immediately he got up from where he was lying, walking over, sizing me up, trying to intimidate me. He shook my hand firmly, saying, "I hear you play ball for Sumner."

As I gave him my résumé in his unwavering grasp, I purposely finished with my accomplishment of making first team all Kansan as a junior, boasting my arrogance. Entertained but unimpressed, he asked, "What college are you looking at?" which froze me for a second.

Being quick on my feet, I answered, "I'm thinking about KU." I had been receiving letters from schools since I was a freshman, but no one had offered a scholarship. Still gripping my hand like he didn't believe a word I was saying, I was saved when Nina's brother, Doug, walked in (thank God). The tension settled as he let my hand go so that I could be introduced to Doug. Nina explained to her mom that she was going to give me a tour of the rest of the house, saving me from his scrutiny. Leading me upstairs, she showed me the four bedrooms on the second level. The master bathroom was bigger than my bedroom. During the tour, I was introduced to her stepbrother, Ian (David's son was special). He wouldn't shake my hand. Nina kept it moving, not wasting our time, leading me down both staircases to show me the basement. In the basement was yet another living room, a wet bar, along with two more bedrooms. The bar was in the "common area." Seven feet from the basement living room couch and big screen television, across the room were beautiful French doors leading to their small backyard.

We sat on the couch in the middle of the room. Talking to her was so easy and natural, just like our phone conversations. We were so excited to see each other just to sit on the couch and do the same thing we did over the phone. She kept my respect the entire conversation, sitting close enough to show interest without disrespecting herself. I placed my hand on her leg to confirm that I wasn't dreaming. She immediately placed her hand atop of mine, taming my aggression without denying my affection. Her comfort level was midthigh before ushering my hand back to her knee as I tried advancing up her leg. She didn't hesitate to articulate that her last boyfriend broke up with her because she wouldn't sleep with him. As revenge she gave her virginity to his friend for her only sexual experience. When her mother announced from the top of the basement stairs that she was starting dinner, she asked, "Chris, are you staying for dinner?" extending an invite. Respectfully I declined, not wanting to overstay my welcome. As I leaned in to kiss Nina, she turned her cheek for me to kiss, denying me her lips. I was a little disappointed. With three months of phone conversations, I had never been denied anything I wanted from any female outside of family. She made me respect her, proving that she wasn't like any other girl I had met. The fact that she didn't let me have my way with her excited me more than anything. She told me she wanted to kiss me, explaining that we had plenty of time for that. After saying my goodbyes to her family, I hurried to my car. The sun was setting on my hour-long ride home. I turned my radio off to think, eliminate all distractions. My demons were focused on the fact that she was no Emily based off the fact that she wouldn't let me kiss her while we were alone. I couldn't believe what she said about her ex. He became more obsessed with the prize instead of seeing her as the trophy. Pulling into my driveway, I called her to let her know that I had made it home safe. We talked for two hours before we agreed it was past the time we should have ended our night, continually refusing to be the first person to hang up, excited to see each other again in two days.

 My second visit was a lot less tense. When I arrived, her parents barely had time for greetings before they headed out the door to their date. Following suit, we left as well. Our evening was wonderful. Both of us were fully engaged through dinner, following it up with a movie. When we arrived at her house before I let her open the door, I leaned in to kiss her. Without her turning her cheek, I kissed the softest lips I had ever kissed. Making sure I wasn't dreaming, I stopped, opening my eyes, seeing that it was real as she kissed me back. Unlocking the door, we made our rounds to say hello to everyone before we headed to the basement. As soon as we hit the bottom step, she kissed me again. It was the most sensual kiss ever, tingling my core, making me feel like I was Akeem that found his Lisa. With our privacy in the basement, our kissing got heavy. Being friends first when she asked me to stop, I complied, knowing that she couldn't resist me forever. Looking at the time, I had to say goodbye to make it home before my midnight curfew.

My aunt Casey and my aunt Harper, who were both ranked officers in our armed forces, talked to me about taking the officer's test for the branches they represented. Casey was in the Army; Harper was in the Navy. Trying to make everyone happy, I told your grandmother that I would try it. My schedule was wide open with the exception of AAU basketball four nights a week at Guardian Angels. Football camp was still a few weeks away. Praying for a scholarship since athletics was all I knew, I retrieved my shoebox from under my bed that had 162 recruitment letters in it from all over the country. Looking at the mountain of disappointment, I decided, what did I have to lose filling out the paperwork that my aunts had sent me.

At summer's end with senior year about to start, your grandma had been working with the lawyer overseeing my trust fund to get my money released early so she could prepare me for my senior year. Her first priority was for me to have a brand-new car. While waiting on the check to be cut, she took me car shopping. The first lot we went to was the Saturn dealer in Olathe. She had read that it was the safest car out, trying to strong-arm the Saturn brand on me even though nothing caught my attention at all. Your grandmother was impressed with a sports coupe that I refused to look at. My height made me feel like it wasn't the car for me. When we left, I didn't see a reason to drive to Olathe again. Our next stop was the Honda dealer on Metcalf. Honda had just released the CRV, which had me interested except for the fact that it looked like a big cardboard box on wheels. Nothing aerodynamic about it at all. After hearing the gas mileage, I was ready to move on. We went to every car lot on Metcalf, Nissan, Kia, Toyota, everything I liked was out of my price range. Tired and frustrated, I refused to settle. After ten different car lots, we called it a day.

Less than a week later, your grandma called me from work to tell me that she was getting off early so we could go to the lawyer's office. I knew what that meant. In my excitement I cleaned the entire house to keep me busy until she got home. When we got to the lawyer's office, your grandmother gave the receptionist our names as I took a seat. I had only been to his office one other time, to sign paperwork for him to release money to your grandmother for me to get a queen-size bed. Immediately the receptionist told us that he could see us now, standing up to open the door to his office behind her. Entering the room sitting down in the two large armchairs, I marveled at the massive desk which sat between us and my attorney. He was sitting in an even bigger armchair. Straight to the point, he pushed the manila folder on his desk toward us. When your grandmother opened it, in detail it explained the initial amount, his fees, necessary withdrawals (things Grandma said I needed money for), the bottom line said $33,364. I was dancing in my chair with excitement trying to go unnoticed. He told us both where to sign, lifting up the page to a check in the amount I read on the top page. We signed. Your grandmother took me straight to Bank of America. I didn't know depositing a check could be so hard. After over an hour with multiple phone calls to verify my check, the bank finally accepted it, allowing me to open my first checking account. They gave starter checks, explaining that it would be seven to ten business days until my debit card would arrive in the mail. I kept $364 for pocket change, planning to take Nina to the Cheesecake Factory since she spoke about it more than once. She subliminally told me what she expected of me to keep her happy.

Sharply dressed, we waited twenty-five minutes in their crowded waiting area to be seated in a small booth on the second floor. Proudly paying our $120 tap, leaving $150 to cover the tip. I made an excuse to stop at Price Chopper, asking her to wait in the car. When I returned with a dozen red roses, she showed me her appreciation. She kissed me so passionately that both our temperatures boiled. When we arrived at her house, she could hardly put the

I COULD'VE BEEN

roses in a vase, rushing to get to the basement. As soon as we were clear of the stairs, she aggressively kissed me again, pulling me into the bedroom, locking the door. Cleaning up in the adjacent bathroom together, our lust almost started things again. Nina again said, "We have plenty of time to do this." After we checked each other over to make sure that we were presentable, she walked me out, stopping briefly in the second living room for me to respect her parents by saying "Good night." They sat on the couch in the dark covered with a blanket. As we stood on the porch, I tried to convince Nina to let me have her again, saying, "Your parents are on the couch trying to do the same thing." Realizing my truth, her jaw dropped, though it wasn't enough to persuade her into sneaking me back inside. Ten minutes into my drive, Nina called to confirm that my intuitions were correct.

Your grandmother wouldn't give up on the Saturn regardless of my opinion, forcing me to drive us to Olathe again. Leaving the house pessimistic, when I opened the showroom door entering the Saturn dealership, right in front of me was a beautiful shiny royal-blue sports coupe with a sun/moon-roof combo that was aerodynamic, futuristic, as well as my favorite color. It could have possibly been there the first time I just didn't see it, or maybe it was there but I didn't want to see it. While your grandma waited for her salesman, I made myself at home. It didn't take long for grandma to find her sales guy. Both of them headed toward me already sitting in the driver's seat. My only reservation was that there was no real back seat. This car's maximum occupancy with me driving was three people. I felt right sitting in the driver's seat so that it didn't matter. Sitting down at the desk, the salesman explained that this car was the sports coupe 2, as he also explained that Saturn didn't negotiate on their prices. The sticker value said $19,000. After he sold your grandma and me on all the bells and whistles, the total price was too much for me at $21,000. I was ready to go. Your grandma insisted that I have a brand-new car, refusing to take no for an answer. After a two-hour stalemate in the dealership, I folded, knowing my opponent. A week later we went to the bank to get a cashier's check for $21,000 (which almost made me cry), then headed back to the Saturn dealer. The car was beautiful, complete with everything we paid for except the tint. It was hard for me to let the check go, knowing my car wasn't ready. Two days later your grandmother drove me out to Olathe. My car was ready, sitting front and center outside the dealership. The salesman was anticipating our arrival, meeting me three steps into the lobby with my keys dangling from his fingers. Handing me the keys, he walked me to my car. I got behind the wheel, turning the key in the ignition. The dash lit up with the odometer reading sixty-nine miles, which was hilarious to me. With my hormones raging, I took it as a sign that this car was meant for me. Opening my sunroof, I had my Puff Daddy CD ready, playing "Can't Nobody Hold Me Down" as loud as my stock system would play it. Indulging completely in my gift, I got a custom license plate that read "TOTIGHT."

A week after my new car with almost twelve thousand dollars still in the bank, I wanted to upgrade my phone like I did my vehicle. Using my salesmanship, I convinced your grandma to start a family plan with Sprint, offering to pay the bill for her to have a cell phone as well. Using the commercials, my angle was "Free from 7:00 p.m. to 7:00 a.m." Once school started, my schedule was packed until 5:30 p.m., with basketball at 6:00 p.m. After strong-arming me into the car she wanted me to have, she gave in to the phone, benefiting in the arrangement. We drove to 119th and Metcalf to the closest Sprint store outside of a mall. In less than an hour we had brand-new phones. I got a Motorola StarTAC flip phone to go with my pager. While your grandmother's phone didn't impress me, she loved it. Up to date with technology, the only thing I needed to start school was a new wardrobe. I couldn't wait to drive myself to the Overland Park Mall with over ten thousand dollars in my account. I had never been to the mall alone. I spent five hours shopping, leaving the mall with sixteen bags ready for the first day of my senior year. Even though I didn't have a clue what wealth was, I felt *rich*, spending money like it was growing on trees.

As soon as I got home, I got a phone call from Bryan. He wanted to ride with me to participate in the senior parade tomorrow morning as well as the scheduled event this evening that missed me until now. Looking at the time, the secret meeting was less than seventy minutes away, forcing me to end our conversation to hurry to his house. Every school year the seniors would get together and teepee Bishop Ward, one of our league rivals, leaving toilet paper hanging from every tree in their school yard. Our class decided it was our legacy to go big, doing our school as well to leave Ward no retaliation. After picking up Bryan, we stopped at Family Dollar so that we could buy shoe polish along with as much toilet paper that we could fit in my trunk. Starting our antics at Sumner, we covered everything on campus, wrapping two cars in the parking lot completely in toilet paper. Content with our school, we headed straight to Bishop Ward with no concern for authorities. After three hours of throwing toilet paper with our classmates, we headed home so we could meet early the next morning for our senior parade. After picking Bryan, I declined two other classmates who called me last minute, saying that my car was full. Having the smallest back seat in the world, we would have looked like sardines with anyone in the back. We met at Blessed Sacrament Church off Twenty-Fourth and Parallel. Everyone's car was decorated with shoe polish except mine. I brought it. I just really didn't want to put it on my brand-new car. I was in my football jersey, as tradition for the first day of school. Seeing everyone else's school spirit made me loosen up, decorating my car windows. Like no other class, our class topped every other, with a police escort fourteen blocks to Sumner Academy. With our lights on, blowing our horns, we drove around our entire high school campus before we all parked in the senior lots, meeting at the corner of Eighth and Oakland. When all 162 of us were together, we marched every hall, letting all the underclassmen know who the school belonged to, knowing that as seniors we represented it to the fullest, raising all bars for the future classes. The parade subsided as the warning bell rang, letting us know that school was about to start.

This year it was a lot of excitement for football after school coach delayed practice for publicity. The *Kansan* scheduled pictures of our returning letterman for an exclusive story on our team. Two weeks later after our first game, the pictures ran in the sports section with three photos highlighting with a bold title "Veteran Backfield Gives Sabers Head Start." Which was the honest truth. With years of playing together, our execution was effortless against an unworthy opponent. It was the first time in school history that we crossed state lines playing against a Missouri team, crushing them 24–4. My defensive dominance continued as I led my team with fourteen tackles along with one bone-shattering tackle on an attempted reverse. I was so deep in the backfield that I decleated the running back as soon as he received the second handoff. After the game, our entire team was so pumped from our effortless victory that a celebration was planned. Not being one to celebrate, I ditched the party, focused on Saturday AAU practice.

The older I got, the more dreams I seemed to have. Instead of embracing them as confirmation I was on the right path, I was afraid of them. They were so lifelike that I always felt like I was living déjà vu. Having a vivid dream of playing football against Ottawa two weeks before our scheduled meeting was the dream that shook me.

In the dream I played quarterback, which wasn't my position. As we lost, disappointed in ourselves, the bus ride to our school was dark, putting almost everyone to sleep. When we got off the bus, heading into the locker room, which felt so real, I was jolted out of my sleep, conscious that it was a dream.

When we actually played Ottawa, we got down early. Getting desperate, right before halftime, Coach Russell called a timeout, drawing up a play on his dry-erase clipboard. Coach Russell had seen me sling a football sixty-five to seventy yards in the air, showing off after practice. He figured the only person fast enough to break away from the defense was Bryson, our quarterback. Coach put me in at quarterback in the shotgun formation to throw a Hail Mary to Bryson, which didn't work because my accuracy wasn't as good as Bryson's. I overthrew him by ten yards. After halftime, we both returned to our regular positions, suffering a horrible loss. The ride back, like my dream, most of the team fell asleep. When we got to the school locker room, almost everyone's locker was broken into except mine. Left confused because my locker was safe holding keys to my $21,000 car in the parking lot twenty feet away. Leaning on luck instead of grace, my rationale found comfort believing that they skipped my locker because I never washed my practice clothes, making my locker reek. I thought it was funny to see them stand up on their own every day before practice, giving credit to myself afraid of any other reasoning.

From the start of courting Nina, I knew she was special, learning that she was equally gifted, blessed as abundantly as I, consistently showing me that she was one of a kind. Emphatically, both of us passionately pursued perfection for whatever we respected, living in the definition of love, sacrificing everything, refusing to make excuses, neither settling for second at anything to anyone. The passions that motivated us created mutual admiration, making both of us respect each other like we respected ourselves, keeping our chemistry magnetic, constantly motivating one another to push ourselves to be our best, equally finding euphoria, asserting our dominance, destroying anyone ignorant enough to challenge us. I was so impressed by her mind, which gave her confidence, which personified her beauty. She was my best friend and confidant. I devoted every Sunday to Nina, removing myself from church completely. I would get up at 10:00 a.m. like I had a scheduled appointment to arrive at her house precisely at noon. Her family didn't attend church either, choosing to sleep in, preparing for their upcoming sixty-hour workweek. Trying not to disturb anyone's sleep in her home would lead us to the basement igniting our lust, driving our passions, indulging our animal instincts in one of the basement bedrooms. Our spontaneity was equally balanced, never having a problem making plans on the fly. Every Sunday we would spend a few hours away from her house as a date, trying whatever restaurant piqued our interest. Both of us had an infinite love of pizza, leading us to travel anywhere to try any restaurants claiming to be better than the rest. After our dates, we would return back to the neighborhood, searching for a new street being developed. Being outside the city, the stars shined bright enough to see the constellations. We always made her curfew early enough to show our faces with her family if they were home.

Some Sundays the evenings would lead to last-minute studying by Nina. Her school district pushed for Monday tests after studying statistics concerning test scores that proved that kids tested bad on Fridays in anticipation of their weekend. In a few hours Nina could memorize verbatim whatever text the test covered. Watching her intensely focused to memorize a full chapter of any textbook amazed me. I struggled to focus reading a chapter, while she could read it, retain it, recite it after reading it once, handing me her textbook to double-check her perfection. To test her, I would pick random places to start reading from feeding her ten words or less being instantly memorized. As she took over finishing the paragraph or chapter word for word. Her passion for perfection upset her anytime she didn't pass her test with 100 percent accuracy, finding disappointment with her 3.9 GPA.

Every Monday after the game was film day, evaluating our play Friday night. After film, Coach Russell would hand out his weekly awards. With multiple bone-crushing tackles, I continued to earn mention in the *Kansan* for my defensive play, which was always followed with Coach Russell's weekly defensive team award. After converting a third and thirty-nine on offensive on our home field, this week I was awarded both. I never set a goal for my season, I just played the same game I had been playing since I was eight, remembering each lesson, never needing to learn it again. I destroyed offensive plays regularly against any new scheme using the basics. After our season ended with three disappointing losses at district finals, I made first team all-Kansan for the second year in a row. Unlike last year, I had two teammates join me for the city newspaper photo shoot, Cole and Bryson. Keeping me humble, Bryson made both first team offense and defense. With love as well as support for each other, we found pride in representing Sumner better than any other class. When the story ran in the paper, they reversed the pictures of the offense and defense, which we found hilarious. It didn't matter to us. Our picture was still in the paper.

My athletic abilities earned respect among all social circles. It opened more invitations to places I had no idea existed along with homes that looked like castles. After four months of dating, I was accepted into Nina's social circle. Making friends with among the elite families of Kansas City, I loved to see the shock on the parents of her friends when she told them I was from Wyandotte County, as the city was known as Crime Dotte. Once I revealed that I attended

I COULD'VE BEEN

Sumner Academy, they would let go of their preconceptions. Your grandma raised me with courage that allowed me to always feel like I belonged anywhere I went. With Nina by my side, they treated me equally, even though they made what your grandmother made in a year in one month.

Clubbing got old, so I dedicated my Saturdays to Nina as well. While her parents planned to binge-watch movies, theater hopping at AMC, going to the theatre for six to ten hours straight. AMC Town Center 20 in Leawood was ten minutes from to her house. Imitating them, we took more interest in going to the movies. We didn't have the patience to watch two movies straight. Paying for one movie watching three was as ghetto as her parents got. Nina refused to do anything criminal regardless of the fact that her parents were both lawyers. Our worst date was to a New Orleans-themed restaurant, where our service was horrible, waiting over an hour after our orders were taken before food arrived to the table. Nina got sick, so I sent her to the car, waiting a few minutes to walk out on the tab. After telling Nina what I did two days later, she went back to the restaurant to pay the tab.

Basketball caught me so fast the talk of college was an afterthought. My focus on the task in front of me was more important, eager for my senior year of basketball. My jump shot was pure. I called it water since I rarely missed. I consistently made seven out of ten shots from anywhere on the court combined with the fact that I was jumping out the gym. Even though it wasn't pretty, I could dunk vertically leaping with no momentum, showing off as the only person on the team that could do it. With a few steps, I could throw down a backboard, shaking dunk in multiple variations. Our high school team really hadn't changed. We lost David Jr., gaining Gavin, his little brother. They played so much alike that it was a natural fit. Both of them were point guards who could shoot the lights out, especially when you pissed them off. Both were five foot nothing with lightning-fast foot speed. Our transition was easy, like our first game against Harmon, easily defeating them 72–47. Winning four straight before we lost to Coach King's former school, Wyandotte, by ten on their home court, Coach King was more pissed at the referees than the fact we lost to the school he used to coach at. Bouncing back, we won seven straight before losing our second game, placing second in the midseason tournament in Topeka. Our only other loss of the season was against Schlagle on their home court, who beat us like we didn't deserve to be in the same gym, prompting our senior class to make a pact not to lose another game having the talent that we had.

The second semester of my senior year I had met all the requirements to graduate, allowing me to participate in an internship program. The program allowed me to get out of school at 10:30 a.m. to report. The lady that took me as her intern ran her own business out of her home. Her small business was all merchandising with logos. She could put your logo on whatever you wanted to help businesses brand their trade. Her apartment office was packed with hats, shirts, pens, cups, coffee mugs, sun visors, anything anyone was willing to pay to have their logo on under the sun. Most days I arrived at her townhouse at noon. Normally she was home alone on the phone, trying to negotiate or confirm a deadline. Daily I was her carrier, picking things up or dropping them off wherever she needed. When I walked in her apartment, she would have the keys to her Lexus SUV sitting on the packages for me to deliver with the MapQuest-printed directions. She was a perfectionist, not allowing me to help her with anything else, letting me leave most days after I finished her deliveries. Typically, before 1:00 p.m. I was finished, which gave me a few hours before I had to be back at school for practice.

With the decline of our student body over the years, our class rank moved to 4A at the beginning of the school year, which took effect just in time to allow us to host the 4A substate tournament. The new class ranking made our competition way too easy, ripping through our opponents like they were junior varsity teams qualifying us for the state tournament being held two and a half hours away in Salina, Kansas. Our first game was against Towanda-Circle. They were good, but we were more talented, controlling the pace of the game. The second game I got two fouls before the game got to be minute old, forcing Coach King to pull me from the game, cursing me out, calling me a dummy as many ways as possible. Frustrated, I sat on the bench until the second quarter playing less than two min-

I COULD'VE BEEN

utes before I was whistled for my third foul. Coach King lost his marbles, tossing his chair into the stands. He was so mad he didn't start me the second half, which pissed me off, making me feel like I had something to prove. When I entered the game again, I was whistled for my fourth foul, making me feel picked on by the referees. I sat on the bench until Derrick fouled out with 1:55 remaining. After a few plays, a foul was called, making me think that I had fouled out of the game, sending them to the free-throw line. Instead it was called on the other Chris, whom Coach King pulled from the game immediately. With the game tied at the line for two shoots, their guard missed both free throws being put on ice with timeouts being called before both attempts with less than thirty seconds on the clock. After the second shot, Bryson got the rebound, spreading our offensive into four corners, choosing to play for the last shot. As the clock hit ten seconds, he made his move, driving to the hole. As he drove to the hoop, the guy guarding me tried to help on defense, leaving me wide open. Bryson realized that I was unguarded, passing me the ball for a wide-open bank shot standing on the square, breaking the tie, sending us to the state championship game.

Our opponent, Wamego, wasn't a small team. I called them cornbread fed and country bred. After my disappointing semifinal performance, I was being ripped by the paper as a horrible player that got lucky in the right place at the right time. Furious, motivated by the headlines, I didn't care who we were playing; I wanted their head. Choosing my shots wisely, I was four of five from the field and one of two from the free throw, which upset me, averaging 84 percent all season from the free-throw line. I didn't dwell on it long, having a double-double with thirteen rebounds. I fouled out as the clock expired in regulation, sending us to overtime. Chris, whom we nicknamed Snow, came in the game on fire as Coach King changed his strategy. In overtime we should have named Snow "Show" after he hit three clutch shots, making two three-pointers. With Derrick and me on the bench being two of our tallest players, Snow and Gavin, two of our shortest players, carried us to a 64–60 state championship win. It was Sumner's first state championship since becoming an academy. The postgame celebration was insane followed by the trophy presentation. Each one of us got to climb a ladder to cut a piece of the net as a keepsake, not being able to split the trophy. The following two weeks were pep rallies, photo shoots, and interviews. It was like we won the NBA championship. Instead of going to Washington, DC, to see the president, we went to Topeka to the state senate. To acknowledge our victory, we were given an honorary day by the state senate. Coach King was so delighted that we brought the title home to Sumner he made sure we got championship rings.

Being selected to play in the Mo-Kan all-star basketball game was an honor that I didn't expect. I wasn't the only Saber to get the privilege of representing Sumner in the game. Chris and Bryson were selected also. Minus Bryson, every other player selected, including myself, played for Coach Edwards as part of my AAU team. At halftime I was one of six selected to compete in the dunk contest. My first dunk was a 180 tomahawk going under the rim, turning around, bumping the ball off the glass before slamming it home. I tried my hardest to compete with Bryson and Mike. With my childhood injury, I could only dunk off two feet. Both Bryson and Mike could jump off one leg, exciting the crowd more. I did a 360 windmill first, which was overscored by their 360s as they both took the ball through their legs while doing theirs. Mike took first, Bryson took second, while I took third. Everyone on the teams were good friends of mine. Being on a winning team all my life, winning was what I expected. I never felt like an all-star because I always left everything on the court. I worked harder for basketball than I did any other sport, feeling like I had the most room for growth in it. The most important lesson I learned was that you can have all the skill in the world and someone with a smarter basketball IQ than you could still defeat you. If you could pick out the other team's weakest player defending them to play to their weakness, you could leverage an advantage. With good defensive combined with a strong offensive threat, you could put a distance between you and your opponent that was insurmountable.

The promise I made to my auntie was called to the table. Isabella and I had made a few trips to St. Louis to go shoplifting, telling your grandmother we were shopping. Through casual con-

I COULD'VE BEEN

versation, she mentioned it to my aunt Harper, who was stationed in St. Louis. Even though I signed a letter of intent to attend Butler County Community College on a football scholarship, my aunt still wanted me to try the test. After hearing that I was making three-hour trips anyway, my aunt Harper scheduled me for the officer's test. Not allowed to give excuses, I committed to the process, skipping a party to drive down on a Friday for my Saturday evaluation. I stayed with my aunt Harper, sleeping on her couch. She was super excited, calling it a night at 8:00 p.m., encouraging me to finish my jack-in-the-box meal and do the same. We both got up at 5:00 a.m. Me to get to the evaluation, while she got up to make sure I got up. After my thirty-five-minute drive, I arrived in downtown St. Louis, using my map-quest directions. Entering the building, I was nervous filling out the paperwork. I learned that the test was in two parts. First came the physical. If I didn't pass the physical, I couldn't take the written test. For the physical, we were placed in a room of one hundred people. The drill sergeant instructed everyone to disrobe completely, squat down so that your butt was lower than your knees, and walk fifteen feet to the other side of the empty white room. I removed everything except my underwear, waiting until the last minute before my group was called to the line. Squatting to the requirement, I beat my group across the room both times. Finishing as fast as I could, I was anxious to put my clothes back on. After several other tests, I was given the stamp of approval permitted to the written exam. It was one of the hardest tests I had ever taken in my life, harder than both the SAT or ACT, which I took less than a year ago. After the fifth question, I felt like the test was ridiculous. I needed a calculator, compass, and map for the math questions, while the reading questions were all carefully worded to test your attention span. I got frustrated, growing short on the ninety-minute time period, wasting twenty minutes on the first five questions and quit trying to analyze every question. Figuring that any answer was better than no answer, I used my last ten minutes to mark C or D on all questions that I skipped, trying to not disappoint my aunt Harper with an incomplete test. When I got back to her apartment, I told her my truth of the experience. Loving me, she understood my honesty, encouraging me by telling me that I could try again in three months.

Through track, AAU basketball, and school basketball, the relationship between Dominic and I continued to grow. He was my little brother and way less trouble than Daryl. Whenever our schedules permitted, we were hanging out. My crush on his sister passed after she graduated, making her a distant memory to Nina. Dominic's mother recruited me to be a participant in the cotillion for Delta Sigma Theta's Kansas City chapter. I didn't have a clue what it was, but I loved Ms. Williams as if she were my surrogate mother, admiring that she represented everything I hoped for in a wife, beautiful, intelligent, and classy, or as I shortened to BIC. Ms. Williams was my liaison, keeping me up to date with the cotillion scheduled events or fund-raisers. The first cotillion meeting had me speechless, honored to be selected among this group of beautiful, prominent people from the metro Kansas City area. While introductions were transpiring, I listened as everyone proudly boasted their accomplishments, learning that most of the group was the offspring of powerful people in the city. With my schedule full of athletic practices or games, I missed a few cotillion meetings, almost dropping out. Ms. Williams refused to let me, so she took over my fund-raising, providing me a list of people to solicit for donations, helping me catch up. After a few phone conversations, all I had to do was get fitted for my tuxedo for our announcement ball, which followed our talent competition. While most of the group decided to sing or dance, I refused to follow the crowd regardless of being blessed with a great singing voice. I wanted to do something that no one else was brave enough to try: preparing in Spanish a speech of my accomplishments as well as future goals. With almost five years of Spanish under my belt, I figured it would be easy, allowing me to stand out individually. Standing center stage under the bright lights in front of the full audience in the Kansas City Community College theater made it difficult. Thank God I was allowed to prerecord it for the event. I moved my lips better than Milli Vanilli for the duration of my speech. Everyone's talent was entertaining as we competed for cotillion scholarships. A few weeks after the talent competition was our announcement ball, held at the downtown Marriot in Kansas City, Missouri. We dressed in our white evening attire in the luxurious suites the sorority provided as the newspaper captured every photo they could once we were presentable. Looking dapper completely dressed in my white tuxedo, cummerbund, accompanied with my white patent leather shoes, you couldn't tell me I wasn't the sexiest thing in the world, especially after the *Kansan* printed a few pictures of me, boosting my ego, making me full of myself.

Dominating every sport that I participated in, it was no surprise to me that I was number 1 in the area for the Prep Track and Field Honor Roll in javelin. The closest competition in the city in javelin was Larry Love. Both of us were throwing it consistently 170 yards. Every week I seemed to always stay a few yards ahead of him in the Kansan Track Honor Roll finishing first or second in javelin at every track meet all season long. I was second in the city in shot put, consistently putting up forty-four feet or better, amazing Coach Break, who joked that I was the little man in the event since I was always half the size of everyone else competing at the meet in shot put. For four seasons straight Coach Break never missed any attempt in any event that I competed in. His respect for my athletic ability combined with my love of hearing my name on the announcements or seeing my name in the newspaper made me go hard every week, leaving blood, sweat, or tears on the field. Our team motto hadn't changed. "Go hard or go home!" was all that I knew. My collection of medals was only second to Kane, who just happened to be Patrick's cousin. He graduated two years before me after four years straight competing on the varsity track team running in five or six events a meet. Knowing that he couldn't be caught, I just wanted to put myself in a close second.

School winding down with a few weeks before graduation, I showed up to my internship like normal at eleven to my boss's husband sitting on the couch reading the newspaper. He lowered his paper, looking me in the eyes and said, "Christopher Drake." The look of confusion must have been written all over my face, prompting him to introduce himself as a Wyandotte County judge. He explained that he read the *Kansan* every day to stay informed of news outside his courtroom. Needing no introductions with a Wyandotte County judge stunned me initially. Having a stranger calling me by almost my full government name was a little shocking, when his wife started our business as usual, giving me my task for the day it disappeared. On my way to track practice, I felt a little violated, being a very private person. Trying to make sure that I wasn't tripping, I called Patrick. After telling him the story, his only words of wisdom were "Get used to it." To which I replied, "I don't want to get used to it!" Before he said, "Let me call you back." Not letting me explain that I didn't want the fame. I was just doing what I loved.

At track meets, each team earned points from each event to determine what team wins the meet. Even though we were all competing individually, if we placed in our events, we were accumulating points for the team. With our team collectively dominating in every event, we easily won substate. Our team had so many people qualify for the state track meet in Wichita the coaches had to rent two fifteen-passenger vans, deciding to leave immediately following graduation, needing almost twenty rooms. Our coaches wanted to beat the rush, making sure that we found a hotel with enough rooms since every qualified competitor across Kansas was heading to Wichita for the state tournament. Some teams traveling farther than our three-hour trip making hotel rooms a limited hot commodity. I was forced to overlook graduating as something expected, which by now it was normal to me, even though statistics of Wyandotte County gave me a 19 percent chance as a black youth. I didn't just graduate; I graduated from the premiere school for the top 2 percent of students academically in Wyandotte County ranked fourth in the nation. My life committed to athletics made it something that I had to sit through to get to the next priority ready with a duffel bag in my trunk with a week's worth of clothes in it. I walked the stage to receive my diploma like so many other awards. I returned to my seat, watching my watch until the last name was called. When the final declaration was made, my excited classmates threw their caps. I was more concerned with passing the congestion to pose for a few pictures, refusing to be late as I was scheduled to leave the school at 10:00 p.m. Focused on myself, I never thought twice of the fact that I had to skip the Grad Night Lock-In with the rest of my senior classmates to celebrate. My desire for perfection kept me on time to everything, trained to believe two consistent quotes from people that I admired: Coach Edwards, "*Winners don't make excuses, losers do!*" and my aunt Vanessa, "*Excuses are monumental mounds of nothing that lead you nowhere except where you already are!*" I arrived early to the school to catch the vans rented to get us to Wichita, chasing records for titles. Arriving in Wichita late after our three-hour ride, it took our coaches over an hour to get all the rooms. Stretching my legs, I walked around while we waited, wandering into the indoor pool with adjacent hot tub, quickly making missing my graduation celebration insignificant.

On my third day in Wichita, my event was up. Excited to compete with the wind in my favor, I set the mark to beat early listed as the second competitor to throw the javelin, tossing it my seasons best of 196 feet, 6 inches, proudly setting the standard. With the wind spiraling like it was trying to create a tornado, I thought it would hurt everyone's performance. It actually did the opposite, as the very next competitor passed my best, tossing his season's best at 203 feet 3 inches. I watched in disappointment as each opponent seemed to be a little taller or wider through the first round of competition as three of the next eleven passed me as well, dropping my best to fifth out of fifteen. There were kids here from schools and towns that I never heard of competing in javelin. My second throw after running fifteen yards with my arm full extended was 209 feet 1 inch, putting me back in the top three. Besting my best of the year while simultaneously throwing my arm out. I had one last official throw for competition that didn't make it eighty feet with my noodle arm. I finished in fourth place, which didn't make me happy since I missed medals. I only found self-pride that when dropped to fifth, I found it in my gut to add distance topping my career best. It didn't hit me until I finished my event that I still had two days in Wichita with no more events to compete in. I was so mad that I didn't drive until seeing other seniors who had made the sacrifices without complaining. As the day was coming to an end, we saw that we were in the running for a team title. Our coaches calculated that if we competed like normal in the relays, we could win state as a team. Sitting in the stands watching our sprinter dominate was amazing, especially as they set new records for the state. It all came down to the four-by-four relay. Yesterday our team dominated the 400 finals. Dominic took the gold medal, Kaden took silver, and Blake placed fourth. Today's relay was really just a formality. With the pop of the starting pistol, Elijah, Dominic, Kaden, and Blake ran the race of their lives. Together they set another new state record, securing our team the 4A state title. I finished my high school athletic career as a two-time first team All-Kansan as well as a two-time state champion.

    Graduating cum laude meant the world to me, especially since Nina ended her year with a 4.2 GPA. With no Division 1 schools offering me scholarships, I was committed to Butler County Community College right outside Wichita. Every junior college in Kansas offered me a scholarship, so I went to visit them all. Butler by far had invested the most in their campus recently, which made the decision easy. Now with two months to report, I wish I had not given my word or signature to go to Butler. The coach that recruited me switched places with a coach from Coffeyville. He was my coach, and I wanted to play where he coached. Patrick along with two good friends from Sumner were all going to Coffeyville, but with my signature on that paper, I couldn't switch schools without repercussions unless I went to a Division 2 or Division 1 school. Daryl was going to Butler also, which made me find peace in my arrangement wanting to compete somewhere. Despite my second thoughts on schools, I had bigger concerns. I was about to be separated from my best friend, my equal. Our commonality was so in tuned we were like twins. We could find comfort and entertainment simply laying out the wool blanket that my aunt Harper gave me and looking up at the stars. With my voice matching Brian McKnight's, I would serenade her with whatever song I could that I felt matched my feelings for her. It wasn't about sex. It was about quality time and communication. We had so much in common we were just commonly opposite. While I sang, she played the piano. I was the best all-around athlete. She was a scholar who stayed on the dean's list. I was big, physical, and aggressive. She was short, sensual, and demure. She was the yin to my yang. The threat of distance with school wasn't the only thing concerning me. Both her parents worked for Sears, who was closing all their Kansas City locations, forcing them to move back to Illinois for work. With Nina having serious academic scholarships on the line, they chose to keep their house in Kansas City until she graduated. They bought a house in the Naperville suburbs of Chicago that they would call home Monday through Thursday, and on Friday evening after work, they would fly to KC to be with the kids until either Sunday night, or they would catch the red-eye first thing Monday morning.

Summer just beginning, my stepfather, Kelvin, got me a job at Kmart working in the photo lab to make extra money for college around our schedule of umpiring. After Ventures went out of business, everyone he knew went to Kmart, making it easy for him to get hired as well. It was on Ninety-Fifth and Metcalf, which was thirty minutes from my house or fifteen minutes from Nina's house. When I worked mornings, I would leave my house two hours early just to go lay next to Nina to hold her before I went to work. Anytime my schedule was open, I was with her. Nina and I delighted on our newfound freedoms, having a quarter-million-dollar home that we were the adults of. Knowing her parents left for Chicago last night while I was at work, I decided to surprise her for a lunch date the following morning. I called as I stood outside the front door with flowers. She woke up to let me in. Seeing the bouquet of flowers, she forgot about her morning breath, kissing me passionately. Following her morning routine, she headed to the kitchen for coffee. I never drank coffee thanks to your grandma. (When I was younger, she told me it would stunt my growth.) Nina's house was always immaculately clean, like they had a live-in maid. Sitting down at the bar top as usual, I noticed an envelope on the counter in front of me. Being inquisitive, I asked about it. She said, "It's cash to get us through the week." She grabbed the envelope, exposing its content, pulling out ten one hundred dollar bills. I couldn't understand why there was two hundred dollars a day for three people, while Nina dismissed it as normal. Instead of letting me buy her lunch, she paid using her own debit card. Having total disregard for the cash her parents left, she purposely left it at home on the counter.

Not including Nina in my college decision, I had to respect it when she told me she was looking at Emory or Duke. With one being in Atlanta and one being in North Carolina. I wasn't in any hurry to be three hours away at Butler for her senior year of high school. My heart wasn't in it, so I didn't want to be three hours away from home. I wanted to play ball. I just wanted to be closer to home, closer to Nina. Living with no regrets, I quit thinking about Butler to enjoy one day at a time of possibly our last summer ever together. I knew that she loved me. She didn't have to verbally say it. My empathic senses never failed pertaining to her emotions. The fact that she passed on her last year of her summer tradition to spend time with me said enough. Even though her excuse was that she wanted a job that she never got. With no adults present to tell us no, I found myself staying later and later or spending the night. Especially after the movie *Armageddon* came out. I constantly found myself singing.

> I could stay awake just to hear you breathing.
> Watch you smile while you are sleeping, while you're far away and dreaming.
> I could spend my life in this sweet surrender,
> I could stay lost in this moment forever.
> Every moment spent with you is a moment I treasure.
> I don't want to close my eyes,
> I don't want to fall asleep 'cause I'd miss you, baby, and I don't want to miss a thing.
> Cause even when I dream of you, the sweetest dream will never do, I'd still miss you, baby, and I don't want to miss a thing!

I meant every word of Aerosmith's song to my core. Her love made me feel better than any victory. As a champion, I had experienced them all. In that moment, it wasn't about winning or losing, tall or short, fast or slow. It was about someone understanding that I had emotions too. On the field I had to be fearless and brave. I had to

I COULD'VE BEEN

always face the best, win, lose, or draw. Right here, right now, it was about someone seeing that I was human too. She wasn't even a fan of sports. She understood that I put my pants on one leg at a time, just like she did. I had tons of fans that I was running from because they only knew me by my athletic ability. Nina didn't even watch sports until I entered her life, taking interest in everything about me. She genuinely cared why I was who I was. Trusting only what I saw, I had no faith in finding someone else who would care to understand me like Nina did.

With no plans for tournaments or competition for our age division with Coach Edwards. Basketball practice was lighter than usual. I guess instead of us all trying to prove ourselves every day, we learned to respect each of our teammates' talents. Honestly, every player on the team was Division 1 ready. Everyone's basketball IQ was through the roof, which only made sense, considering we spent on average 250 days a year either playing or practicing for the last five years together. Playing ball was easy if you could pay attention and correct your ignorance immediately. Listening to the coaches taught us quickly. Learning to never make the same mistake twice, as if the whole team had eidetic memories for the game. Our execution was so flawless we could kill teams five years older than us, barely breaking a sweat. The only thing we did individually that made us a winning team was care. We cared to show up three to five days a week to learn from the coaches who made things easy when we followed instructions, learning from their lessons. Being basically an only child, all my life it was all I knew how to do. I followed my coach's instructions like they were your grandmother's. All of which became my father figures and role models. I guess deep down I had my own daddy issues. I did whatever it took to find acceptance from my coaches and my team. At my size, I just wanted to fit in somewhere, which was athletics, because almost everywhere else I felt out of place.

All summer there were so many people calling me my phone wouldn't stop ringing. The saying "you've got to pay the cost to be the boss" hit me hard. My cell phone bill was a thousand dollars, forcing me to try everything to reduce my bill. If someone called between 7:00 a.m. and 7:00 p.m., I only answered to say, "I'll call you after seven." Jumping through all the hoops didn't change a thing. After paying my bill to a zero balance, I was sent another thousand-dollar cell phone bill. After months straight of thousand-dollar cell phone bills, my money from Bill's life insurance was gone with college a few weeks away.

Saturday evenings I loved hanging out with my AAU teammates. With our popularity, we didn't wait in line to enter in Westport clubs. Showing our real IDs, we received wristbands or stamps to signify that we were old enough to drink. The name CMH carried weight that broke rules. At eighteen it was normal to be standing on the dance floor with a professional athlete that played for our city or Tech-9, rubbing elbows in elite circles. As the summer was winding down, starting preseason games for the NFL, my respect for the league I dreamt of playing was tarnished. Preparing for my freshman year, hoping to lead the state in tackles, without fail one of my role models who played cornerback for the Chiefs was in the club nightly, always seeming to close the club down regardless of practice or game. He knew better than we knew what club was jumping seven days a week.

Buco Juco

To prepare for my upcoming football season, I started going to the track at Kansas City, Kansas Community College to work on my speed. According to scouting reports, my lack of speed was the only thing that prevented me from going to a Division 1 school. Not really knowing the track side of things, with field events being my forte in high school, I hated to stretch before working out. I felt like only old people needed to do that, and I wasn't old. I was pound for pound, the best all-around athlete in Kansas City. I set a schedule to run on Mondays, Wednesdays, and Fridays, being self-motivated, competing with myself. I knew I would be timed on the forty almost immediately when I got to school, so I wanted to run ten hundred dashes a day. I desperately wanted to bring my time of 4.7 down to something more compatible with NFL players of my size and position. Two weeks before the day I was to report, I strained my hamstring. Knowing there would be over a hundred players competing for fifty-five positions, I took the last two weeks off, trying to recover by camp.

Your grandma and I stuffed my car to the brim with whatever she thought I would need being three hours away in school. My car was so packed that I could barely see out the back window. Marcus, a childhood friend from Twenty-Fourth and Wood whom I played peewee football with, was attending Butler as well. His mother and your grandmother got along well when we lived on opposite corners of our block. His mother took on foster kids, trying to help them have a stable home, like Patrick's mother with plenty of kids at his house. I loved when his mother would watch me. Me and Marcus grew apart when I left Eisenhower to go to Sumner. His parents moved into the Schlagle schooling zone right around the corner from Patrick. Marcus was influenced by his older siblings who were living the gang life, reppin' flags, influencing him. When I hung out with him, he was just Marcus, forming our bond like cousins. He was that friend that I could watch from a distance. I didn't want to get too close to his fire. Our mothers got together and coordinated the four of us carpooling to Butler. With extra space in their van, Mrs. Lead, Marcus's mother, let me load my bigger items with them, which wasn't much. We followed each other down I-35 south, stopping in Emporia for gas. Marcus rode in the van with his mother, and your grandma rode in the Saturn with me. After the three-hour ride, our destination looked desolate when we got off the highway to pay our toll. The only sight we could see waiting in line to pay at the booth were huge oil rigs and silos. I was disappointed with the smell in the air, knowing that the air pollution was a product of the oil farms. The school was three miles from the highway according to the school website. Driving what appeared to be the main strip, we passed a Walmart. It was the only thing that resembled the city life that I was used to. Pulling into the dorm parking lot was like driving down to Fifth and Quindaro in the middle of the summer. The weather was nice, so there were people outside all over the place.

Some of the team reported early taking summer school. Most arrived yesterday or earlier today. Everyone who had already unloaded and unpacked was standing outside, watching all the newcomers. When we arrived, there were easily thirty people standing around the small stoop outside the old dorm. I recognized most of the faces as premier athletes at their high school, like me. Growing up in the inner city playing sports all my life, the size-up my teammates were doing from the stoop didn't bother me. I hadn't lost a fight in years and was trained to look the enemy in the eyes before I beat them. I made my way through the crowd to find my room. My roommate, Peyton, was a sophomore. He arrived the day before and was already unpacked. Seeing your grandma helping me bring my stuff in the room, he immediately got out of bed to help too. His willingness to help me made me feel like I was with family. I unloaded my things as quickly as I could so your grandma and Mrs. Lead could be on their way.

I COULD'VE BEEN

Peyton gave me the "grand tour." In the old dorms, each unit had two hallways with five rooms on each hallway upstairs and downstairs with the center area of the dorm being the common area / washroom. Half of the common area was toilets; the other half was showers. The only place to have privacy was in the bathroom stalls; otherwise there was always someone in your face. We had a new dorm that was built two years ago as well, along with four four-unit apartments that were like double-sided duplexes. After the quick tour, I decided to join the other guys on the stoop to see who my competition was. Butler talent for the upcoming season was quickly turning into a who's who of Kansas football. Familiar face after familiar face, Butler quickly made me feel at home among all the players like me who really should have made it to a Division 1 school.

We got to school the Thursday before classes started. I was scheduled to report Friday at noon. Our team meeting was my first opportunity to see Coach Tully in action. From the beginning, I was not impressed. Something didn't seem right, other than his chewing tobacco. I never understood dip. Bill chewed tobacco, which disgusted me. He would leave spit cups all around the house or car. Listening to Coach Tully address the team, you knew he was from the South. He told us he came from the University of Arkansas. Trying to motivate us, he bragged about how he had a lot of Division 1 friends. Being the warrior I was disappointed. I never bragged about my friends. I never tried to use my connections to make me look better. I guess it was the whole "show me" state attitude that Bill taught me. After giving us a rundown of what to expect until classes started, we ended the day early so we could rest for our 7:00 a.m. start tomorrow. We had to start early with coaches wanting everyone to run the forty-yard dash three times.

Having just healed from my hamstring injury, I made sure I stretched long and good before my group was called to the line. In order for our coaches to get an accurate time, we had to run three sets for the average. My first one I ran a 4.58, which wasn't bad for my position but overall was slower than average for skilled positions (excluding lineman). My second forty was slower, running a 4.72. Being overcompetitive, my third attempt I pressed like I was running for my life. Twenty-five yards into my forty-yard dash, I pulled my hamstring. The trainers responded immediately, racing to me, picking me up off the track. At my size, I had never been carried before. Three of them helped me to my feet, struggling in their attempt to carry me to the head trainer. Coach Adams, our head trainer, laid me down on my stomach. He put his hands as deep as he could under my butt muscle, making me feel a little uncomfortable. After a few seconds, he said, "It's strained, not pulled." He also told me he recommended a couple days of stimulation, or stim as he called it. It was the electronic pulse machine. He promised that it would fix me right up.

Practice began two days later on Monday with me less than 100 percent. I was able to make it through the drills with no problems and only a slight discomfort. When it came time for conditioning, I didn't think it would be wise to sprint across the field, so I sat out when it was time for linebackers and defensive backs to run. Coach Tully saw me sit out and lost it, acting worse than I'd ever seen Coach King act. He berated me in front of the entire team.

"Christopher Drake, are you too good to run with your team?" With his tone raised to be heard across the field. I tried to open my mouth to explain, but Coach acted as if I wasn't speaking loud enough for me to hear him dismissing me, raising his voice over mine to say, "You're giving me excuses! Champions don't give excuses!"

He threatened that for every one sprint I sat out, the team would run ten more. He purposely put a target on my back for the whole team. Despite the trainer's recommendation of taking it easy, I started running with my team. Finishing last was good enough for him, raising the stakes, saying that he would add ten more for every sprint I finished last. He threatened that if anyone slacked off to let me beat them, that we would run until there was no sunlight. Hating to be publicly challenged, knowing the repercussions of not standing up for myself on my childhood block, I sprinted with my team. Without time to fully heal, aggravating my injury over and over, I stayed with the trainers after every practice. Unintentionally I got to know some of the trainer's team on the first name basis, which was better than I hoped for. A few of the bullies on the team started talking about how

I COULD'VE BEEN

I was the only person to see the trainer daily, which was true, but who were they to judge me. The knot in my hamstring was really needing time to heal, but that didn't exist with less than ten practices to make the team roster. I wasn't using it to get out of practice. We still hadn't made the cut to fifty-five, so I refused to sit out.

Not even a full week into camp, we lined up for skeleton drills, playing two on two. One blocker for the runner on offense, one lineman and linebacker on defense. Having done this drill for years, it was a breeze. For twenty minutes straight I dominated the drill. Everyone in the drill had to lay on their backs. Both the lineman laid helmet to helmet, and the skilled players would lay three yards behind their feet on their backs. Coach would stand in the middle with the ball. Once he tossed the ball, it established the offensive side and the defensive side. We all had to make it to our feet. The offensive players tried to get past the defensive players, staying within the five-yard boundary set by the pad dummies. I was so skilled in one-on-one combat that no one could stop me from making the tackle. My confidence became arrogance. I lined up against the smallest player on the field. Instead of the normal distance from the line, I chose to move closer. Listening to my teammates talk trash, I was late on seeing Coach's hands empty. Just as I got almost to my feet, I was trucked by the shortest player on the team. Our helmets collided, and with the force of impact, I blacked out. Feeling like I was in a car wreck, the next thing I knew the drill was over, and three trainers were in my face. Faintly I could hear Jacob Shade still talking shit in the background. I called him the leader of the mentally challenged. He was the loudest and the biggest. Everyone who followed him should have been playing at a Division 1 school. Their raw talent was obvious; they just didn't have the grades. Gathering my senses, I heard the head trainer say "concussion" to his students. I had never heard it called a concussion. In high school we called it a blackout because that was what happened. Everything would go black after contact. One of the student female trainers broke it down further, saying, "Concussions are when you impact someone so hard your brain swells." Which wasn't something I needed to hear as I was dealing with the aftermath. I sat out for about ten minutes as the team started a new drill. Fearful the team would pay for my lack of practice, I sat out until my vision was no longer blurry and my head stopped ringing.

Physically and emotionally exhausted, I was frustrated with the worst start to any of my ten seasons of football. Coach Tully wasn't helping me adjust at all. His in-your-face coaching technique was a little too aggressive for me, expecting perfection every play while trying to learn a new position. Watching him getting in other people's face with a mouthful of tobacco made me nervous. The whole time he was fussing, he was spitting in their face with his frustration. If he had had spit in my face, I can't say what I would have done. Marcus decided that he didn't like anything about Coach Tully. He thought he was racist, and he refused to play for a coach that called him *boy*. Marcus packed his stuff, calling his mom, leaving school just as fast as he got there. Knowing nothing in life other than sports, I thought he was crazy for leaving. Him being like family to me made me start looking at everything differently.

Classes started, which changed my focus. Football was still life. It just had me confused. I thought you couldn't play football if you didn't make the grades. I also thought that you had to actually go to class in order to get the lessons to make the grades. Less concerned with the true reason Marcus left, life moved on once the campus came to life. So many people would travel for miles to get a Butler education. Monday through Friday there were every bit of nine thousand students in the rat race for education. It amazed me to see the logistics of the crowd commuting the campus to class. I would sometimes show up to class just a minute or two late, watching what I called the ant migration. Every day on campus we had someone trying to sign us up for something like credit cards. It sucked being harassed on the way to class. We were still trying to figure life out, and they were busy trying to help us ruin our credit. Loving people always searching for understanding made me try to have compassion for my teammates. Every time I thought I was making progress, it would get used against me. Teaching me quick that while I thought I was in college, I was really in the jungle, where "only the strong survive." Everyone seemed to be looking for any weakness they could use against you. Being nice was considered a weakness to the mentally challenged. They would all get together to call you sweet or make a big deal out of nothing just to see if they could get under your skin. I would always stand up for myself, forcing them to pick on someone else. We had teammates from the small country towns across the state of Kansas that only played seven on seven because their school's populations were so small. I couldn't stand a bully, so I stood up for them too. I didn't understand what reason people had to pick on someone. It got to the point that I became the protector of those that couldn't protect themselves. It was only words, but I learned at a young age that they hurt just as much as fist. I started to see the group that I called the mentally challenged as a group of hyenas. Sitting around, waiting to bully the weakest person around. Their same mentality carried over to football, which was the only place it belonged.

The purple-and-gold game had so much talent on the field. I was still trying to acclimate myself to playing middle linebacker. I played the first half against the sophomore running back. He was the tallest running back on the team. He was so arrogant, and he was always talking shit. His height made him easy to wrap up. Rotating groups of linebackers every fifteen play, I got to prove myself worthy of our possible six linebackers spots on the roster. Second half, Coach Tully switched to a freshman running back no one knew anything about. I heard that he was sent to Butler by Clemson because he was academically ineligible. It didn't take long for Obu to confirm the rumors with his athletic ability. He broke a run of thirty yards, prompting our defensive coordinator, Coach Q, to have me pulled by the linebacker coach. Coach Q chewed me out with the intensity of a drill sergeant at war. I didn't understand his aggressiveness since it was an intersquad scrimmage. He pulled me from the field to watch Obu do the same thing to Carlos the next play. The difference was Carlos was a sophomore. When Obu broke for thirty yards on Carlos without Coach Q giving him the same treatment he gave me, he lost my respect.

Sitting on the sideline was not something I was used to. When I got back in the game, I was determined to stop Obu, mirroring him like I was coached, seeing the hole develop right before me. I took off at full speed, colliding in the hole with Obu like two full-steam locomotives. Blacking out again for a brief second, being helped to my feet by my teammates, I refused help from a trainer determined to finish the scrimmage. I spent the rest of the evening feeling like I had a brain freeze, afraid to go to sleep. Blacking out scared me more than any dream ever did. Initially my vision would be blurred. After a few blinks of my eyes, my sight would return hazy, like a fog was blocking my vision. Desperately wanting to make the team, I kept my mouth shut. Less than three weeks in with two concussions made me forget my hamstring since apparently my brain was moving in my skull.

    The team was cut to fifty-five, which I made it, despite my personal adversities. Back and forth on the depth chart with Carlos made practice competitive. Our linebacker group cut in half after our fifty-five-man roster was announced. A week after cuts, we lost another linebacker to injury, reducing us to five linebackers that could suit for game time. Running a 4–3 defensive, three of the five were always on the field. I was being groomed to play the most important position on the defensive side middle linebacker, the captain of the defense, the formation or scheme caller. Carlos made it hard for me to stay on the field with his year of experience ahead of me. He played the position more natural, identifying the play a lot faster than me. I played it like a rooster in a lion's den. I wasn't afraid to get out there, but I couldn't focus on what was in front of me because I was afraid of what was happening behind me. Not wanting to let a play pass behind me, my change of direction on grass was horrible, so play-action passes embarrassed the fuck out of me. Once I started in one direction, I was committed. Our coaches saw my weakness and loved exploiting it in practice, trying to correct it so it didn't happen in a game. Most of practice time was split into our specialty groups. Preparing for our first game, the coaches started introducing schemes. In order to execute our defensive schemes, we had to bring our three defensive groups together to explain responsibilities. Standing in a huddle, listening to Coach Q, I realized that the entire group that I called the mentally challenged were on our defense. Watching the offense practice across the field, I didn't see near the circus that we had going on since all the clowns were on our defensive. Every single one of them were on their second or third year at Butler from out of state. Out-of-state athletes didn't get recruited by Kansas community colleges; they got sent from D-1 programs, which made me try to respect them. They acted as if it was tradition to heckle our teammates from small towns all the time. I understood that they didn't look like everyone else. I just refused to be a part of reverse racism. I found myself constantly speaking up for anyone who wouldn't speak up for themselves.

My life off the field was nothing like the craziness that I dealt with for four hours a day. With one thousand people in campus housing, it was easy to avoid our seven team bullies. Individually they weren't as bad, but together they fed off each other's energy. I spent most of my time hanging out in rooms of people that I wanted to understand. With people from all over the state of Kansas, I wanted to try to understand what life was like for them. We had the offspring of farmers, cowboys, and coal miners. Everything I watched on television as a little boy. I met a young lady whose father owned 250 acres, having 105 people that worked for him daily to support their families, while her roommate came from a family that bred pedigree horses that sold for a minimum of twelve thousand a horse. Listening to them compare life stories showed me money outside of sports. On our football team, we had two actual cowboys whose families raised cows for profit, teaching them how to wrangle cattle. All of it was endearing to me, considering my past. I made so many friends it was like I was the mayor of Butler. I never learned discrimination, so I would talk to anyone. The only thing that kept me in line was my responsibility focused on our 9:00 p.m. curfew with coaches doing room check every night. I had to give the respect I wanted so never missed a curfew, reaching my room every night fifteen minutes before the coaches made rounds.

Every day in practice we did tackling drills with our specialty groups. For moral confidence building, we ran the skeleton drill with just linebackers. Laying us on our backs helmet to helmet, waiting for the ball to be given to one of us. Coach paired me with Carlos. Coach Lawton, our position coach, dropped the ball in my hands, and we both worked to our feet. With literally two yards between us, we collided good enough for me to black out again. Superstitious about numbers, the third time I blacked out, it really got my attention. Not knowing who I could trust talking to about it, I started leaning on the hamstring strain to pick or choose what I felt was safe. Coach Lawton didn't see it, but Coach Tully did, so he started using me on the dummy offense as a running back. Playing running back most of my life, I loved it. Coach Tully sarcastically said, "Your leg seemed to be fine whenever you play running back!" Running the ball against the first team defensive line wasn't easy with substitute lineman blocking. Jacob beat his blocker quickly, tackling me. I fell on my ankle with all his 320 pounds in the process. The severe pain I felt made me think initially that I broke something. After being checked out by Coach Adams, it was diagnosed as a sprained ankle. Coach Tully seem disgusted with my injury, like it was my fault. Seeing the disgust on his face, I tied my shoe as tight as I could, getting back on the field, practicing through the pain. When practice ended, I removed my shoe. My ankle was so inflamed I couldn't get it in my tennis shoe to drive to my room, so I headed to the trainer since they were twenty feet from our locker room. Coach Adams seeing me hobbling with my ankle double the size gave me crutches with a mandatory week out of practice.

Caught up in my emotions, frustrated by my injuries, I made a trip to Kansas City. Nina's nurturing, caring approval gave me a feeling that I had been missing. After consoling me venting my frustrations, she made love to me like it was our first time. Limited by my ankle, she showed me her love. Putting on her favorite group Dru Hill, we had a meeting in the downstairs bedroom. So consumed with football with a lack of privacy in my dorm, it had been a couple of weeks, so it wasn't long before I erupted like a volcano. My mind was completely clear. Nothing even mattered, like Lauryn Hill said. I wanted to stay right there forever. Sitting on the couch in the common area of the basement, trying to replicate how she made me feel through song. Going away from my comfort zone, I sang Goo Goo Dolls' "Iris." I felt like I was being misunderstood by coaches who could care less. My loyalty to the program made me need their approval to feel like I belonged at Butler. Their only concern was numbers, treating me like stock, only caring to invest for me to produce. Feeling like just another pawn in their game. I headed back to school with a heavy heart to get a good night's sleep to be ready for class.

On the sideline, not even practicing was depressing. I felt like a failure. The only positive thing was we won our first game. The saying "If it isn't broken, don't fix it" came to life with Carlos, who gave the team what they needed. Practice after practice, game after game, I became a relic riddled with anxiety standing on the sideline without full speed repetitions. The game was passing me by. I lost my confidence in the game I dreamed of playing professionally from the age of eight. The hardest thing I ever had to do was watch the game I loved from the sidelines, knowing that I wasn't going to play. After I returned to practice, my only chance in playing in a game was if Carlos got hurt. I cared more about winning than I did my own selfish goals. Game after game we won, while weekly I watched Daryl lead the team in sacks and Obu run for almost three hundred yards a game. Learning competition over jealousy playing sports, I was happy for both of them. The thought of a blackout happening in the back of my mind I still wanted to play. I didn't even care where I played. I just wanted to be on the field.

Three-fourths of the way through the season, I got my first opportunity on a road game against Highland. It was raining like a cow pissing on a flat rock. It was no problem for our offense. Obu made light work of Highland defense, giving us a two-touchdown lead early. Carlos struggling in the rain with his footing and came out of the game to change his cleats. Instead of wasting a time-out, Coach put me in the game. My first play I called the defensive huddle. When I finished calling our defense, we broke huddle. Lined up ready, waiting for Highland to do the same. The quarterback ran cadence, and the ball was snapped. It was coming right at me in the One Hole. I took three steps forward and slipped in the mud. Luckily for me the ball carrier fell right in front of me after tripping over his own lineman. I jumped up like a WWE wrestler celebrating like I made the tackle. The coaches watching from the box sent the message down to keep me in the game. I looked great on the play. For three quarters of football, I had the same cleat issues Carlos had. Loving the fact that I was on the field, I kept celebrating whether I made tackle or not. With our offense doing their job, we cruised easily to victory.

Monday. just like every Monday, we got together in our offensive and defensive groups to break down the film. As soon as I saw Coach Q, I knew something wasn't right by the glare in his eye when he looked at me. After everyone was seated, he dimmed the lights, and the VHS began. Coach Sands was running the VCR, Coach Q running the pointer. Everything seemed normal until I entered the game. On film it was obvious that I didn't make the tackle. It was obvious exactly what happened, and Coach Q lit into me, clowning me in front of the team, asking, "Did gnomes make the tackle?" rewinding the tape over and over and over so he could make sure he didn't miss an opportunity to call me incompetent. He overcriticized everything I did after my ghost tackle. For a good hour straight he said everything he could to piss me off. In my frustration of being singled out, not able to defend myself, I wanted to whip his ass when I started shaking in my anger, but a calm came over me knowing that I made several real tackles during the game, so I sat waiting for him to acknowledge them. Never once did he. Every time I made the right play, we only watched it once, moving on to the next play he could berate me more. Refusing to cry, I died from embarrassment as he focused on me the entire film session. My cavalier attitude enraged him, and by the end of film, he was nose to nose with me, spitting chewing tobacco in my face, telling me how he felt. I didn't understand what his problem was with me. He antagonized me, trying to make me punch him. My nonconfrontational decision in the seventh grade made me stand to defend myself, but I refused to hit a man half my size who was my elder. Knowing that he overlooked my good plays, I stood in solidarity. I didn't see what the big deal was since we won, and they didn't break any big plays. Having committed treason as far as Coach Q was concerned, my season was done, with only five linebackers eligible on the roster, Coach had to suit me up, but he probably would have put anyone in the game before me. Watching from the sidelines, we went undefeated, winning our national championship on the Smurf Turf at Albertsons Stadium, the home of the Boise State Broncos.

Again reaching a pinnacle, another sport in my athletic career. With my third title in sports, this one felt bittersweet. I was on the team, but I had about as much involvement as the water boy. I was happy for the school and the team. I felt like I didn't earn it. Carlos tried to pick my head up, telling me that I made him better in practice. I told him that he would forever be a brother to me for his words. Knowing that he was a sophomore broke my heart even though he was my competition. He was one of the only people on the team that would try to explain things to me instead of just worrying about himself. He understood the concept of team.

Quickly distracted with my grades, which started to drop as I beat myself up about my season. Being my own worst critic, I was harder on myself than Coach Q could have ever been. With Cs in all my classes, I watched my biology grade drop from a C to an F. Knowing what your grandma would say, I couldn't let her find out. Not grasping the concept of biology at all, it became my complete focus, trying to improve my grade. I created a study group that met every evening from 6:00 p.m. to 7:30 p.m. It started with three people. Putting our brains together, we started to make sense of the course. It took all our minds to understand the seven steps of photosynthesis or the different terms involved in a cell. It slowly started to click for all of us, getting excited for our weekly quizzes, thinking we were prepared to still only make a C or D. Honestly we were proud that we weren't in the group of Fs anymore.

With the season over, we had football conditioning after school to prepare us for next year. While running the halls of the athletic building, I was stopped by Coach Sands telling me that the basketball coach wanted to see me in his office. After taking a seat, he wasted no time asking me if I would be interested in playing basketball for Butler. He said, "We need some nonscholarship athletes that could give us minutes off the bench." Offended by the words he chose, I didn't like his presentation. When he said "bench," I really quit listening. Having created a study group for biology with all the stuff already on my plate, I quickly ended our meeting, saying no for the first time in my life. I felt like my grades needed my focus more than I needed to sit on the bench again. Declining the opportunity, professionally sabotaging my chances to make up for my shitty football season, I knew I could benefit the team playing with over half of them in AAU basketball. His presentation made me curious if he had ever seen me play, or did he just have knowledge that I helped Sumner win a state championship in basketball. Knowing that I watch countless films on schools or opponents to see if someone had talent, I wasn't even a coach. I also became curious if he had asked Daryl. He was gifted with a great leaping ability as well as being left-handed, which wasn't easy to defend if his presentation was as innocent as he claimed. After finding out that he never did ask Daryl, I felt like a part of a game that was being played with me making me feel like I made the right decision turning it down.

My biology teacher started to use the bell curve to try to fix the fact that her entire class was failing. Used to making As and Bs I wasn't happy with the Cs or Ds I was making despite the study group. Being a fixer I devoted an extra hour leaving the study group to focus by myself until it clicked. Overnight I went from Ds and Cs back to As and Bs, forcing her to toss my grade to make her bell curve work. My teacher used me as an example that everyone could turn their grade around. Two of my classmates confided in me that they would pay for my help. Trained to never leave someone on the team behind, I invited them to the original study group as I joined again. It turned into me tutoring four students understanding the lingo to help them make sense of it. Being the mediator between textbook and understanding, we all started passing the test regularly. My teacher, taking notice of how I changed our grades around, invited me up to teach the class, hoping that I could help everyone in the class understand. Three days a week I was the professor in biology class, breaking things down into life instead of text as slowly everyone's grades started to improve. Excelling in biology made me proud, which carried over to my other classes. My computer teacher, whose primary lesson plan was PowerPoint was so amazed with how fast I got it over everyone else that she nominated me for Who's Who of junior college stu-

I COULD'VE BEEN

dents. I didn't even know something like that existed. I thought she was pulling my leg when she told me she wanted to nominate me, asking for a picture. It was my light at the end of the tunnel, giving me hope that I was on the right path. She told me after she sent it that it would take a few months for the results.

Dorm life was great. When we returned from winter break, Daryl and I were upgraded to the new dorms along with our roommates. The design of the new dorms had two rooms that shared a bathroom between them, only having four people share the same bathroom. Our neighbors, who had spent a semester in the new dorms, shared that we could put foil on the windows to keep the sun out with them facing the east on the flat taurine with no foliage to break the beams that started at 7:00 a.m. every day, allowing us to sleep past sunrise. The size of our room was almost double that of the old dorms. Having more room and an actual desk to do homework made me really comfortable during the week on the weekends I went home to Nina. Confiding in her my discernment, still trying to fill that void of connection with the program, she recommended that I take a weekend to stay at school, suggesting that it might help me. My first weekend at school, Henry wouldn't leave me alone. Henry was a sophomore who was on his way out the door. He had to finish the semester before he headed to the University of Florida. All season long he talked trash, calling me a square, telling me that I needed to loosen up. He promised me smoking with him would change my perspective on everything and remove the stick from my ass. Living with my stepfather for the last four years, I wasn't interested in a word Henry was saying. I shot him down daily until he quit asking. In an effort to bond with my teammates, we piled five people in the Saturn to go to the country bar in Wichita. When I saw the mechanical bull, I felt out of my element. My teammates were all fishing, so I played wingman to entertain myself. The night ended up with us heading back to Butler with seven people in my car. I didn't ask any questions, but I did make it clear that I wasn't the ride back to Wichita. I was very entertained with how bad the two young ladies wanted to be with my teammates that they liked so much that they packed my back seat like sardines. Spending time with some of my teammates outside of practice made me feel a brotherhood that I needed.

Off-season conditioning was fun without the daily stress of winning, especially having my health returned back to 100 percent. I was competing on a very high level across the board. I finished first or second on the team in every drill we did. I wasn't competing against my teammates. I was competing with myself. To be the best on paper on our team so packed with talented athletes was a big statement. The only thing I didn't make the top two in in the weight room was bench press. My squat was six hundred pounds, my leg press was nine hundred pounds. Doing combine test, my vertical, while great at forty-two inches, I was second only to Daryl at forty-two and a half inches. I was able to claim the crown for the fastest ten-yard start. I ran a 1.29 for my ten yards. The closest to me was Obu at 1.32, giving me the vindication I needed besting our best. Off-season conditioning started to iron out some of my issues of feeling inapt. Being in the top of each category granted me a little acceptance but not enough to make me feel like I was part of the football family.

With my grades back in line, I figured track would put me back in the Butler spirit. I joined the team to throw javelin. College track was totally different than high school. I met the coach, who gave me two javelins with a schedule of the meets with his name and phone number on the bottom. After telling me team procedure, he informed me that we didn't have a coach knowledgeable in javelin, so I was on my own. The day of the meet we would all meet by the locker rooms for uniforms before catching a ride in the school vans to attend the meets. Being self-motivated, it didn't bother me. After class three days a week, I would go to the football practice fields, running myself through the same routines that Coach Break did with me. No announcements to be heard, no glory to be won. It did nothing to put me back in school spirit. It left me more confused, wondering if anyone cared, feeling like Butler County cattle, just there for them to make a quick buck off my athleticism.

One night cruising the old dorms, I stopped upstairs to challenge my teammate to a game of Madden, trying to double the money your grandma sent me gambling. I hadn't lost in Madden in years, figuring that I could live taking fifty dollars from the dorm weed man. With a good lead approaching halftime, the room got real quiet with my performance, talking all the trash I needed to talk. I heard a strong "Forty-seven, forty-eight, forty-nine" that sounded like it was in the room we were in. Intrigued, I asked the room, "What's that?"

He said, "That's just Obu."

A few minutes later, I heard it again. "Forty-seven, forty-eight, forty-nine, one."

After winning my game of Madden, collecting my profit, I went next door, searching for the counting, curious to see it with my own eyes. It was Obu, and he was doing push-ups. In amazement, I stood watching as he kept going. He was so focused that he didn't notice that I was standing there. I patiently waited, listening, gathering my thoughts, as he said "thirty," wondering why he went from forty-nine to one. With no break or pause, he did it again right in front of my eyes. He said "forty-nine" and again started at one without pausing. Now really intrigued, I made my presence known, clearing my throat. Obu realized that he wasn't alone, stopping his workout to sit in the chair in his room. I must have watched him do one hundred push-ups straight before he took a break to acknowledge me. Dumbfounded because I couldn't do twenty-five push-ups straight, I asked him as genuinely as I could, "Why do you start over at forty-nine?"

He said, "I don't know what's after forty-nine."

I thought he was joking at first, but the sincerity was written all over his face. Lost for words with my mind blown, I didn't know how to respond, so I changed the conversation to the only picture I saw in his room. It was him and his daughter. He told me that everything he was doing was for her. Evaluating what I witnessed, I knew there was no way he was passing his classes. I knew our coaches were in collusion to cover it up. Our program wasn't about developing us to succeed in life; it was all about winning on the field. Our talent was more important than we were because winning generated money. Our athletic ability was being rented for the profit by the school being patronized with a steak-and-shrimp buffet three days a week. I was raised that to truly care about something, you should always do it right no matter the consequence. Discovering that standards were different based on ability, I was disgusted. I knew that I had just as much athletic ability as anyone in the school. My respect for the integrity of the program was only as good as our weakest link. With no blame to Obu, I realized that our coaches were borderline criminals. Because he could rush for three hundred yards a game, they ignored the fact that he couldn't make the grades. My discovery blew my mind and really put me in a "fuck it, what do I have to prove at this school" mentality. The next time I saw Henry, I asked him where the weed was. The program's lack of integrity made it easy for me to sacrifice mine. He was in such disbelief that he called eight people to his room to smoke with us to witness me smoking weed.

"Come watch Drake lose the stick up his ass," he said. When we were done, I returned to my dorm, eating all the little Debbie snacks in the room before picking up the room phone to call Nina. Immediately she knew something was off with me. I could sense the panic in her voice as she asked, "Chris, what's wrong?"

Always being honest, I said, "I'm high," and giggled. She was pissed, chastising me.

"I will not be with someone who smokes pot!" she said. Without reverence, she lit into me for twenty minutes straight. The only way she would let me off the phone was to promise that I would never do it again.

That night I slept like a baby. All dreams seemed to be held at bay. Peyton had gone home for the weekend, keeping the room quiet. The foil on the windows kept the room pitch-black. I slept so good I slept halfway through the next day. I woke up after sleeping fourteen hours just in time for dinner starving. I ate like I had never eaten in my life. I had two steaks, two baked potatoes, three orders of fried shrimp with two trips to the dessert bar. I couldn't believe what I did last night. I was hanging out. Bonding with my teammates was cool, but it was bigger than that for me. I went against my morals, losing my integrity that I wasn't sure if I wanted back. The only thing to make me question yesterday was the way I felt about Nina today.

As school was just days from ending, my ring collection was looking good. The best news was being informed by my teacher that

I COULD'VE BEEN

I was selected Who's Who of Kansas freshman academically. She told me that I should have my picture in their book. She said, "I ordered an edition, it was mailed last week." It made me so happy I almost kissed her. After I got in gear with biology, it turned my entire academic life around. I finished freshman year magna cum laude with a 4.2 GPA. Not pressed to compete with Nina, it did feel good to prove that I was equal.

Where Do I Belong?

Home for the summer, my reality was surreal. Everything that made me comfortable or happy was changing or already changed. Your grandma had moved after my spring break. Now we resided on Tenth and Quindaro, which I didn't like at all. Combined with Nina's leaving with her brothers for Illinois after her graduation, which was two weeks away. The only person in life other than your grandma that ever asked me "What makes you happy" or "What do you want to do" was leaving possibly for good. She got accepted at Duke in Raleigh-Durham, North Carolina, planning to attend in the fall. Knowing school was Grandma's bottom line, Nina encouraged me to apply to every school that I could in the Raleigh-Durham area. I applied to all twelve traditional colleges near Duke. Knowing I had Nina's support, the only other person's support I needed was your grandmother's, which wouldn't be easy. The first thing I needed was an acceptance letter. Talking to her about it without one would be a total waste of time. I thought everything would be a breeze. I would get accepted somewhere starting the fall with Nina, and we could continue our relationship.

Reality hit in to the tune of silence. No responses or letters of acceptance at all. I kissed Nina goodbye, telling her, "If it's meant to be, God will make it happen."

"I won't give up."

Without a tear, I watched the woman who taught me what it was to love someone other than blood get into the car. The driver from the limo service closed the door. As she looked at me through the tinted windows, I grew determined to ensure this wasn't the end. The driver walked around the car, and with the slam of his door, she was gone.

I COULD'VE BEEN

My new living arrangement was uncomfortable to me. Without paying any bills, I had to keep my mouth shut. Our new house was obviously built in the early 1900s. The design was horrible. Downstairs was the living room, dining room, kitchen, and two bedrooms. In the hallway at the bottom of the stairs was a full bathroom. A staircase in the hallway led to my room. My room was divided in half, split by the staircase. My queen-size mattress could barely fit on either side of the stairs, having just enough room to get to my closet or half bathroom. I had two milk crates for my television stand that I preferred. I could put the wires through the holes, making it more practical than an actual television stand. On the other side of the stairs was equal space to the side I put my bed on. With that side having a half bath, it made me decide to sleep across the room so I wouldn't have to smell the toilet all night. I used the other side of my room as my personal gym. I brought three full-length mirrors from Family Dollar so that I could see myself from multiple angles to watch myself doing sit-ups or push-ups. Keeping to myself at home, I brought a baby gate to block the top of the stairs, keeping the dogs out my room while making it difficult for my parents to enter my room unnoticed.

Looking for distractions, I went back to the photo lab at Kmart, trying to keep busy. I didn't return to umpiring baseball. My heart was hurting, needing something new to occupy my free time. I found the only thing that could keep my mind off Nina—*basketball*. A new gym in North Kansas City had just opened with four full-length courts. It was the new hot spot for pickup games that a few of my friends named Hooper's Paradise. My first day at the gym I stood on the sideline through three games. There were so many people in the gym with only one court designated for full court play.

KT was home for the summer from UCLA as well. I watched as his handpicked team ran the court (with all friends we had been playing with for years). After watching from the sidelines, I saw their weakness. I was fifth to be captain, so I had to wait for the chance to pick my team. Instead of sitting, waiting until my turn, the captain of the next game let me run with his team. Fresh to the court, we started on defense. As we were still trying to figure out who we were holding, KT nailed a three-pointer from almost half court. Having played against him in school ball as well as AAU basketball, I knew what to expect. The captain told me to hold Justin, who also played on our AAU team but was three years younger. Our height match-up was the only comparison. Justin was 150 pounds soaking wet, while I weighed 220. Using my size along with my jumping abilities, I dominated Justin in the paint. Halfway through the game, KT jumped in Justin's shit, saying, "THIS GAME IS TOO CLOSE, MAN UP!" Frustrated with trying to stop me after being humiliated by someone we both looked up to, Justin couldn't get his head together. Realizing his lack of confidence, my team started feeding me the ball in the post.

Down 11–7, I played with Justin like I was a Harlem Globetrotter. I got the ball on the box with Justin between me and the goal. With right pivot along with a ball fake, I went around him, making the easiest reverse layup ever. Running back down the court to play defense, I knew I made Justin looked silly. KT, trying to give Justin a chance to "man up" passed him the ball. With defense being my specialty, I got so close to Justin (what we called "in his pocket"). He got so nervous that he dribbled the ball off his foot out of bounds. Everyone in the gym was feeling the mismatch. My captain got the in-bound pass, looking over the entire team to feed me in the post again. I turned around and pulled up for the jump shot. Justin was caught flat-footed. expecting the ball fake again. Standing there in disbelief that I shot the jumper, Justin didn't have time to react to my miss. I knew I missed as soon as I shot it. The ball didn't roll off my finger like all my made shots. I rushed around him, got my own rebound, scoring a quick lay-up with the put back. At 11–9, KT feeling like he had nothing to prove, forced the ball on Justin again. Heading him left, he tried to prove his dominance. Trying to force his way right, he dribbled the ball right in front of my face. Quick handed, I stole the ball on the dribble, creating an easy fast break as my team captain took off down the court. KT was so mad about the turnover he let him go, watching me pass the ball in stride with no defense to stop him. As my captain got to the three-point line, he pulled up for the shot, nailing it, making the game a tie at 11–11. The look of disgust on KT's face permeated the court. Refusing to lose, KT took matters

I COULD'VE BEEN

into his own hands, making a three from almost half court to put us off the court ending the game 13–11. A tie at eleven required a two-point win.

Having played as well as we played, the captain of the next game picked me and two other players that just came off the court to join his team. Seeing the mismatch from the previous game, they started early and hard, feeding me in the post, allowing me to score the first seven points for our team against Justin. Each point I scored seemed to make KT more disgusted that Justin couldn't stop me. KT scored when he wanted, realizing the score he pulled up nailing a three to put his team on the board. Everyone in the gym knew the ball was coming to me in the post. After I got position on the box, my captain threw me the ball. Using my pivot, I turned left, dribbling with my right hand, seeing Justin's teammate coming to help. Tired of watching him get used, he left his man, allowing me an easy bounce pass for my teammate to make the wide-open layup. KT's championship mentality took over. He started raining three-pointers, putting his team back in the game. On our next possession, I ended the game 11–9, pissing KT off completely. Not saying goodbye to anyone, KT walked straight out the gym. The rest of his team grabbed their stuff, reminding the gym that they were 6–1 for the day as they followed behind him. Always up for the challenge, I started going to the gym daily, trying to make sure the next time someone said they ran the court all day, it was me or someone on my team.

As summer was winding down, the upcoming fall school semester had totally slipped my mind. Your grandmother being good with schedules reminded me that I had a few weeks to report. I wanted to play football. I just never wanted to play linebacker ever again. Obu just broke a junior college record for rushing yards in a season, eliminating the coaches from looking any other direction. Being a true competitor, Coach Tully didn't bother me, but the mental abuse I took from Coach Q was scarred in my mind. Understanding coaching is correcting, I still didn't understand why Coach turned drill sergeant on me for over an hour straight, overlooking anything I contributed positively. I would always adjust quickly to show my coaches that I understood. He never gave the chance. I tried calling Coach

Tully multiple times at Butler, which was the only number that I had for him. Every time after six rings, the answering service picked up.

"Coach Tully, this is Christopher Drake, could you please call me? My phone number is (913)-766-3645." I wanted to talk about changing my position. I constantly checked my phone every hour for days. I couldn't make a decision without talking to our head coach. I never got a call, which made me feel like I wasn't important enough to the program to deserve a call back. My decision was brought to a standstill once I heard the rumor that Daryl had been arrested for armed robbery and kidnapping. I took his arrest personal, feeling like the program failed him. It was making six figures with the title, while he was robbing a restaurant, getting less than four hundred dollars. After looking at the capitalism of the program, I didn't want to play football at the junior college level anymore.

Talking to Nina long distance didn't help in my decision. Her grandfather passed, devastating her family, so she needed me for strength. When I flew into Chicago, it had been almost two months since the last time I saw her. When I walked up the Southwest gateway, I saw my angel immediately. The glow of her soul illuminated her, smiling from ear to ear. The fact that death brought us together slipped both our minds. Making it to the car, I met Nina's father as he got out the Mercedes to greet me, watching as I put my bags in the trunk. She was staying with him for the summer, doing an internship in the city less than fifteen minutes from his home. Nina, excited for my first trip to Chicago, turned instant tour guide on our way to his condo. He was remarried, living downtown with his new wife and child. He dropped us off while he found a place to park. Inside his condo, he joined us just long enough to make introductions before he headed back to work being on call at the hospital. Nina gave me the tour of the condo with her stepmother in accompaniment, holding Nina's stepbrother. The tour didn't take long, but everything was lavish and advanced. When we finished, her stepmother told me where I would be sleeping, asking Nina to make me comfortable, while she tended to the baby. Nina decided we should go for a walk so that we could talk without listening ears. Holding hands, having a face-to-face conversation, we lost track of time until she got a phone

I COULD'VE BEEN

call for dinner. With the funeral tomorrow morning, we called it a night after dinner, respecting the loss of life more than the fact that we hadn't seen each other in two months.

Dressed in all black, wearing my Nehru suit with my black patent leather shoes, I looked like I belonged in a *GQ* magazine. With Nina by my side, we looked like we should be headed to a red carpet event. When the car service picked us up, Nina explained that we were going to her grandparents' high-rise to ride in the limos with the family. During our ride across town, she busied herself navigating the things she felt important. When we arrived, Nina walked me in the lobby, showing me a side of wealth I had never imagined. There was a lobby with a reception desk like in a hotel with no chairs. There was a bar with barstools centered in front of a huge flat screen television. Just as she headed toward the counter, a gentleman came from the back, asking, "Whom may I announce is here to visit?" I kept my mouth shut, letting her do the talking. After she announced who we were there to see, he told us we could proceed. When Nina pressed the button for the forty-ninth floor, I noticed there were only fifty floors. Nina, aware of my fear of heights, knew I was nervous for the elevator ride up. She looked me in my eyes, grabbing my hand as the elevator whisked us up so fast and smooth. With her midride kiss, it was over before I knew it. When we got off the elevator, the hallway was immaculate. Following her, trying to behave myself, I got nervous as she knocked on the door, knowing that I was about to meet the entire family. When we entered the apartment, the first thing I noticed was the glass window seventy feet across the room. It spanned the entire width of the room in view. It was the most luxurious apartment I had ever seen in my life. I couldn't help myself singing "Moving on Up" in my head. The view across Lake Michigan was breathtaking. Bombarded with introductions, I forgot how high I was in the air. There were so many people in the apartment I couldn't imagine how many limos were coming. When the limos arrived, it took eleven elevator trips down to get everyone outside. I counted nine limos before I was ushered into a limo with Nina. The limo rides to the church made the reality set in for everyone, witnessing grief fall all over everyone's face in our limo. Knowing that nothing

I could say would help, I sat quietly, strongly holding Nina's hand until we arrived at one of the largest churches I had ever seen in my life. Ushered to my seat, immediately I faced forward in the third row in the center aisle of the church as it filled to capacity. The service adorned with fire chiefs, police captains, as well as television actors showed me just how respected her family was, making me want even more to be her partner for life. The ride back to her dad's house was somber. After talking to her dad's wife about the service, things seemed to slip back to normal. With me flying home tomorrow, the rest of the night we held each other while I sang "The Only One for Me." Holding strong to our love, we said our goodbyes, knowing that in just a few weeks she would be in North Carolina.

When I got home, your grandma was on me about school, forcing me to tell her how I was feeling. In truth I laid everything out, explaining how I felt exploited for my talents with no concern for my life after I couldn't statistically produce. Sharing my fear of blacking out to your grandma, I told her about my efforts to call Coach Tully to talk about me switching to play offense. During our conversation, she made the mistake of saying, "I don't care if you play football, but you better have your ass in school!" Having fourteen junior colleges in Kansas City, I argued that I could attend a local college to play basketball while working to keep me from the money issues I had at Butler with my athletically-approved job that only produced forty-four dollars a week as leverage. Your grandmother knew she couldn't afford to have another year of sending me five hundred dollars a month. I impulsively decided my new path instantly focused on getting to North Carolina, knowing that I needed to try to finance it myself. Your grandmother left me, saying, "Life is about choices. Make your decisions wisely." Two days later I missed the day to report to school for football at Butler. Not one coach called like I witnessed them doing my freshman year, which made me feel like I made the right decision.

My intentions were to play basketball at JCCC, but life had me so busy I never made time to talk to a coach or enrolled in classes. Waiting till the last day of enrollment the Friday before school started, I enrolled at Johnson County Community College, determined to prove that I would be fine without selling my soul for steak-and-shrimp dinners depending on wire transfers from your grandmother. In my ego I did the stupidest thing in the world, choosing all my classes without talking to a counselor. I wasn't really interested in school. I just knew that I had to go in order to play basketball. I wasn't really interested in basketball. I just wanted it to distract me as I worked toward the trophy that I wanted, believing that no one was competition for what I loved.

My perception of love was blended while maturing through playing sports. Watching the sacrifices your grandmother quietly made making the impossible possible just to see me smile, never giving me any excuses while juggling her life around what I wanted. My victories taught me that winning was faith following growth, learning from teachers that constantly evolved with new lessons surrounded by those that set my growth as a priority to be around them, teaching tool for advancement rewarded by self-effort, which made me outwork all competition for what provoked my passions, tossing gasoline on my fire making my definition of love a completely excuseless sacrifice, as if nothing else in the world existed.

Nina and I were still together even though we had only seen each other for three days in the last three months. She was my weakness at six foot two weighing 235 pounds of solid muscle blessed abundantly with athletic abilities. The killer mentality that sports taught me seeing everyone as competition until I defeated them dissolved to try to love someone as much as your grandmother loved me. There was no mountain high enough or river wide enough to change my love for her. North Carolina was just a formality that God could eliminate if we were supposed to be together.

The first day of school I arrived at Johnson County CC five minutes before class started. The parking lot was packed as I drove up and down the aisles, looking for the first empty parking spot. In the same dilemma with me was a black-on-black Acura that you could hear two aisles away with their bass vibrating through the cars. They were avoiding the aisles that I went down, as I was avoiding the aisles that the Acura went down. After ten minutes, I decided to look for a parking on the other side of campus. My schedule was nice,

Mondays, Wednesdays, and Fridays in by nine and out by noon. When I finished classes for the day, I forgot that I had to park on the other side of campus. I walked to the lot that I drove around all morning. Standing on the curb to the parking lot, I saw this guy losing his shit on the phone in my peripheral. He was yelling at the person on the other end of the line like they were ignorant as fuck. You could hear him halfway across the parking lot. Always wanting to help, I walked up to him to ask if everything was all right. He told me that while he was in class, someone stole his car. Stunned I asked, "What car?"

He replied, "The black-on-black Acura on 20s."

I realized this was the guy that I was jockeying with for a spot earlier. Feeling rude with no proper introductions, I said, "My name is Chris." Extending my hand.

He looked at me with his face all wrinkled up, saying, "No disrespect, but I don't know you, for all I know, you could have had one of your friends steal my car."

Being tried as a thief, I immediately pulled back my extended hand, turning around walking away.

A week later we crossed paths again. The first thing he said was "I'm sorry about last week. My name is Cameron." Through conversation I learned that he was here from Baltimore on a soccer scholarship, needing to pass two core classes to earn his Division 1 scholarship. Knowing that he was carless, I offered him a ride home after he shared with me that he lived less than five minutes from the school on 119th and Quivira. Approaching the corner of 119th, he asked to stop at the 7-Eleven gas station across from his apartments. I sat in the car waiting. When he got back in the car with nothing in his hand, I was confused by our stop, curious to why he wasted my time to return empty-handed. Making the U-turn to turn into his apartment complex, he asked, "Do you smoke?" pulling a green tube out of his pocket as I simultaneously said, "Yes." Cameron was rooming with his friend Antonio from Baltimore as well, who played professional soccer for the Wizards. Observing my environment on his living room couch, my curiosity kept me distracted until he lit the blunt, grabbing his notebook with pen. As we smoked, he recited and repeated the bars he was working on. He loved music, dreaming of rapping more than playing professional soccer. I found myself hanging with Cameron like I hung out with Patrick or Dominic.

As school progressed, my conversations with Nina weren't as frequent, but at the end of each call, she told me she loved me. That was all I needed to stay focused on getting to North Carolina. With the applications submitted months ago, I started calling the schools that I applied to, searching for information on my application, with each phone call I seemed to hit a dead end. I was determined to be closer to Nina, refusing to give up having faith that it wouldn't be long before I found out something, I was just too anxious to wait. I could not concentrate in class. I was too busy thinking about what school would accept me first. My choice was UNC based on proximity. Close enough without smothering each other and its athletic program was top of the line. Every night when I closed my eyes, I prayed to get accepted to any school in North Carolina.

Antonio's apartment was an extreme bachelor pad. He and two of his teammates split everything four ways with Cameron. They had one of the second-biggest flat screen television I had ever seen. They had both the Xbox and PlayStation gaming systems side by side. I thought it was the coolest man-cave I had ever seen. While we smoked, we played Madden, which was something I did almost daily at Butler. Jumping out to a good lead, I knew when Cameron lost interest. He stood up from the couch, going over the huge fish tank in the corner that was covered with a bedsheet. Cameron removed the sheet, turning on the bulb light that sat atop the fish tank. Seeing a snake that was at least six feet, I slid out the front door without a word. I stood on the stoop, thinking, *What the fuck!* The door opened with Cameron standing there with a Burmese python on his shoulders. Lost for words, I thought, what if the snake wrapped around his neck, choking the mess out of him?

Cameron said, "This is Damien."

I looked at him, like, why do I care. He asked if I wanted to hold him. Petrified, I said, "Hell no, he's good right where he's at." My high was completely blown. I just needed my keys off the coffee table. I was ready to go. I thought Cameron was cool, calling himself a Filipino Jew. Anybody that can make light of themselves doesn't care what others think. The snake made me wonder if we could be friends. Both of us were easy on the eyes, and the two of us together could pull all the women in any bar in Kansas City. I just wasn't interested in that. His love for snakes bothered me. I was raised to kill them, while he was keeping one as a pet. The quality of people coming to the apartment made me accept Damien as long as he stayed in his cage. Antonio's apartment was *Love and Hip-Hop* Kansas City before the show was even thought of. It was three minutes from the school if the lights didn't catch you. The more I hung out with him, the more pot I smoked. I started getting up early to go to their apartment so we could blaze before school. After classes we'd head back to his apartment for video games and more smoking. Even if we weren't playing video games, we were still smoking. With the schedule that everyone else kept in the apartment, Cameron had the place to himself until 6:30 p.m. to 7:00 p.m. almost every day unless he was working. Whenever his roommates got home, I would leave, knowing they had enough people in their face or space all day long. Sitting on Antonio's couch baked as a potato one afternoon, your grandma called me to tell me I had a letter from North Carolina State University. Being a student of sports, my first thought was Jimmy Valvano: "Don't give up! Don't ever give up!" All I could see in my stoned mind was Coach V running around the court, celebrating, prompting me to race home during rush hour traffic. Opening the envelope, I learned that I had been accepted for the spring semester at North Carolina State University. My Butler grades gave me what I needed to get accepted.

    Overcome with joy, I had to share the news with the reason I applied in the first place. I called Nina, and she told me she was happy for me. Even though her tone said otherwise. Cutting our conversation short, she said, "I'm studying for a test tomorrow." Left to celebrate by myself, I stole some of my stepfather's pot along with some aluminum foil. Cameron had taught me how to make a makeshift bowl to smoke out of. I went in my bathroom upstairs so I could blow the smoke out the window to keep your grandmother from finding out. Stoned, I lay in the bed, drifting to sleep. My

I COULD'VE BEEN

phone rang. It was Nina. She had finished studying, calling to confirm she heard me and was happy for me. Almost asleep with my speech blurred, I mumbled less than five words before Nina said, "Are you high?" Instinctively I said no. She wasn't buying it as she started reading me the riot act. My conscience caught up with her question, and I admitted that I was. It was the first time I had ever lied to her. She was so beside herself she hung up on me.

The insurance check was finally processed for Cameron's stolen car. The only problem was it went to Baltimore. Cameron's mom was like your grandma, loving Cameron with all her heart. Wanting him to be happy, she offered to pay for me a ticket to fly home to Baltimore with Cameron so that he could get a new car to drive back to school. Fall break was next week, so Grandma couldn't study long. Once I told her the ticket was paid for, her only request was that I call every day.

From the moment we left the airport, I was enamored with Baltimore. When we got to Cameron's house, I was introduced to his mom. She was home hosting a party for Cameron's younger brother. Cameron's brother was a soccer protégé as well, being recruited by tons of schools as a sophomore. By the front door was a gold fish bowl, and everyone who walked in the door willingly dropped their keys in it. I didn't understand because Cameron's brother was sixteen. Seeing the fish bowl nearly full, I followed the crowd, hearing the music. When I got to the bottom of the stairs, I saw two kegs behind the bar. With Jell-O shots covering the bar from one end of the bar to the other. I was in love with Cameron's mother. My friends and I were drinking at sixteen, but we hid it from our parents, playing stupid if asked about it. To have a parent understand that she couldn't stop it but she could protect us made me never want to leave. Skipping the party, Cameron wanted to see some of his friends and drove us to their neighborhood bar/restaurant Sonoma. Everyone greeted him like he had been away for years, which certified to me that he was just like me.

Cameron's dad had already been scouting, narrowing it down to three cars for him to choose from in his price range. The next morning bright and early we got up to go check out the cars. The first car we looked at Cameron pulled the trigger. After paying for the car, the first thing he did was take it to Jiffy Lube. Thinking he was here to get it checked out or an oil change, I patiently sat there while he got out of the car, talking to one of the Jiffy Lube employees. Twenty minutes later, Cameron comes to the car, saying, "Get out, they are about to put some rims on my shit." Despite the line of cars, they went right to work. The whole time I kept thinking, *Isn't that what got your last car stolen?* The rims were just the beginning. Determined to replace everything that was taken from him, Best Buy was next. I tagged along as Cameron walked straight to the car stereos, knowing exactly what he wanted. After stopping a sales associate, it didn't take long to get the Chameleon detachable face radio he wanted checked out in the audio department. We bypassed the lines again. The tech explained that the harness was complicated, but if he wanted it done right now, he could pull around, and they could install it in less than an hour. Awed by the fact that lines didn't seem to exist, we sat for a little over an hour. Making it to his parents' house was loud, already testing out his new radio. Once he added the speaker box his brother got for him, it was deafening.

On our third day in Baltimore with Cameron's car fully returned, he was committed to putting it through a series of tests. Driving the city from place to place, he ran into some of his soccer buddies who were having a pickup game. I knew he wanted to play bad. I also could tell that he felt guilty that I didn't play. Being selfless, I said, "Bro, it's cool, I'll watch, I would love to see you in action. With all the shit talking you do, I won't believe it until I see it with my own eyes." Feeling challenged, he couldn't refuse the invitation. In the parking lot of Oakland Mills, he got a jersey from the team captain. As I stood on the sidelines watching, I didn't quite understand the rules. I did understand that every time his team got the ball, they made sure he got a touch. His footwork was impressive, I watched as he split five people with one foot missing the goal with a very solid kick. He did score the only two points, which certified him my equal athletically. After the game, he took me to a house party in DC with beautiful women all around. I was more impressed with the indoor pool that I saw as soon as I walked in the front door. The entire night

I COULD'VE BEEN

I sat by the pool, listening to the music, while Cameron socialized with his friends. When we left the party, I hadn't said more than hello to anyone there.

Waking up to the smell of breakfast in the air, I stumbled into the kitchen, finding a small all-you-can-eat buffet. Cameron's mom was still cooking when she noticed me, saying, "Help yourself, Cameron will be back shortly." He had gone to get us weed for our ride back, but knowing she wouldn't approve, I said nothing except "Okay."

Grabbing a plate, fixing small portions, his mother noticed, saying "You're 6'4", why are you eating like a bird?"

Being finicky about food, I couldn't be rude, so instead I lied, saying, "I'm just not a big breakfast eater." I sat down at the table to eat. Cameron returned fifteen minutes later, heading straight to his room. Wanting to escape the pressure of eating more, I followed. Cameron had scored an ounce of what he called Kind Bud's. Being new to pot, I was ignorant to different types. Seeing these little green cone nuggets blew mind. Each cone was equal to the next in size with no loose weed whatsoever. Eager to get back to Kansas City, he started packing, telling me we would leave at 10:00 p.m.

Goodbyes said, car loaded, we got on the highway heading back. Cameron refused to preroll, saying it's more time if we got caught. He passed me a CD case, the bag of green with some papers, instructing me to open the case to break the weed up in it. Only having rolled blunts or used a glass bowl until I met Cameron, I struggled with the papers in the passenger seat. Waiting anxiously for me to finish, he kept asking, "Are you done?" When I finally said yes, he told me to put the weed in the hiding spot behind the radio, speeding up as soon as I was finished. Petrified by speeds of 115–125 that he was doing, I was afraid to light the joint, fearful of being pulled over for speeding. Cameron talked shit until I gave him the joint. Once he lit it, I smoked with him. The entire time I was looking in the rearview mirror for red-and-blue lights. Whenever I got the bag out, he would slow down to ten miles over the speed limit, but as soon as it was back in his hiding spot, he got up to crazy speeds again, flying around traffic, switching lanes back and forth. I couldn't sleep the entire ride, anxious, worried, wanting to know if I was going to jail. We only stopped for gas, making it from Baltimore Harbor to Kansas City in a little over nine hours. Seeing Cameron drive with total disdain for the law scared and excited me at the same time. Hearing Coach Edwards in my head, saying, "It's only a crime if you get caught."

For the next two months, Cameron and I drove in tandem, weaving in and out of Kansas City traffic, both of us driving speeds of one hundred-plus, switching four lanes to come back four lanes. Following Cameron made me fearless on the road. Day after day it was like practice for driving. Both of us being athletes, we pushed the limits daily on I-35 and I-435.

School ending, the semester over, the excitement for North Carolina State had me preparing early. I figured it would be cheaper to fly, saving my money to buy my own plane ticket. The reality sat in that this was really about to happen. Two weeks from now, I would be with Nina again. I called to tell her the good news even though we were not talking as much as we used to. Her roommate answered the phone and told me she was studying and would call me back. Thirty minutes later, my phone rang. It was Nina, I could tell that something was wrong as she said, "Chris, I need to tell you something… I found someone." Demanding an explanation that she didn't seem to have, I hung up. I was upset that I had worked so hard to make this happen. I felt like she could have told me two weeks ago, when I told her that I was finished with all my financial aid paperwork, or a month ago, when I told her that I got accepted. Knowing that I risked everything for love trying to get to get to North Carolina, I was going. Me and the new guy could fight it out when I got there.

January 6, I arrived at NCST campus. The beauty too vast for my cab ride, prompting me to drop my things in the room, leaving to explore the campus. Before leaving, I noticed that there were things in the room already in one of the armoires, but no one was in there. My first destination was the football office. As I walked across campus, I asked everyone I saw for directions just to confirm that I was heading the right way. Excited about the new coach and quarterback, I walked proudly in the football office at six feet, three inches, weighting 235 pounds, with my National Championship ring on. I asked if I could speak to Coach Amato. The gentleman who greeted me said, "The coach is unavailable, can I ask what this is about?"

I said, "My name is Christopher Drake, and I would love to play tight end for his football team."

Still not knowing who I was talking to, the gentleman said, "The team meeting was yesterday. You didn't make that meeting you can't come out for the team." I quickly tried to explain that I just flew in today. The gentleman wasted no more words with me, walking away, ending our conversation. Holding back tears, I walked outside, looking to the sky. Lost, feeling it was my destiny, I stood there for an hour, praying a coach would walk past. Hot and hungry, brand-new in a foreign place, I lost hope for the day, heading back to my room.

My roommate and I hit things off instantly. He was a junior from Charlotte. Sizing him up like I did all opponents, he was six feet tall, weighing about 120 pounds. Despite the fact that he looked like he had never played a sport in his life, we got along well. I spent the evening explaining to him how I was off to a bad start being shot down for the team, needing to play as part of my plan to get Nina back. Trying to help me adjust, he took me to meet our neighbors. The two ladies on the right of us were cool. Admitting to drinking, my roommate went back to the room, retrieving a small bottle of Crown, saying, "I don't really drink, but we can do a shot." Cheers to the new semester. Spending about thirty minutes with the girls, I was ready to move on, knowing that neither were Nina's caliber. Left of our room, there were two guys. Knocking on the door, you could smell the pot outside the room. The door opened to a cloud of smoke. My roommate reminded them that if the smoke alarm went off, they would be fined $1,500 and kicked out the dorms before making a suggestion.

"Yawl should smoke in the bathroom with the door closed. When yawl finish, you need to turn the shower on hot and let the steam clear the air." Amazed with his knowledge and compassion, I felt like I found a new home with a new friend. It wasn't hard to get distracted with my neighbors' help. A few days later, they invited me over to test my roommate's theory with them. Wanting so bad to say no because I knew Nina wouldn't approve, I didn't know why I still wanted her approval, so I rebelliously accepted. When I entered their room, it reeked of weed. I thought, how could we test his theory if the room already smells like pot? After rationalizing the reality of the situation, I volunteered our bathroom. I figured that if it was so full-proof, my roommate couldn't object. All three of us made our way to my bathroom. They sat on the side of the tub as I sat on the toilet. After shutting the door behind us, I put a towel on the floor to cover the crack, we lit the blunt. We passed it around the cipher at least twenty times. When we finished, I was so stoned. I stood up to let my neighbors out, shutting the door behind them. After they cleared the bathroom, I started the shower and exited, closing the door behind me. My roommate was right. Twenty-five minutes later, the room was odorless. Starving, not really sure how to get to the cafeteria, I decided to wait for my roommate. Once he arrived, his explanation confused me, so he decided to join me.

The cafeteria was impressive in size, looking like a gymnasium. The food, however, was not. Satisfied by nothing I saw on any of their five buffets, I wasted three dollars with no refund, still starving on the way back to the room. Charles pointed out a wing spot directly across from the room. We stopped in so I could see the menu. Looking up at the wall while waiting in line, I inched forward as each order was complete. It took ten minutes to settle on fries. When I got to the register, there was this beautiful Asian girl working the counter. Amazed by her beauty, when I went to pay, looking at her face instead of her hand, I missed, spilling the money on the counter. Realizing that she was looking at my eyes and not my hand, we shared an awkward giggle. Here to be with Nina, I took my change and had a seat to wait. Watching and waiting while this obviously shy girl, out of her comfort zone, worked the counter and register like a boss. The more I watched, the more I thought of Nina. I couldn't call her high because she would know. Needing to wake early the next morning for enrollment, I grew more concerned with sleep than calling Nina to tell her I was in North Carolina.

Up early like a tourist, I was couldn't wait to get to the enrollment office. Walking down the streets of North Carolina, I felt like

I COULD'VE BEEN

I was living in George Orwell's *1984*. With cameras everywhere, the closer you got to the heart of the campus, the more cameras you saw. Going to Sumner with all the mini geniuses, I thought nothing of it when I walked past this parked car. The driver was wearing the biggest pair of noise-canceling headphones holding this big bowl-looking antenna. Minding my own business, I kept it moving until I reached my destination. Outside the enrollment office, there were aids helping guide us in the right direction. Using my charm, I stepped to the female aid, playing lost. Being sweet and helpful, she told me that if I knew what classes I wanted to take, I could take the short line, but if I needed to talk to a counselor, I needed to take a ticket. Young and dumb again, I bypassed the counselor, enrolling myself in psychology, biology, math, and English, thinking it's only four classes. Three of which I'd had before. Rushing through the process to keep my plan of calling Nina at three o'clock, after receiving a printout of my schedule, I was given a check for my books. Following the line, I asked the person in front of me why I got a check. He asked if I got financial aid, and after I told him yes, he told me that I would get a bigger check in a couple of weeks. In college, broke, I quit asking questions, counting my blessings. I was enrolled in class with almost $500 for four books.

The first bookstore I went to only had one book that I needed, being late to the draw. I was told I could buy it new for $80 or used for $55. Being a spoiled only child, I went new, thinking I still had plenty of money for the second bookstore. Walking across campus, I felt like I was on a movie set. Everyone and everything was beautiful. In the campus bookstore, I was stunned when the lady told me $240 for three books even with one of them being used. With the line built up behind me, I had to decide quick. I really didn't want to buy them, but I knew I needed this for class. I spent over three hundred dollars in books without a pencil, pens, or paper. Refusing to pay any more campus prices, I went back to the dorm. Venting to my roommate my frustration with the inflation on campus, he told me that if I walked two miles off campus, I could find everything I needed. Still plenty of time before three, I dropped my books on the bed, heading out the door. Crossing the street, walking past the wing spot, I peeked in to see if the young lady was there today. Not wanting to look creepy, I didn't look too hard, trying to stay on task. I walked down the street for two miles without seeing what Charles was talking about. Taking out my phone, I called him. All he could say was "keep going." After almost another mile, I found the CVS. Upset by Charles's perception of distance, I didn't care to walk any farther. I was almost to downtown Raleigh anyway. The prices were cheaper than campus. I bought everything I thought I would need as well as food that I could prepare in the dorm. Spending another $60. I walked back feeling accomplished. The smell of food permeated the air the closer I got to campus. Having walked almost six miles, I decided to treat myself to wings and fries, hoping to see her again.

Walking in at two o'clock, the place was dead. Right across the street from my dorm, I felt like I had enough time to eat in today. Disenchanted by the guy taking orders today, I ordered anyway. Sitting down to patiently wait for my food, she rushed in the door as if she was late, dropping her book bag behind the counter. She put her hair in a ponytail before washing her hands. Apologizing to her coworker, she asked him, "What can I do?" The guy working told her that he was just waiting on my food. Not even looking in my direction, she said, "You can go home, I got it." Gathering his things without hesitation, he left.

A couple of minutes passed, but instead of calling my order number like last time, she came around the counter and brought it to me. Staring intently as she set the food on the table in front of me, I froze in her beauty. As she started to walk away, I said, "Excuse me, what is your name?"

"Joy," she said.

Making her way back to the counter, I watched as she pulled a book bigger than her out of her book bag. As she was standing at the corner of the counter studying, I asked across the empty room, "Why aren't you sitting down to study?"

She said, "My boss doesn't like us to study at work. I'm supposed to be working, not studying."

Losing track of time, enchanted with her grace, when I looked up it was 2:58 p.m. I rushed out the door to my dorm. My next-

I COULD'VE BEEN

door neighbor was walking up the stairs as well. Always taking time to talk to people, I tried to keep it short. Making it in the room at exactly three, by the time I finished dialing the number, it was 3:01 p.m. Ring after ring, my call went unanswered. I sent a text last night before I went to bed, telling her that I would call her at three today. Never in eighteen months of dating did Nina miss anything we scheduled. Heartbroken, lost for words, I called Teagan because she and Emily were friends with Nina. She didn't answer, but she sent a text saying she would call me right back. Looking at the time, I realized that Teagan was not on Eastern time, so she was still in school. While I waited for Teagan, I tried Nina once more to again no answer. Feeling rude to my neighbor for cutting him off, I went next door. He opened the door, letting me in before sitting back at his desk. Opening the top drawer, he pulled out a shoe box lid. It was flipped upside down. In it was about a quarter ounce of some really beautiful pot. Breaking it up to roll, he asked me if I wanted to smoke. Still hoping to talk to Nina, I told him no, I had someone to talk to that could tell when I was high. Jokingly he asked, "Who, your mama?" Before I could answer, my phone rang. It was Teagan. Before I could get out hello, she started apologizing.

"Chris I'm sorry, I'm really sorry."

Curious I asked, "What are you apologizing for?"

She said, "I know you've flown all the way out there to be with Nina, but she's dating someone else now, and she doesn't want to see you."

I knew that she said she'd met someone, but she didn't tell me they were dating. Telling my neighbor to give me a minute, I stepped out into the breezeway. Trying to gather my thoughts, I asked Teagan the stupidest question in the world, "What do you mean?" (Hearing clearly what she said just stunned me in disbelief.) She said it again.

"She's dating someone else, and she doesn't want to see you."

Not caring in the least, I asked, "Who is she seeing?"

Teagan said, "Chris," and I said, "huh." The second time she said, "Chris Duncan."

Jokingly I said, "What did she do, replace me with my twin?"

Teagan scoffed as she said, "Yes."

"What do you mean?" I asked, and she went on to tell me that the new Chris was my same height and stature. He also was black, with freckles, and to top it off, he played halfback for the Duke Blue Devils. Mind blown, I got off the phone.

My neighbor's door was still cracked. When I walked back in I must have had a stupid look on my face, prompting him to say, "You look like you're ready to smoke now."

Pissed, not able to talk to Nina about it, considering her a coward, I said, "Yes, I think I need to." Sitting on the toilet while he sat on the side of the tub, we smoked as I vented. Some of the best advice in the world comes from potheads listening while smoking the blunt. The only thing he could say was "*Fuck her*, you're in North Carolina with tons of beautiful women around!" At both ends of the campus, there was an all-girls school. Reflecting on my situation, my confidence reminded me that there were plenty of fish in the sea. Stepping out of his room onto the breezeway, I noticed the door to my room slightly cracked. Thinking my roommate had made it back, I walked in my room. From the door, I saw my top drawer pulled out. I called out to my roommate because the bathroom door was closed, but no one answered. Walking in, I headed straight to my dresser. Moving my sock, I looked for my National Championship ring. I wasn't finding it where I put it. I started tossing everything from the drawer. It was gone. Emotional, I sat on my bed and cried over the events of the last hour, not because of what Teagan said, more because in the midst of what she was saying, I must have unlocked my room, opening my door for someone to rob me. Not wanting to believe I could be that stupid, when Charles arrived an hour and ten minutes later, I asked if he had been in the room about 4:15 p.m. to 4:20 p.m., and he said no. Having nothing to hide, he proved it by calling the person he was with. Upset, facing my truth, I walked next door, asking where I could get some weed. My neighbor wrote down a number. His name Tank spelled with a *G*. I called the number, explaining how I got it twenty minutes later. Gank was knocking on the door to my room. Telling me he couldn't serve anyone he hadn't seen smoke (with a blunt in his hand). I said we had to smoke in the bathroom. Half my size, he looked at me over his glasses like I had lost my mind.

He said, "I got a better idea, come with me."

In the parking, he had a beautiful Mitsubishi Eclipse sitting on rims. We got in. He popped the sunroof slightly and passed the blunt to me to light. After puffing it twice, I went to pass it, but he said, "Hold on." Starting the car, he explained that smoking on campus made him nervous, so he pulled off through the neighborhood behind my dorm. Still venting, he listened as I told him what happened to me. Intrigued, he listened as we smoked while he drove. When the blunt went out, he was jumpy, trying to leave immediately, almost forgetting to sell me my dub. I went back to my room, knowing my roommate still had half a bottle of crown since I couldn't buy it from the store yet. I offered to pay him for the rest of the bottle. After a couple of shots, I couldn't remember anything as I faded to sleep.

Oversleeping for my class, I woke up as my roommate closed the door on his way out. Brushing my teeth but forgetting to wash my face, I grabbed my book bag and ran out the door. Jogging to class, I got lost, arriving twelve minutes late. Sneaking into class, my biology teacher explained that this class was so many credits because it was two parts, half classroom, half lab. Drifting in my thoughts off to why Nina couldn't tell me herself, I missed more than half of class. All day long through all my classes, I felt like I deserved to hear it from Nina. Having left my car in Kansas, I called the only person I knew in North Carolina with a car, Gank. He said he had too much homework to do as I could tell that he had no interest of driving me to Duke to see her face. He confirmed it, saying, "Maybe after I'm finished we could smoke." Frustrated I thought, *I don't want to smoke, I want her to look me in my face and tell me she doesn't love me.* Being raised not to beg, I said okay.

Instead of trying to do my homework, I sent a text to Nina. To my surprise, she responded, saying, "I'm sorry, I tried to tell you before you came out here."

In my desperation, I responded, "Can you tell me to my face?" I watched my phone for twenty minutes, checking it to make sure it was working but received no response. After over two years with all my efforts, I felt that I deserved closure.

Emotionally a mess, knowing that I didn't have class the next day, I talked my roommate into buying me some liquor. Not knowing what I wanted, I went with him (it was right next to the wing spot). After looking for a minute, I told him I wanted Hennessey. He stepped to the counter, asking the cashier for a fifth, even though it only left me with fifty dollars. Passing the wing spot, I decided to take a shot at Joy. Walking in straight up to Joy, saying, "I think you're beautiful, I would like to call you."

She said, "I have a boyfriend, but I will give you my number, we can be friends."

Riding my emotional roller coaster, I took her number, heading to my room. More than halfway through my fifth, Gank called, offering to come get me, saying that we could smoke if I brought the cigar. Drunk, I said okay, walking back to the store to buy two cigars. Just as I made it back to my dorm building, he was pulling up. Running upstairs to grab my Hennessey, I told my roommate that I'd be back. With the events of yesterday, I totally forgot about my ring. As we arrived at his apartment with me being drunk, it was all I could talk about. Once Gank found out that I played ball, the only thing he could talk about was beating me in basketball, swearing that he could beat me on the court, talking shit as we smoked.

His phone rang for a booty call, so he told me to hang out in the living room. Sharing his apartment with two other guys, everyone had a lock on their door. The only thing in the common area was a couch. The kitchen had a table and chairs, but unlike Mike's place, where everyone trusted each other, here it was like everyone acted like their roommate was a junkie waiting to rob them. Gank appeared sharply dressed, saying "Let's go," and dropped me off back at my dorm.

As I got closer to my door, I noticed my neighbor's door with the two ladies cracked. Neon lights had the crack lit up like a club. Knocking the door open, I saw six shot glasses on the desk with four ladies and two guys. Desperate to feel attractive, I walked in, saying, "Why are you in my room?" Stumbling to sell my joke. Everyone laughed as I joined the party in the middle of their drinking game. Wanting to fit in, I played my first drinking game, losing bad. I got so drunk that I stumbled next door, passing out for fourteen hours. When I woke, I still felt drunk. I had never played a drinking game before. Trying alcohol young, I didn't like the after-effects in practice, keeping me away from it. My drinking experience was Mad dog 20/20, Sysco, wine coolers, or beer. Using my day out of class to recoup, I didn't even look at my notes about homework, accomplishing nothing until I microwaved some ramen noodles to eat before going back to bed.

Having slept all day, I woke up at 7:00 a.m. not having class until 10:00 a.m., I opened my notes. Trying not to wake my roommate, really not interested in the homework, I kept laughing, thinking in my head, *Be very, very quiet,* like Elmer Fudd. Distracted, unable to focus, time passed with me, not getting anything accomplished. Not wanting to run to class, I quit early to make sure I had time to take a shower, wash my face, and brush my teeth. Arriving at biology class to a chalkboard full of notes, my teacher wasn't in the classroom. As people finished writing down what was on the board, they packed their bags and left. I hurried to write them down as quickly as I could. Packing up, I still wanted to understand. I waited outside class until I found someone who looked approachable.

"Excuse me," I said as she looked at me, eager to hear why I stopped her.

She said, "You must have missed the lab yesterday." I must have looked confused as she explained that it wasn't on the printed schedule. "You needed to log in to the online portal to see the scheduled labs." I must have had my jaw on the ground as she continued to tell me that the teacher explained yesterday that he would be grading the labs today. I stood alone, disappointed in myself that my attention span was short in class on Monday. Finishing the rest of my classes, I learned all my homework was online, checked daily. Choosing not to see the counselor, I was totally oblivious, asking my roommate about the portal. After he told me where the computer lab was located, he explained how to log in. I grabbed my book bag, heading downstairs. At 2:00 p.m. when I arrived, the place was already busy. As time passed, it got busier and louder. By 4:00 p.m., it was more like a club than a computer lab. Unable to concentrate, I left frustrated at 7:30 pm., five and a half hours in the lab. I was able to finish my homework for two of my classes, planning to use Thursday for the other two. Something told me to check, making sure I didn't have a lab tomorrow. Running back downstairs, I logged in again, seeing that there wasn't a lab. On my way back upstairs, I started talking to this hilarious guy named Donny, sounding like what I expected to hear from a North Carolina native (a little country, a little city). Learning that we both shared the third room just on opposite sides of the building, Donny wanted to see if I could hear him through the wall. Both of us headed to our bathrooms. I listened in my bathroom for twenty minutes before there was a knock on my door.

Donny standing there obviously stoned said, "What was I supposed to be doing?" I laughed hysterically because it was his idea. I listened as he explained that he walked into his room, and his roommate had a blunt ready to smoke, so they started talking and smoking. He knew we talked about the third room, so he came to knock on my door. It was a reason to laugh. I laughed so hard that I cried a little. Donny stood there looking at me like I was crazy. Hearing my laugh, he started laughing. Prompting me to ask, "What are you laughing at?"

He said, "Your laugh, you laugh like Eddie Murphy."

Immediately my laughter stopped. Stone-faced, Donny started laughing so hard he started crying a little, managing to say, "Don't make that face." Not knowing what he was talking about, I walked to the mirror without changing facial expression. Seeing what he saw, I started laughing again. I needed that. It had been hard to find humor. I hadn't laughed since I got to North Carolina. Donny went on to tell me that he and his roommate were interested in comedy, telling jokes to each other all the time. Intrigued, I became curious if his knock on my door was genuine or if it was a practice for his comedy stick. Needing laughter for my soul, I didn't let it concern me long. Donny and I became instant friends. He treated me like his little brother even though I was a good six inches taller than him.

Used to having a curfew at Butler, invoking my own at your grandma's house while I attended JCCC, this was my first real freedom. Curiosity kept me standing on the breezeway, people watching late into the night. I got to see regular people, not just students being on the end of campus. Lost in my thoughts, riding my roller coaster of emotions with the reality that football and my relationship was not going to happen. In North Carolina, 1,300 miles from home, alone, my ring stolen, my girl gone. Calling Grandma for advice didn't help. She told me I was out there for school anyway, so suck it up. Knowing she was blind to how deep I loved, I tried to reason for closure. She said, "You want closure, it's over, move on."

Focus was hard. Drifting in and out of my thoughts became my daily curse. I would go to classes just most of the time. I would be so amazed by the size of the class that I would end up counting the seats by rows. In psychology class while I was half listening to my professor's lecture on Sigmund Freud, my head was in math class, keeping statistics. There were seven hundred seats in the auditorium. Class averaged 612 on Wednesdays. Monday and Friday attendance was down 12 percent. Trying my hardest to focus, I would hear pieces, but my heart just wasn't in it.

Spending hours in the computer lab with all the distractions, I spent three hours a class on homework. Breaking it down, I realized it would take approximately thirty-six hours a week in the computer lab. I realized the only thing I've ever given that much time a week was practice. Doing it for class made me wish I had seen a counselor. Feeling like I set myself up for failure, I reverted to my social life. My neighbors were always playing drinking games, making me joining them occasionally. Trying to fill the void, looking for guidance, I thought I found it in the bottom of the bottle, using their motto, "Alcohol kills everything." Four to eight people shared shot glasses, playing the craziest games. Feeling under the weather, I missed class the rest of the week. My roommate told me about this thing called the infirmary, which was a hospital on campus for students that didn't require insurance. I made my way there with reading material, thinking it would take a while. Thinking I had caught a cold, I waited for the results of my test. The nurse came back quicker than I expected, telling me I had mono. She told me that my saliva was a real risk to spreading it, insisting that I stay out of class to sleep and hydrate myself. The nurse told me to expect to be out of class for two weeks, making me really regret playing the drinking games.

Out of class, I wasn't even trying in school anymore, Fatigued from my illness, depressed with how my life seemed to be going, I laid in the dark for two weeks. My roommate wasn't afraid of getting mono from me, continuing his normal life. Every day he would walk in the room, flick the light switch by the door, and say, "Are you alive?" making me laugh, lifting my spirits. Lord knows I needed it. Not believing in quitting, as soon as I felt back to strength, I started going back to class. Thinking the storm was over, I tried to salvage my opportunity, fixing my grades like Butler. Going hard, I woke up early to go to the lab. Getting out of class, I spent my evenings in it until it was time for bed. On Friday I wanted to let off some steam, feeling accomplished with my week. I chose to hang out with a different group of drinkers from down the breezeway. All night long they kept trying to convince me to sleep with one of their friends. She was pretty, just not my type. As they conspired to get me extremely drunk, I passed out where I was sitting, waking up at 2:00 a.m. to everyone gone or sleeping, with everything seeming in order. I gathered myself, heading to my room. While taking a shower, I had regrets from my decision to drink with them, feeling like my throat was sore again as I headed to bed. Waking up the next afternoon to a little soreness, I thought I was tripping, creating an illness in my mind. Trying to dismiss it, I went to get wings for dinner, expecting Joy to be off, knowing her schedule from our brief conversation. As soon as I opened the door, I saw her sitting at a table with an order of fries doing homework. With it obvious what she was doing, I asked anyway, "What are you doing here?"

She laughed, sensing my sarcasm. She said, "Homework." Placing my order, I sat down at her table. Realizing her class was one I took at Butler, I started explaining her homework to her. Knowing she had a boyfriend, I just wanted to help. Beautiful women normally have beautiful friends. Figuring maybe she could hook me up with someone. As I ate, I helped her finish her homework quicker than she expected. She was so excited she hugged me, jumping into my arms. It was my first physical contact in months, so it caught me by surprise. I asked her if I could walk her back to her dorm, watching as she gathered her stuff to leave. Her whole focus the entire walk was why I came all the way from Kansas, asking me again for every answer I gave. She found empathy in my story, saying jokingly, "I hope my boyfriend loves me that much." We sat outside her dorm, talking for a few hours before saying good night. I walked back to my dorm on cloud nine, unconcerned with her boyfriend.

My dreams were pleasant even though they were all about me and Joy being together. When I awoke Sunday, I was not able to talk, with my throat feeling swollen. The infirmary was closed, so I rushed down the street to CVS for cough drops. Not able to talk at all, I made my roommate call Joy, writing down my message. She was expecting me to come to her job and walk her home when she finished. I was in no position to be in her face or space, not knowing if I was contagious. Going to bed early to wake up early the next day, trying to be the first person in the infirmary. I arrived as they opened. This time the nurse took the popsicle stick, sticking it on my tongue, and said, "Oh lord."

Not liking what I heard, I mumbled through my suppressed tongue, "What?" as she was still holding the stick on my tongue.

She replied, "It looks like you have strep, but we will have to run tests to confirm." As she took a swab of my throat, she told me that step would grant me a withdrawal. Still wanting to be here, I prayed for anything but strep. Fifteen to twenty minutes went by before she returned with a look of disappointment, telling me instantly without words that it was strep. She told me that strep was highly contagious, and I could not go to class. She immediately asked what dorm I was in. She contacted the dorm director to see if my roommate could be relocated. With the dorms full, my roommate decided he would take his chances. She gave me a mask from the infirmary, instructing me to wear it unless I was eating. Feeling weird wearing it in public, I would fold it and put it in my pocket if I left the room, making sure I stayed six feet away from everyone.

Listening to the nurse's advice, I refused to withdraw, confident that if anyone can pull this off, it would be me. Believing so much, I convinced Grandma that if I had my car, I could get to the library easier, which wasn't true. I left two days before spring break, flying back to Kansas City. Working on Grandma to get my car most of the semester, I kept in contact with a friend from Butler named Stacy. Through sparse conversation, she told me that if I came back to Wichita that she and her friend wanted to sleep with me, making my focus passing through Butler on my way back to North Carolina. Looking at a map, I saw Highway 40 was a straight shot once I got to Oklahoma, allowing me the opportunity to go by Butler on my way back to school. I stayed in Kansas City less than thirty-six hours, eager to get to Butler, trying to see my friends before heading to Wichita to spend the night with Stacy. Swiping a little pot from Starr for my ride, your grandma gave me a thousand dollars cash. Needing it, I asked no questions, kissing her goodbye, heading south to Butler. Making it to Butler around 9:00 p.m., the campus was empty. Knowing my way around, I poked my head in the new dorms. Half the football team was in one room watching a movie, floored that through the adjoining bathroom, their neighbors were girls hosting half the softball team, watching a movie. Knowing Butler had a Vegas theme, I didn't ask questions, saying goodbye as fast as I said hello.

Calling Stacy, she directed me to her apartment. When I arrived, she and her friend were standing on the balcony so I could find them. After parking, I made my way upstairs as quickly as I could. My allergies took off as soon as I sat on the couch watching the cat hair settle in the air around me. Knowing what Stacy said, I kept giving her the eye, not sure if this was the friend or not. With no subtleness about her at all, Stacy said, "Yes, she wants to fuck you." Taking my shirt off, Stacy suggested that we all move to the bedroom so the cat wouldn't interfere. Following her lead, we walked to the bedroom, thinking I was living a dream that quickly became a nightmare. They started fussing that I wasn't equal in my time, and neither of them were into women, making me work harder to keep the time equal between them. Falling to sleep with exhaustion, as soon as I woke the next morning, I was ready to go. I still had eight days before class, but I didn't want to be here. Asking Stacy if she could get me some pot, she told me a deal I couldn't pass up. Not knowing how long my drive was going to be, I bought two boxes of Philly originals, twist-

I COULD'VE BEEN

ing ten blunts before I said goodbye. Car loaded, map on the front seat, I hid ten blunts over my visor for easy access. Driving for about two hours, I had just made it to Oklahoma when I decided I could light a blunt. Smoking while driving, I swerved in the next lane as I choked. Seeing red-and-blue lights in my review mirror, I panicked. Opening my sun roof before I put the blunt out, riding almost a mile before I pulled over. Taking his sweet time, an Oklahoma state trooper walked up to my car.

"Where are you headed?"

Always being honest, I said, "To school."

This made him step back to observe the situation. Seeing my car fully loaded, he stepped closer to the window, seeing my map, realizing that I was genuine. "I'm going to let you off with a warning," he said, walking back to his car. I pulled off with my nerves fried. I couldn't believe that he didn't say one word about pot. It dawned on me that he never said why he had pulled me over. Not wanting to go back and ask, I set my cruise control. Being the rebel that I have always been, after twenty minutes I lit the blunt back up again. Refusing to stop for anything but gas, eight hours into my ride without making it out of Oklahoma, I realized that ten blunts wasn't going to make it to North Carolina. Still having plenty of weed, I bought three boxes of Phillies, my next stop for gas. Figuring it was better to have them and not need them than to need them and not have them. Looking at the map, I realized I would go through Forrest City, so I could possibly see my grandma. Watching the time disappear, it seemed like forever before I hit the Arkansas state line. Underestimating my drive, it was too late to stop when I got to Forrest City. I didn't want to wake my sixty-one-year-old grandmother at one in the morning, Knowing she would know I was high, I kept going. Determined not to spend money for a hotel, I kept driving. Every time I felt tired or complacent, I would light up a blunt, turning up the radio as loud as I could, before rolling the windows all the way down to let the air whip my face. Mentally tough through sports, I had been driving almost twenty hours straight when I hit the mountains, leaving Tennessee. Near delirious, I was forced to find my concentration through the curves, fearful of the eighteen wheelers and the curves, waking up completely after thinking that I was about to drive off the mountain. Seeing the end of the line, I kept pressing to the thought that I could sleep when I got there. Fatigued, dozing off behind the wheel, after I got far away from the mountains, it started raining. The rain woke me up with fear because it was raining so hard I couldn't see twenty feet in front of me, making me concentrate. All the way through North Carolina, it rained on and off, like it knew when I was passing out behind the wheel. When I finally arrived in Raleigh the next morning, the sun was shining beautifully. Exhausted, I parked illegally in the dorm parking lot, passing out immediately. Luckily, it was spring break, so I didn't get a boot on my car my first day there.

Waking in a ball of sweat, still out of it, I moved my car to the street. Heading to my dorm room to sleep some more, I passed out again, sleeping sixteen hours. When I finally woke up, I was starving, making me head straight to the wing spot for Joy to fed me. Overjoyed that I was back, she kept hugging me, making me wonder if I still had strep. Trying to protect her, I cautioned against the affection, making her say, "I don't care, I'm so happy to see you, I missed you. Campus has been dead, work's been slow. If I had known, I would have gone home for spring break." Pausing to breathe, she continued, "I say that, but I really need the money." Happy to be missed, I left a fifty-dollar bill under my trash, knowing she would see it when she cleaned up. Going back to my room to unpack my car. On my last trip from, I heard my name.

"Chris! Chris!"

Looking from the breezeway, I saw Joy running in my direction. Knowing that she had found the money, I went to my room, shutting the door. Yelling at me through the door, she said, "I'm still on the clock, but I'm not going back to work until you open the door!"

Not wanting her to lose her job, I opened the door, smiling at her. I asked, "What's wrong?"

She said, "I can't take your money."

For five minutes we went back and forth before I started unpacking my bags, staying stern in not taking it back.

She said, "Okay, I don't know why we're arguing." She headed back to work. Turning back my covers to lay down, I found that fifty-dollar bill on my pillow. Calling the restaurant immediately, I asked how she had done it because I saw her walk out the room with money. "When you weren't looking, I took a bill out my bra and put your money under your blanket."

Happy to see her intelligence, I started spending all my time with her. Her boyfriend would call, and she would talk to him with me in the room, telling him about me, ensuring that I was just a friend. As spring break was almost over, we decided to watch a movie in my room. The dark room with a slow movie wore on both of us, and I don't know who fell asleep first. I woke up at 4:00 a.m. with Joy cuddled up next to me. I always walked her to her room, so I was happy that she didn't leave in the middle of the night without me. Confused but happy that she trusted me enough to stay the night with me, I fell in love with someone else's woman. Thinking of what happened to me with Nina, I started avoiding her, knowing the way it made me feel. Not 100 percent healthy, just knowing it was now or never, I went back to class on Monday. All day I tried to convince myself that I could catch up. Listening to the teachers, it sounded like they were all speaking Italian. I was too far behind, forcing me with great regret to withdraw from all my classes.

Just getting here with my car less than a week ago, dreading the drive home, I focused all my energy and free time on basketball. Every day I grew in popularity on the outdoor court. My dominance made some of the players trying to get me off their court tell me that the school team was always in the gymnasium scrimmaging all worthy comers in the gym. Wanting to play for the school, I switched to the indoor court every day. By the first of May, half the NC State team knew who I was, watching me dunk on multiple players on the team. With my current academic standing, I never approached their basketball coach, knowing their roster was so deep. Secretly I was hoping he would find me. Half his team knew about me catching hoops from half court, dropping sick no-look dimes daily for weeks or dunking on any fast break that I got showing out. Realizing that it wasn't going to happen, I had no purpose in North Carolina. Staying as long as my ten-thousand-dollar student loan supported, I left on Nina's birthday, May 21.

Stopping to see my grandmother on my way to Kansas City, I learned the power of her legacy. I got off the highway in Forrest City, Arkansas. Driving as far as I could remember from my earlier trips to visit, I stopped at a gas station on the main strip ten minutes into the town. I entered the gas station, asking if anyone knew how to get to Ernestine Weaver's house. Instantly three different people tried to give me directions. I knew my grandmother was a big deal in her city, just not that big. Staying overnight, I got to spend time with the matriarch of our family with her sweet Christian values. The whole evening, she preached to me to seek God in my new decisions. Seeing her legacy, I felt pressured to be as great as her, especially being her oldest grandchild. Knowing I still had thirteen hours to drive until I was home, I hit the road the next day, heading back to Kansas knowing that there was no place like home, and I didn't have any ruby-red slippers.

Life is imitated, or as I continue to say, "Life is a learned experience." We imitate what we admire with the desire to duplicate our perception of *perfection*. I love to say that ignorant people don't know they are ignorant, when actually they have imitated their role model to better them until they contently feel that they have succeeded. I say this with proof. I'm not the smartest person in the world. In reading my story, I hope that you understand that I followed in your grandmother's footsteps. I recreated her circle in our circle of life, completely, trying desperately to walk a different path all my own. I was rooted in love. Gifted prodigy with an eidetic memory, there was never anything in life that I didn't excel at when my heart was in it. Cursed as an empath, I have always absorbed other people's energy, making me introverted. In understanding my gifts, I had to live as a student and a professor. I know that on this journey, I have died without a physical death. Quoting Fifty Cent, "Death is easy but life is hard, it will leave you physically, mentally and emotionally scared. You can die in your flesh and still breathe tomorrow. Blessed, I testify with certainty that tough times don't last but tough people do."

Athletically or physically, my accomplishments taught me what it feels like to be king. I died from that. What good is being king if you murder the people who love you with envy. Raised genuine, my teachers taught me to never beg or never cry. As I matured, my attitude became, I was born to live, don't live to die, making me reserve my judgment without experiencing it for myself. Trying to share my gifts, I have offended more people than Dr. Phil, being misunderstood, explaining my perception through my lessons learned in life. There is a fine line between talent and ego. I've learned that talent speaks for itself, while the ego needs reassurance. Failure is never an option. As your father, know that I never lost, but I learned when to quit giving my time to things that didn't deserve it. My perspective became that I owe nothing to no one, having nothing to prove. The only thing to rekindle my fire, bringing me back to life, is love. I love you… I'll love you forever. Realistically I know that your success without a two-parent home can be restricted. I fought so hard to stay, sacrificing myself with no excuses, trying to make sure that you were balanced in perspective. After years of watching your tears, I saw that staying wasn't helping you more than it was leaving you emotionally scarred. Knowing my scars, knowing the time it took to heal, I left, but I didn't give up. I write this to you first with all my heart because I know that nothing is built without building material. The world that I was raised for doesn't exist anymore, so I struggled with my legacy for you, making sure that in life or death, you have building materials. God helped me find my path. I know that your mistakes are yours to make. I've made plenty. Baby, understand that after me, no one owes you anything. You owe yourself to go out and manifest your dreams into your realities. Everyone has a unique story that no one else can tell, like a fingerprint. You are the ink to your paper for your story. Every day you wake up is a chance to rewrite it. Live fearless, accept change, try new things regularly, because then and only then can you form your own opinion. A wise man once said, "Doing the same thing over and over expecting different results is the definition of insanity." I dare you to be crazy, reassuring that your heart beats. Don't let crazy drive you insane. Love the things that love you while chasing your dreams, knowing that people come and go. Living your dreams is the only fairy-tale love that you can hope for. Everything that's right for you will find you on your path.

CHRISTOPHER DRAKE

My final thoughts of perspective for you, baby. First is a quote from someone that I love and admire because there is no one more honest than him, parallel from a different universe. Mike Tyson said, "Everyone has a plan until they get hit in the mouth!" My blackouts made it relatable. Having dreams of playing professional football, that to me became a battle of life or death. Second comes from the late great Tupac Amaru Shakur backed by the movie *The Hate You Give*. The only reason that thugs exist is because instead of you trying to understand why or lending a hand to help, the fact that you see me as your opposite, you convict me guilty of living. Unfortunately, a lot of times, it's based on the color of skin. His brand was Thug Life, an acronym meaning, The Hate U Give Little Infants Fucks Everyone! No one is ever born preprogramed to be anything in life. It's learned from our living role models. Hate in any degree is reverberated energy from someone significant in our life. I pray that my hate of ignorance didn't rub off on you like it was rubbed off on me. Every culture has a gang. Every culture has a militia, appropriately learned imitating the development of our systematic systems. There is no greater militia than a group that gets a pass with "legal" murder, saying, "I was in fear for my life!" Imagine if that liberty was extended to the common public with no penalties.

Loving you made me do the unthinkable. Against all odds, raised in the enter city without a real two-parent household until I was almost fifteen. I'm not in prison. I'm not on drugs. Your daddy wrote a book. Following my faith using all the gifts that I have accumulated, I present to you proof that all black men aren't gangbanger. I bleed and love just like everyone else. The difference is that I have you to love, making me limit my excuses, knowing that you love me win or lose. Excuses to myself have as much value as pencil shavings, something that doesn't matter. Your love has made mine limitless.

I love you forever, my written rebuttal to *I love you more*.

Your father, your daddy,
Chris

About the Author

Christopher Drake quietly resides in Atlanta, Georgia, working in the film industry at one of the largest studios in the world. His love for crafting creativity was captivated when he found his career. Studying everything as he has always done throughout life, his respect for the executive producer / writer / director of the studios, he works at inspired Christopher to write his story. Winner of two state championships in high school along with a Junior College National Championship. Christopher always valued the results of hard work reaching the pinnacle of all his endeavors. With an abundance of successful acquaintances, his hunger for success pushed him to never settle, using his off time between productions to travel back home to Kansas City to write. Self-motivated through Faith Christopher's "never quit, never surrender" mentality has produced this completion of his first novel to this trilogy.

www.ingramcontent.com/pod-product-compliance
Lightning Source LLC
LaVergne TN
LVHW042018291224
800129LV00008B/269